The Cultural Politics of
European Prostitution Reform

The Cultural Politics of European Prostitution Reform

Governing Loose Women

Greggor Mattson

Erkki (as you would be in my
pseudo-homeland), you have
long been one of my best
friends in Ohio, and beyond,
Hey sister, soul sister,

[handwritten signature]

palgrave
macmillan

First published 2016 by
PALGRAVE MACMILLAN

The author has asserted his right to be identified as the author of this work in accordance with the Copyright, Designs and Patents Act 1988.

Palgrave Macmillan in the UK is an imprint of Macmillan Publishers Limited, registered in England, company number 785998, of Houndmills, Basingstoke, Hampshire, RG21 6XS.

Palgrave Macmillan in the US is a division of Nature America, Inc., One New York Plaza, Suite 4500, New York, NY 10004-1562.

Palgrave Macmillan is the global academic imprint of the above companies and has companies and representatives throughout the world.

Hardback ISBN: 978-1-137-51716-6
E-PUB ISBN: 978-1-137-51718-0
E-PDF ISBN: 978-1-137-51717-3
DOI: 10.1057/9781137517173

Distribution in the UK, Europe and the rest of the world is by Palgrave Macmillan®, a division of Macmillan Publishers Limited, registered in England, company number 785998, of Houndmills, Basingstoke, Hampshire RG21 6XS.

Library of Congress Cataloging-in-Publication Data

Mattson, Greggor.
    The cultural politics of European prostitution reform : governing loose women / Greggor Mattson.
        pages cm
    Includes bibliographical references and index.
    ISBN 978-1-137-51716-6 (hardcover : alk. paper)   1. Prostitution—European Union countries.   2. Prostitution—Government policy—Europe.   I. Title.
    HQ184.A5M38 2015
    363.4'4094—dc23

                                                                2015020283
A catalogue record for this book is available from the British Library.

To my parents.

Contents

List of Figures and Tables   ix

Acknowledgments   xi

1   Governing Loose Women: The New Politics of Prostitution   1

2   States of Anxiety: Prostitution Reform as a Symptom
     of European Integration   27

3   Dutch Pragmatism and the Difficulties of Professionalizing
     Prostitution   51

4   Legislating Peace for Women: Sweden's Sex Purchase Act   77

5   German Consensus for Sex Work, Compromise over
     Sex Business   97

6   Finland on the Fence: Abolitionist Compromise at
     the Edge of Europe   127

7   Seeing *as* a State: Transnational Problems through
     National Lenses   155

8   The Truly Trafficked Woman, and Other
     Globalization Anxieties   167

9   Methodological Afterword: Identity Work and the Interviewer   181

Notes   193

Bibliography   219

Index   235

List of Figures and Tables

Figures

1.0 Lone Women on the Move   1

2.0 Fortress Europe: Welcome to Entropy   27

2.1 DAPHNE Project Poster Portraying Women as Victims   39

2.2 Logo of the DAPHNE Project, 2005   42

2.3 European Women's Lobby Campaign against Prostitution   45

3.0 Red Light Districts Are for Everyone   51

4.0 Vulnerable Women as Object Lesson   77

5.0 Frankfurt Brothel   97

5.1 Berlin Brothel   103

5.2 Frankfurt Brothel   104

6.0 Erotic Bar/Fresh Meat   127

6.1 Erotic Bar/Fresh Meat   132

6.2 Saigon Massage   133

6.3 Finnish "Entertainment Lines" Sex Ads, 2002   143

6.4 Finnish "Secretary Academy" Banner Ad   144

7.0 Police/The Secrets of Love   155

8.0 The Traffick in Talk   167

9.0 Reflections   181

Tables

1.1 Parliamentary Prostitution Debates in the EU-15, 1999–2004   8

2.1 The European Union Creates the Field for Prostitution
Conflict, 1990–2006   30

3.1 Dutch Prostitution Reform Timeline   52

4.1 Swedish Prostitution Reform Timeline   78

5.1 German Prostitution Reform Timeline   98

6.1 Finnish Prostitution Reform Timeline   128

Acknowledgments

Any project that takes so long accumulates debts that are impossible to repay, daunting to recall, but a pleasure to acknowledge. Many interviewees gave generously of their time and knowledge. Most are not directly acknowledged in the text, yet their time and assistance was vital. I hope all feel fairly represented.

Generous funding made a four-country comparison possible, including a Fulbright Scholarship to the European Union and a National Science Foundation Graduate Research Fellowship. From the University of California, Berkeley, I received Fernström Foundation Travelling Grants from the Scandinavian Department and the Leo Lowenthal Prize in Sociology. At Oberlin College I was fortunate to receive the Andrew Delaney Fellowship in the Social Sciences, an OKUM Faculty Development Grant to the University of Michigan, a Powers Travel Grant, and a Class of '57 Research Grant.

At the University of California, Berkeley, I benefited from the guidance and mentorship of Ann Swidler, Neil Fligstein, and Claude Fischer. Many dear colleagues and friends provided key insights and read early drafts, including Corey Abramson, Hana Brown, Phillip Fucella, Christel Kesler, Hwa-Jen Liu, Isaac Martin, Damon Maryl, Darren Modzelewsky, Gretchen Purser, Sarah Quinn, Amy Schalet, and Lisa Stampnitzky.

I received insider knowledge, hospitality, and places to sleep from Kris Clarke, Jukka Hartikainen, Jan Helten, Teemu Kärnä, Jim Valio, and Jan Wickman. Translation assistance was also provided by Anna and Jarno Paavola, Richard Podgorski, Mika Torvinen, Sirpa Tuomainen, and Mattias Zinn.

At the University of Michigan, I benefited from the hospitality of Elizabeth Armstrong, Alice Goffman, David Halperin, Trevor Hoppe, Rostom Mesli, and Genevieve Zubrzycki.

My friends and colleagues at Oberlin also read drafts and provided moral support, including Ann Cooper Albright, Jan Cooper, Jenny Fraser, Harry Hirsch, Daphne John, Amy Margaris, Libby Murphy, Gina Perez, and Rebecca Whelan. Undergraduate researchers also provided valuable assistance as part of Prostitution Research: Understanding Debates in European

Societies (PRUDES), including Christophe Beaumier, Cindy Camacho, Taylor Field, Kat Lamp, Daniel Ljungberg, and Amanda Wysk.

Ken and LaDene Mattson also did lots of nice things for me, including copyediting my dissertation and raising me. All children should have such curious and supportive parents.

I

Governing Loose Women: The New Politics of Prostitution

Figure 1.0   Lone Women on the Move Governing loose women is the challenge for European prostitution reformers.

Source: author photo

Olympian Cultural Politics

Between 1998 and 2004, contentious debates about prostitution increasingly disrupted international events ranging from the World Cup and the Olympics to meetings of the International Labor Organization, the European Union, and the United Nations. These debates took a harsh edge amid rising global concern about human trafficking, an issue whose relationship to prostitution was itself sharply contested. This time period at the start of the millennium marked the beginning of what I call *the new prostitution politics*. I argue that very different ways of doing prostitution politics reflect very different understandings of community protections against vulnerability that are embedded in welfare state regimes. Prostitution became the focus of widespread cultural politics: disputes over the meanings of fundamental aspects of social life. Amid widespread anxieties that globalization eroded national cultural differences, prostitutes came to symbolize the ability of nations to preserve their values and police their borders, and the efficacy of transnational politics to solve global problems. Harsh intergovernmental criticism, broad media coverage, and public interest are just some of the emblematic features of these new prostitution politics, epitomized by the events before the 2004 Summer Olympics.

Athens was a flurry of construction and scrubbing in the run-up to the event. One press release among the steady flow in July 2003 noted the city's intent to enforce the 1999 brothel ordinance that had never been implemented. Fifteen brothels that did not comply were to be closed immediately because they were too close to other brothels, schools, or churches. An additional 400 or so would be shuttered because they exceeded the maximum number of permits (215) allowed under existing regulations or the 200-meter restriction from schools, churches, other brothels, libraries, playgrounds, nursing homes, etc.[1] Urban watchdogs and the newly formed Movement of Greek Prostitutes (KEGE) protested the move as part of a general whitewash before the international festivities. In compromise, the city council offered to increase the permit threshold to 230. This move was decried by KEGE for banishing 370 brothels, but the Greek Orthodox Church added its own objections to the plan for "legalizing" an additional 15.

The debate about brothels in Athens might have been everyday urban politics only five years earlier, as they had been for other Olympic cities before. Unluckily, however, Athens hosted the Olympics at the peak of European anxiety over prostitution. An international fracas ensued when other countries publicly accused Athens of tolerating the oppression of women by licensing any brothels at all. These two views on prostitution—as manageable, or inherently oppressive—became a struggle not only of the best solution to a particular urban social problem, but as a litmus test for different visions about Europe.

On July 23, the deputy prime minister of Sweden, speaking on behalf of seven Nordic and Baltic countries, convened a press conference to express "abhorrence" over Athens's plans. "It is with indignation and surprise that we have learned that Greece plans to increase brothel activities during the Olympics in Athens 2004. This will lead to more women being exploited and abused," declared Deputy Prime Minister Margareta Winberg of Sweden's ruling Social Democratic Party. These seven ministers from other social democratic or socialist parties thus joined the conservative Greek Orthodox Church in objecting not to the enforcement of the brothel cap, but to the city's recognition of any brothels at all. As the joint statement declared, the Nordic–Baltic initiative aimed "to stop the expansion of the brothels, but also to start a discussion if this is in line with Olympic ideals, using women and girls in this way."[2]

This Nordic–Baltic communiqué was carried by major international newswires, prompting KEGE to escalate its street marches. Global newswires flashed photographs of prostitutes with their faces covered by sacks or hidden by parasols while they demonstrated outside Greece's Interior Ministry and Athens's City Hall. As one KEGE member complained, "We are licensed and they won't let us earn a living; they don't do anything about illegal prostitution."[3] The group protested the city's inattention to illegal migrant sex workers and complained they were punished by this unhindered competition as well as onerous registration requirements.

Athens's mayor now had to defend city actions against local detractors and an international gallery of critics whose ranks grew to include the Vatican, the United States, and Greece's own European commissioner. The mayor had a potent defense for Athens's actions, however: her gender. The capital city's first female mayor defended not only her city but all Greece by asserting that "as a woman politician who has fought for years against human trafficking in any capacity, I am extremely sensitive to this issue." As fast as her press office issued rebuttals to charges of sexism or insensitivity to gendered violence, the Greek Embassy to the United States translated them into English and published them on its website. These reached a wider readership than their previous press releases, whose topics had been confined to such mundane issues as construction timetables, toilet availability, and reassurances about Athens's ability to complete the main stadium in time for festivities.[4]

European Union (EU) member states typically respect a norm of non-interference in domestic affairs among themselves, making the willingness of so many countries to criticize the city of Athens notable. By the close of the event, however, no increase in prostitution demand or sex trafficking materialized, though it was unclear whether this was the result of overblown hype or effective prevention measures.[5] Though Athens was the first time that foreign ministers criticized a host city's treatment of domestic citizens, today the Athens episode is forgotten. It has been buried by the stream of hyperbolic claims about prostitution at every subsequent international sporting event—and by the surprising international consensus around the concept of human trafficking despite disputes over the meaning of prostitution.

The New Prostitution Politics

The controversies surrounding the Olympics in Athens contains all the elements of what I call the new prostitution politics, the contemporary resurgence of interest in prostitution, human trafficking, and conflicts over what to do about them. I use the term prostitute because, as I show below, there are sharp disagreements between reform movements angling to redefine prostitutes as "sex workers" or "victims." Advocates of different definitions of prostitution reach across borders for allies, creating both a transnational civil society *and* international discord. Issues that until recently would have been local—closing 15 brothels in a city where they were otherwise permitted—now balloon into international struggles over the definition of prostitution, the kind of social problem it represents, and thus the proper state actions to address it. These are framed in various moral terms, raising the domestic stakes of the solution and highlighting transnational differences.

The first such wave of international activism over prostitution occurred over a hundred years earlier, at the end of the nineteenth century. Then "white slavery" captured the international imagination, sparking innovations in policing, journalism, and transnational social movement activism.[6] Abolitionists, as they called themselves, drew on the networks and meanings of the international movement to abolish slavery, successfully co-opting socialist movements against wage slavery.[7] That wave of activism, which lasted roughly from 1888 until World War I, transformed prostitution from a taken-for-granted aspect of urban life into a social problem that demanded a national solution: the removal of prostitution from the public sphere through criminalization of female delinquents.[8] This activism founded new organizations—ranging from women's courts, city social work offices, and Traveler's Aid to the US Federal Bureau of Investigation (FBI)—and transformed the interests of professions, including journalists, social workers, doctors, and police.[9]

After World War II, some of the fruits of the first wave's zeal were undone when new activism, inspired by universal human rights, agitated for prostitution's decriminalization so as to not punish the victims of poverty or coercive pimps.[10] In the latter half of the twentieth century, prostitution was decriminalized in most Western industrialized countries, with the notable exception of the United States (save Nevada).[11]

Three aspects characterize the new prostitution politics from the old: women in positions of political power, policy polarization, and the way these politics are embedded in robust civil society organizations and transnational ties. The gender of government officials marks one stark difference between the old and new prostitution politics. While the government and police officials who presided over the first wave of prostitution activism were almost exclusively men, this time around the main players are overwhelmingly women. In 2003 this included Athens's mayor, all seven Baltic and Nordic ministers, the prostitutes' spokespersons, and Greece's EU commissioner. Although these women spoke from many sides of the conflict, they spoke as if their gender justified their point of view, as if there was only one position that women could take.

A second way in which the new prostitution politics diverge from the old is that policy positions are polarized between strategies of legalization and those of abolition. At the turn of the twentieth century, old regimes of managing prostitution through municipal ordinances and red-light districts were swept away as middle-class women claimed the city streets as their own. Prostitution was criminalized and banished from the public sphere. Then, activists largely agreed that the old system of regulated brothels had to go.

Now, however, debates about legalizing or abolishing prostitution represent a new consensus: dissatisfaction with prostitution's post–World War II decriminalization. Replacing that convergence is the current *divergence* between two policy poles: legalization or abolition. These are framed in broad philosophical terms as two opposed alternatives that obscure both the messy realities of everyday life and the common ground that partisans share. By highlighting women's agency or victimization, legalization and abolition map onto much-critiqued modern disputes about structure versus agency. This policy polarization is also reductive, collapsing a continuum of actual policy frameworks and levels of enforcement into two neat categories that obscure more than they reveal. Only sex workers' rights activists advocate for the "old" decriminalization, but they had no impact on policy.

A third realm in which new prostitution politics differ from the old is today's involvement of a dense web of civil society and government organizations: state agencies, international governmental organizations, and domestic and international nongovernmental organizations (NGOs). In the old days, it was mainly middle-class social movements calling on the state to do something—sparking the first international conferences for feminists and police, both in 1899. An explosion of smaller NGOs serving everything from neighborhoods to continent-wide issues has outpaced the rise of intergovernmental organizations like the International Olympic Committee and the EU. The state agencies involved in prostitution are not merely the police or municipal "women's offices," but now range from borough welfare offices and hospital emergency rooms to the military and diplomatic corps. This means that, today, an NGO opposed to its government's policies can receive support from other governments or international organizations that share its views, while states use diplomacy to sway other countries toward their preferred policy. KEGE received support from sex workers' rights groups around the globe, while abolitionists added their voices to those of the Nordic ministers.

If domestic struggles feature competing local justifications, the international struggle is so heated because partisans justify their policies in the high-stakes rhetoric of human rights. Legalizers who advocate for sex workers' rights cite United Nations (UN) resolutions guaranteeing the right to work, a position recently endorsed by the 1998 International Labor Organization's recognition of sex work.[12] Abolitionists cite UN statements against prostitution dating from the early days of the League of Nations and the 2001 Palermo Protocol to "prevent, suppress, and punish trafficking in persons, especially women and children."[13] The increased public concern over human trafficking has become tangled in these debates about different ways to regulate prostitution, spreading Europe's conflict over prostitution still wider. At the transnational level, prostitution abolitionists and legalizers face off at otherwise-unrelated international conferences on poverty, migration, women's issues, and sexual health. In the face of interstate conflict, local groups make common cause with other governments and intergovernmental bodies, receiving financial and other support.

From 1999 onward, the new prostitution politics divided allies into legalizers, abolitionists, and wishy-washy fence-sitters in international clubs and bilateral diplomacy. Starting in 2001 under the George W. Bush administration, the United States initiated a name-and-shame approach of ranking countries by their achievements in stemming human trafficking in the annual State Department Trafficking in Persons (TIP) Report league tables. This continued under the Barack Obama administration. These TIP reports sharpened disagreement over the specific definitions of prostitution and human trafficking used by the State Department to evaluate successful policy.

The TIP Reports caused consternation among American allies for sometimes conflating legalized prostitution with tolerance of human trafficking, or misclassifying local actions or contexts as evidence of national tolerance for victimization. Finland, for example, received a Tier 2 rating in 2003 alongside Uganda and Albania based on rumors of "enclosed prostitution camps" in Lapland. The Finnish minister of justice protested, "If we do not have a law that comes under the same precise name as that in the United States of America, it hardly means we do not recognize the crime in question."[14] Other allies that did not receive favorable "Tier 1" ratings rebutted these by charging the United States with hypocrisy given how late it came to the issue, even as they scrambled to regain privileged Tier 1 status.

The Olympics were not the only international sports event tarnished by the new prostitution politics. The 2006 World Cup in Germany featured a similar cast of plaintiffs opposed to temporary brothels erected in host cities in anticipation of increased demand. Headlines blared: "Germany Backs Bigger Brothels to Fight World Cup Sex Explosion," "Scoring in the Soccer Love Shack," "Vatican Laments World Cup Prostitution," "Ahead of World Cup, U.S. Warns Germany about Sex Trafficking," "Feared Surge in World Cup Prostitution," and "Nun Puts the 'Red Card' on Forced Prostitution at World Cup." Prostitution partisans lined up along predictable lines in this naming and shaming.[15]

Much of the concern about prostitution reflects broader fears that globalization is eroding the ability of states to control their affairs. An unintended consequence of all this transnational conflict about prostitution and human trafficking is that the solutions to address it strengthen, not weaken, state control by increasing border staffing and surveillance measures.[16] The new prostitution politics are most vigorous when the decision to legalize or abolish prostitution becomes salient to national identity. The three aspects of the new prostitution politics— women in power, policy polarization, and the involvement of dense webs of domestic and transnational organizations—became crystallized by the emergence of two new national strategies to address prostitution in 1999.

Polarized, Polarizing Reforms

The origin of this state of affairs was the divergence in European prostitution policies that occurred following two 1999 reforms. In that year the Netherlands completed its legalization of prostitution begun a year earlier, recognizing sex work as an occupation and legalizing contracts between employers, employees, and customers. In that same year, Sweden declared its intention to abolish prostitution by criminalizing the purchase of sex, defining prostitution as violence against women akin to rape.

During the initial discussions about the meanings of the Dutch and Swedish reforms, national identity was often cited as the ostensible cause of reforms often described as the "Dutch way" or the "Swedish model." Dutch legalization was explained as an extension of Dutch tolerance and pragmatism, while its detractors used the analogy of tolerance for dirty streets or public urination. Likewise, prostitution abolitionists around the world lauded Swedish conscientiousness, while its critics condemned the same quality as hypocritical Swedish sanctimony. The Swedish and Dutch promoted these understandings themselves, describing their national laws as the logical next step in their defense of human rights. In Sweden, the "sex purchase law" was likened to the 1979 law prohibiting the spanking of children, drawing an analogy between the helplessness of both prostitutes and children and the harm done to society by the exploitation of vulnerable citizens. The Dutch highlighted their work to combat human trafficking, with governments supporting the first efforts in Europe in 1981, and their pragmatic approach to managing ineradicable human dilemmas, like drugs or euthanasia.

Between 1999 and 2004, prostitution reform proposals swept Europe. Eleven of the then-15 European Union (EU-15) countries debated policies along these lines (see Table 1.1). Paris endured sex worker protests

Table 1.1   Parliamentary Prostitution Debates in the EU-15, 1999–2004

	Legalization	*Abolition*	*Decriminalization*
Austria	x		
Belgium	d	d	x
Denmark			e
Finland		e	
France		d	x
Germany		e	
Greece	e		
Ireland		d	x
Italy	d		x
Luxembourg	e		
Netherlands	e		
Portugal			x
Spain			x
Sweden		e	
United Kingdom	d	d	x

Key: d, debated; e, enacted; x, existing policy

in 2002 when France attempted to sanction clients and make the most sweeping curtailments to prostitution since the Revolution. Belgium saw competing measures in parliament: one to legalize and tax brothels to bolster sagging tax revenues; another to further criminalize the sex industry to drive it out of existence. Scotland weighed a proposal to criminalize the purchase of sex; the British Parliament mooted legalization. While Italy debated legalization, Milan cracked down on prostitution by prohibiting cars from stopping to pick up prostitutes. Sex workers donned sneakers and ran alongside to jump inside still-moving vehicles.[17] Denmark decriminalized prostitution, reflecting its actual practice on the ground while still hosting one of the world's most successful radical-feminist-run prostitute help center, *Reden*, which means nest.

The first two countries to enact reforms after Sweden and the Netherlands were Germany and Finland. In 2000, the Berlin federal court ruled that prostitution was not immoral, prompting the formation of a parliamentary committee to write legislation to legalize it. The ruling leftist Social Democratic and Green Parties sponsored it. Meanwhile, Finland amended its Aliens Act in 1999 to allow border officials to refuse entry to suspected prostitutes and speed the deportation of suspected prostitutes within the country and, in 2000, prohibited streetwalking. Finland also debated Swedish-style client criminalization in 2002, 2003, 2006, and 2012 but criminalized only the purchase of sex from victims of pimps or human traffickers in 2006, also with the support of the Social Democratic and Green Parties. With these newly formalized but competing conceptualizations of prostitution, the Swedish and Finnish delegations clashed with the Dutch and Germans whenever international organizations took up the issue of prostitution or trafficking in women, especially within the EU itself. German and Finnish delegates also worked to defend their national policies—as they currently existed and as they hoped they would become.

This striking divergence was surprising because of the degree of European unity during those years. These same European countries had been pioneers in decriminalizing consensual sexual relationships, taking adultery, homosexuality, and prostitution out of state purview starting in the 1950s. The 15 EU countries had just harmonized their monetary, economic, and legal systems, programs part of an ambitious program "in anticipation of the creation of a European cultural area."[18] Based on these successes, a new European Constitution was being formulated and proposals were being floated to harmonize criminal justice, immigration, and social welfare policies. These were being packaged in a historic document, the European Constitution, which was to be voted on in 2005.

Using national culture to explain the divergence of European prostitution policies could not explain the similarity between the German and Dutch policies, the polarization of the proposals in parliaments across the continent, nor the presence of the same parties on opposite sides of the polarized policy divide. There is, after all, nothing inherently Dutch about legalizing prostitution as an occupation and crafting prostitute pension rules just because Amsterdam has a historic red-light district. Neither is client criminalization the only policy solution to bring about the abolition of prostitution, nor necessarily a Swedish one. If national culture alone could not explain why the harmonious club of like-minded countries became divided over prostitution, what could—and why did only four quite-similar northern European countries enact changes so differently from each other, by ruling left-wing parties, in such a short five-year period?

The Ongoing Project of the Nation-State

The answers to these questions tell us about the ways that national identities not only persist amid globalization, but differentiate and thrive. These disputes between prostitution legalizers and abolitionists starkly dramatize contemporary debates about national belonging and the relationships among state bureaucracies, national identities, and civil societies. Appeals to national culture to explain policy contrasts can do so only in tautologies: Germans reform prostitution in German ways, Finns in Finnish ways. These simplistic understandings of culture and national identity cannot explain the similarities among countries, the differing positions taken by ostensibly transnational political parties like the Greens, or the polarization of the debate into two alternatives framed and understood as opposites. My use of the term "cultural politics" highlights the patterns in these struggles over the production and change in meanings, whether within conventional political institutions, broader cultural "common sense," or interpersonal contexts.

Europe's prostitution reforms reduced prostitution from multiple forms, ambiguous meanings, or local compromises to a single, national standard. This aligns with other ways nation-states impose standards for more efficient governance, ranging from last names, measurement standards, and passports to that domain of mathematics devoted to governance: state-istics.[19] Scholars routinely use the term nation-state to describe modern countries, but treat it as a taken-for-granted achievement of the distant past rather than an ongoing project that must be explained.[20] Nation refers to the group feeling of shared identity over a territory, what Benedict Anderson famously characterized as the "imagined we." State, on the other hand, refers to the institutions of governance, the organizational-chart architecture of government bureaucracies.[21] The compound concept "nation-state" has become a Western commonplace that its lack can only be be understood, with horror, as failures: failed states without rule of law, those where transactions across ethnic lines can only be accomplished by bribes, or governments that engage in ethnic cleansing.[22] The assumptions implicit in nation-state failures obscures their ongoing achievement.

I introduce the concept of *nation-state project* to capture the way prostitution reforms represented this ongoing project of articulating national identity through cultural politics. In those countries in which prostitutes came to exemplify a collective vulnerability, reforms were popular because they buttressed national identity with the power of state institutions by prosecuting sex buyers who victimize women, in Sweden, or protecting sex workers in the Netherlands. Thinking of the nation-state as a project best describes this ongoing process of articulating national identities with the state agents who have the power to enforce meanings throughout a country's territory. It describes, in effect, an attempt at limiting the potential range of meanings within a nation—the bureaucratic administration of equal treatment over a territory comprised of a people with a shared identity.[23]

Seen through the lens of nation-state projects, European prostitution reforms are far more similar than their partisans perceive them to be. For one, these legal reforms represented the first comprehensive attempts by states since World War I to intervene in prostitution at the national level, overriding the decriminalization consensus that ushered in decades of de facto municipal control. Previously, most countries had decriminalized prostitution, allowing large domestic variation as municipalities had worked out their own compromises to regulate the gray areas of sexual commerce. In the Netherlands, this included the free-wheeling red-light district of Amsterdam that seemed too brazen to be illegal, while other Dutch cities simply prevented brothels. Similarly, cities on Sweden's west coast had a more pragmatic approach to prostitution than did legislators in the national capital, and their norms were swept away by the new policy.

Another similarity is of standardization. All of the new national regulations demand that the prostitute be detected, scrutinized, counted, inscribed, and assessed—whether mentally, financially, or territorially. Each is an attempt to reduce prostitution to a single cultural meaning—worker or victim—and impose this meaning throughout the range of state bureaucracies, and across all cities in a country. The solutions may be framed as opposites, but they share the logic of extending state responsibility—and power—over prostitution, an authority the state had shunned when national legislatures decriminalized prostitution after World War II. Prostitution, once not a relevant or legitimate state concern, now became key to the defense of national morals from external threats, whether from a nebulous globalization or from erstwhile-allies in the European Union.

European Integration and Globalization Anxieties

My project focuses on what prostitution reforms mean for nation-states engaged in the project of European integration, which has general implications for understanding the impact of globalization and vulnerability for other countries as well. Sociologists of culture have long observed that meanings take on a heightened significance in "unsettled times."[24] This unsettlement comes from the shared definitions of a situation as mobilizing or disorienting: A war can prompt national solidarity or collective dismay, as can sudden economic prosperity. Nation-state projects seem necessary when globalization is perceived not as an opportunity, but an unsettling threat. As I show in the next chapters, prostitution reformers often cited vague external forces as causing the need for sweeping new prostitution policies. This is despite the fact that scholars over the past 20 years have consistently debunked this notion of globalization as a homogenizing force that erodes national sovereignty and local traditions.[25] The fact that these notions persist among policy makers and popular publics, prompting their own very real effects, is what I call *globalization anxieties*.

Globalization anxieties, perceived as real by governments, reformers, and national populations, justified new prostitution reforms in a Europe that was integrating. European integration can itself be seen as a particularly strong form of globalization in that it institutionalizes and exemplifies many of these fears about globalization: lost national sovereignty, porous borders, the imposition of impersonal standards, the overweening importance of economic markets, and uncontrollable migration. During the period 1999–2004, European integration came to be unsettling to Europeans, a shift in opinion from the successes of the new currency in 1999 to the utter defeat of the European constitution in national referenda in 2005. Prostitution reforms demonstrated the ability of nation-states to guarantee and enforce this identity in the face of popular understandings of globalization as a threat, reinforcing national ways of doing things before the European Union imposed an unwelcome compromise.

Protecting prostitutes reassured populations that *themselves* felt vulnerable to forces beyond their control, I argue. Prostitution reforms represent the heightened role that images of vulnerable women took during those times, unsettled as they were with the implications for the extension of EU integration from the legal and economic realms and into social policies of welfare, criminal justice, and migration. Prostitutes, as vulnerable women caught between the market and the state, exemplified a general feeling of vulnerability that afflicted all national citizens. These European politics became polarized around the question: Are prostitutes vulnerable workers or abused women?

Partisans on both sides claimed the answer was to extend human rights protections to prostitutes. Yet at issue were not excessively different protections for universal human rights, but which protections took precedence: workers' rights or women's rights. The answer determined which set of human rights laws applied, which state agencies had to respond, which client NGOs assisted, and which feminist groups engaged. Implementing an answer set a country alongside ready-made allies but across from opponents who were erstwhile friends within the massive, voluntary project that is the European Union.

Yet most of the prostitutes in EU countries are not citizens but denizens and thus ineligible for the newly proffered protections for sex workers or prostituted women. Some were non-EU nationals in the Union without permission; some were in the EU on tourist visas and thus not allowed to work, others had overstayed their visas.

The EU illustrates, moreover, the way that international agreements are part of nation-state projects. Contemporary countries do sign on to international agreements over universal human rights, but local interpretations of these rights means they are enacted differently. Given such deep divisions between otherwise-close friends, Europe's prostitution reforms illustrate the ways national identities are institutionalized by the state, encoded in the rights and responsibilities of citizenship, and communicated transnationally by means of (not despite!) ostensibly universal values.

Can Sexuality Be Rationalized? Citizenship and Vulnerability

Proponents of Europe's two new legal systems for prostitution each claim the mantle of rationality for managing a difficult social problem, whether defining it as an occupation like any other, or as violence against all women. They rationalized prostitution in both senses of the word: redefining it precisely, and justifying the new policy responses based on this redefinition. National prostitution reforms illustrate the inherent ambiguities of trying to collectively shape and enforce something that feels so private. Two social theorists can help us understand the ambiguities involved in trying to rationalize sexuality: Max Weber, and Michel Foucault. The dilemmas of rationalizing sexuality—and the insights gained from putting these two thinkers in conversation with each other—have implications for how we think about the relationships among national cultures, state bureaucracies, and social movements around gender and sexuality that arise to change them.

Max Weber famously analyzed the dilemmas of rationalization in modern society. A German jurist who wrote mainly in the first two decades of the twentieth century, he is remembered for his analysis of the rise of scientific and government standards over hidebound traditions or rulers' whims. This rationality opened up freedom for many, especially for those who had little of it, by disrupting patronage networks and extending the rule of law. But Weber noted that it also stripped life of its meaning by reducing us to numbers in the queue of government bureaucracies or statistics in a population register. His famous metaphor was of an "iron cage" in which modern citizens become trapped in the inhuman rules that we ourselves built in the name of fairness and efficiency.

"Disenchantment" was Weber's description of the result of living in this iron cage, built by banishing emotions and sexuality into the private sphere, away from considerations of how jobs, educational credentials, or resources are allocated. These efficiencies strip away the meaningfulness of life:

> The fate of our times is characterized by rationalization and intellectualization and, above all, by the disenchantment of the world. Precisely the ultimate and most sublime values have retreated from public life either into the transcendental realm of mystic life or into the brotherliness of direct and personal human relations.[26]

When we no longer accept subjective whims and gut feelings as legitimate reasons to hire or vote, we have also set aside something of what makes us human.

If rationalization in general leads to disenchantment, sexuality poses a particular challenge because it epitomizes those "direct and personal human relations" so intrinsic to being human. Sexuality is one of the primary places where modern individuals "re-enchant" their lives with meaning, desires, and stories. French theorist Michel Foucault reminded us that these meanings are still social. They may seem and feel intensely personal, yet they are derived from and bind us to larger communities and their ways of doing things.[27] Norms about marriage and relationships all shape the desires we have for ourselves, for our loved ones, and the metaphors we use to describe the relations between the rulers of families and nations.[28]

Scholars over the past 20 years have explored the ways in which sexuality is the metaphor by which modern individuality is couched and the political language of citizenship is articulated.[29] Traditionally, sexuality was the product of public concerns for family property and inheritance.[30] Contemporary debates about national belonging are framed in individualistic sexual terms, whether about marriage and adoption rights for gay couples, the status of transgender citizens' relationships, control over reproduction, and responsibility for offspring conceived through technology or surrogates. Each of these issues defines the limits of community, the responsibilities individuals owe to society, and the kinship ties that bind the nation. Now that sexuality is curled at the core of a private self, these individualized (and individualizing) desires seem even less amenable to coercive policing or government control. Rationalization through some bureaucratization of sexuality is only possible if such government action is supported by cultural norms.

Because sexuality feels so deeply individual, yet is shared so widely, perceived threats to its realization resonate at the individual and national levels. Prostitution is made problematic because, like sexuality itself, it implicates our notions of the good society, our hopes for the future, and the collective actions we take to preserve traditions. Yet these conflicts are rarely about the sale of sex alone. In the chapters that follow, I show that the meanings of prostitution vary widely among policy administrators: a draw for illegal immigration, a blight that lowers property values, a public health threat, a reflection of men's unreformed attitudes toward women, the incursion of economic forces into sexual relationships, or a threat to the socialization of children. Missing from these debates is any explicit discussion of gender because prostitution is invariably defined by female sellers and male buyers, illustrating the way that vulnerability is gendered. When I asked about men selling sex, I was rebuffed and the conversation was redirected to *real* prostitution. For Europeans, the perceived vulnerability of female prostitutes articulated fears about the market to desires for state protection. These were addressed in differently patterned ways across countries, as this book attempts to explain.

The European prostitution reforms that arose in the early 2000s are novel because they formulate prostitutes as full citizens for the first time. Up until these new prostitution reforms, prostitutes existed in legal gray areas that varied by country: workers without workplaces, sellers without legitimate products, women without gendered protections, employees without contracts, citizens without taxation, beneficiaries without benefits. The reforms broke with the old definitions of prostitutes as criminals or as morally deficit, and the gray areas introduced by decriminalization, but fully incorporated prostitutes into the "we" by which their nations were imagined.

The extension of citizenship to prostitutes was a nation-state project, a shift in definition of the collective we of the nation and the directives to state agents. Including prostitutes in the full protections of the state reaffirmed national values for the majority by extending the umbrella of community membership to the symbolically most-vulnerable. These vulnerable, however, were controlled further and more effectively through state control than either the old coercive ways of policing or the don't-make-a-fuss decriminalization.[31] The policies of the new prostitution politics conferred upon prostitutes the rights of national recognition but also responsibilities to comply. Not since the nineteenth century had prostitutes been so recognized as citizens, deserving not merely of judicial noninterference and the right to reside in the community, but now also entitled to the state's occupational and legal protections and the generous welfare provisions that are the hallmark of northern European countries.

Welfare states provided the *inclusion roadmap* by which prostitutes were extended citizenship, the care society grants the deserving vulnerable.[32] Welfare policies are one of the most important ways that states institutionalize national values through the protections afforded to the vulnerable: minor children, the poor, pensioners, workers, and victims of harm. Welfare states institutionalize, reward, and sanction commonsense moral notions of vulnerability and community membership, excluding outsiders and disciplining criminals.

Weber and his contemporary heirs portray bureaucracies as a basic expression of human mastery over the environment, an arena where social groups compete for power.[33] It was this same belief in the primacy of the state that underwrote the dramatic expansion of the welfare state in Europe after World War II, where social benefits would inculcate social cohesion and reduce domestic conflicts.[34] If welfare states provide an institutional repository of past political fights over fertility and women's work, they also serve as an inclusion roadmap by which individual sexual desires are incorporated into national ways of doing things. Prostitution regulation in the Netherlands, Germany, Finland, and Sweden show that rationalization is, at best, a state-bounded phenomenon underpinned by feelings of national identity rather than some perfect enactment of an abstract, homogenizing, philosophical idea, of either abolition, legalization, or community itself. If this means the replacement of local nuances and longtime practical compromises with a new national standard, these newly nationalized standards soon butted against conflicting standards institutionalized by neighboring countries.

Comparative studies reveal how otherwise-similar Western European countries can yet differ widely in their conception and implementation of other social concepts as well. Citizenship, for example, can privilege bloodlines and ethnicity, or abstract belongingness through law.[35] The upper middle class in all countries draw symbolic boundaries around themselves to explain their privileged status, but the French do so based on cultural appreciations and personal integrity, while Americans refer to occupational status and hard work.[36] Amy Schalet's research shows that Americans and Dutch have very different expectations about how well adolescents can regulate themselves, reflecting very different ideas of what constitutes "the individual"—an economically independent one, in the United States, or a self-aware family member, in the Netherlands. Different conceptions of government underpin contrasts in abortion policy: in America, the protection of individual rights but not the provision of services, in Germany, the provision of services that balance individual and societal interests.[37]

These examples show that even within the industrialized West, where there has been much institutional convergence,[38] there are still deep differences over core concepts that are reproduced in national contexts, in part by the expectations of state benefits and sanctions. This makes the enthusiasm by which Western citizens subscribe to universal human rights agreements a puzzle to be explained, rather than the natural progress of cosmopolitan enlightenment.

Civil Society and the "Many Hands of the State"

Complicating attempts by governments to shape national standards are the fact that *the state* does not speak with one voice, nor do its multifaceted institutions pursue the same goals. Welfare states, described by one scholar as "the capacity of a society or social group to pursue a set of higher moral values," can be sidelined by bureaucratic apathy or civil society sabotage.[39] Bureaucrats can invoke service to "the system" to justify their own immediate desires, while state contractors and NGOs receiving state funds may bend the rules to pursue professional or organizational goals. Social workers may emphasize their solidarity with their female clients as women, even when this interpretation may not be in the client's best interests. State attempts to impose social control from above may not penetrate the social worlds of professional bureaucrats or state-funded NGO workers.

Citizens do not blindly receive cultural meanings from the state, nor is the state the sole source of meaning from which they craft their everyday citizenship. Nation-state projects in Europe regulate sexuality for the common good, crafting national consensus over the *terms* of the debate exactly because definitions cannot be imposed upon everyone. For example, attempts to impose a single meaning upon prostitution were opposed by prostitutes in each nation. Swedish prostitutes countered government claims that no one could consent to prostitution by organizing a prostitutes' rights movement on a US model, arguing that the right to sell sex is a fundamental act of self-determination.[40] In the Netherlands, the government's move to legalize citizen prostitutes but treat foreign prostitutes as illegal workers was vigorously opposed by the union of prostitutes and Evangelical Christian campaigners. The union prioritized their solidarity as sex workers over distinctions of citizen versus foreigner. When no provisions were made to provide a legal status for migrant sex workers, the union did not endorse the legalization for which they had long fought, privileging their solidarity as sex workers over their inclusion as full Dutch citizens.

Prostitutes realized how the law defined them had ramifications for their rights as citizens and their solidarity with noncitizen sex workers. Extending citizenship to prostitutes only recognized domestic nationals, excluding the majority who are undocumented migrants, as the majority are in northern European countries. In countries where prostitution is now classified as labor, prostitutes are deported as illegal workers. Where prostitution is categorized as gendered oppression, victims are repatriated to receive care back home. Either way, their place in the country is eliminated when the gray area of the demimonde is no longer an informal affair, but an affair of state.

Prostitution rationalization is one contemporary example of the historical trajectory of nation-state projects: They expand their jurisdictions and construct local standards of what is rational to underpin their rule.[41] Common to historical and comparative sociological theories of the state is a model of culture as a set of tools for action.[42] In my research, such a model highlights the need to see prostitution reforms as disputes influenced by the institutional and conceptual tools at hand,[43] key among them welfare institutions. The five-year wave of reforms from 1999–2004 is interesting not only for the laws that passed, but for the continent-wide popular concern, both of which testify to the unsettlement of fundamental concerns of national life, such as citizenship and vulnerability. To put it another way, laws are the result of redefinitions of the meaning of vulnerable women affirmed by appeals to one set of human rights laws over others.[44]

My cases, the first four countries to standardize prostitution,[45] dramatize Weber's insight that rationalization in modernity does not succeed in imposing a single meaning across all cultures. In fact, even with the institutional resources of the state, prostitution rationalization cannot even enforce a standard meaning within a single society. This highlights a problem with thinking about *law, the state,* or *the government*: It is really a collection of competing institutions, none of which are themselves univocal.[46] The rule of the state can only pretend to be absolute within its borders, and no citizens are better positioned to subvert policy than the bureaucrats charged with enforcing them. This illustrates how the simplified understanding of abolition and legalization as opposites understood them as rational, when really they were local compromises predicated upon tacit understandings of citizenship and vulnerability laid down by the inclusion roadmaps of the welfare state.

Welfare State Citizenship

I argue that the similarities and differences among the four countries that first enacted prostitution reforms can be explained by understanding their welfare states. Scholars have characterized "three worlds of welfare capitalism" to describe the ways that states provide benefits for their citizens: corporatist, social democratic, and liberal residual.[47] Each of these regime types distributes resources in different ways, framing vulnerability in different ways.

The *corporatist* regimes of the Netherlands and Germany were designed to manage social conflict among workers, incorporating citizens by virtue of their work status. For the Nordic *social democracies*, however, gender egalitarianism was the way in which these sparsely populated countries mobilized their labor capacity by implementing policies that helped mothers be full-time workers, such as generous parental leave and childcare. Mothers were not just appendages to male citizens, but full citizen-workers in their own right. Under this model of gendered citizenship, Nordic policy makers framed prostitutes as victims of male oppression and state neglect. Understanding prostitution as *sex work*, as it is in the Netherlands, is virtually impossible because sexuality was removed from workplace concerns to enable women to work. Nordic sex workers' rights activists, as I show in the chapters that follow, struggled to be heard—if silent, they were victims. If they spoke, they weren't representative of victims. Meanwhile, in the Netherlands and Germany, sex workers' rights groups were consulted about the legislation, although less about its implementation. Both models represent ways to incorporate prostitutes into citizenship via the state: liberal-residual welfare regimes such as the United Kingdom's, which privilege incorporation via the market, debated but did not enact prostitution reforms.

Welfare regimes also provide the inclusion roadmap upon which feminists organized. In each country where national prostitution regulation was enacted, the dominant feminist movements were organized in ideological alignment with their welfare state's model of incorporating citizens. Because state bureaucracies recognized certain feminist philosophies over others, a hegemonic "state feminism" gained resources and legitimacy, in stark contrast to the American range of plural feminisms that have had limited impact on state structures.[48] In Germany and the Netherlands this is a commonsense liberal feminism focusing on women's choices to work, while in Sweden and Finland there is an emphasis on national solidarity to eliminate women's oppressions.

As I show in the case study chapters, Finnish and Swedish supporters of sex workers' rights had difficulty being recognized as feminist, just as feminist opposition to prostitution was much less common in the Netherlands and Germany, where feminist NGOs accepted a distinction between free and forced prostitution. These national feminisms parallel the relationship between women and the state that is institutionalized in the welfare protections for vulnerable workers. The liberal feminism[49] in the Netherlands and Germany draws upon the resources of a welfare state that incorporates vulnerable citizens as workers, recognizing prostitution as a form of women's labor that had been unfairly excluded from state protections. Radical feminists of Sweden and Finland, drawing upon the welfare state philosophy that the state must vigorously protect each individual's autonomy, argued that no woman would consent to prostitution if not for the corruption of male violence or unhindered capitalism.[50]

For this book I interviewed policy makers, state agents at the bottom of their respective hierarchies, and community activists outside the state's purview to see how the new prostitution regulations were being implemented at the street level. I also reviewed policy documents and news accounts of prostitution reforms. Though the activists and officials staffed very different organizations with very different purposes, they shared a mission to goad government to protect individuals against the diminution of their autonomy, whether temporary (illness, childhood, imprisonment) or chronic (drug abuse, mental illness, disability, old-age). Prostitutes, for both legalizers and abolitionists, lack autonomy, though for different reasons—either because of the violence done against their gender, or because of their difficult conditions of work. The administrators I interviewed thus justified the new policies as helping to restore autonomy to vulnerable women, implicitly framing the policies in the moral language of vulnerable citizenship.

Doing the Research

In 21 months of fieldwork over nine years, I conducted 100 interviews in Berlin, Frankfurt, Helsinki, Stockholm, Amsterdam, as well as at the EU institutions in Brussels, Belgium. The experts who shared their experiences and viewpoints with me included key government and community figures involved in crafting or managing these policies, such as police, aldermen, bureaucrats, neighborhood organizers, feminist campaigners, and prostitute rights' activists. In these interviews I probed to understand these activists' and administrators' views on: the need to bring prostitution under state control, conflicts over other domestic social problems, and competing visions of prostitution control within the EU. I used these interviews to figure out why it was important to institute a new common sense about prostitution and the source of these new meanings. I also tracked these meanings in a comprehensive analysis of documents including policy proposals, newspaper debates, and organizational reports and newsletters.

I focused on the institutional custodians of social problems,[51] interviewing the elites who shaped the conceptualization of prostitution and framed or implemented the solutions to its problems. These included researchers at state-sponsored institutes, managers of state offices, officials who drafted white papers on behalf of their organizations, and nonprofit organizations working on issues of prostitution and human trafficking. Although the reforms were passed at the national level, they were implemented at the municipal level, and it was municipal controversies that seized lawmaker attention. I describe these broad, national and transnational stories through case studies of individuals who, if not representative in a statistical sense, represent the range of stories told about prostitution in their country. This focus illustrate the complex ways that policy stakeholders interweave personal feelings, organizational duties, and national ideologies in their work.

I conducted the interviews in English, the language of international conferences and international media requests. Only a handful of interviewees were unwilling or uncomfortable being interviewed in English. For those contacts I contracted with translators or, more frequently, was provided a translator by their organization. For example, the city government of Frankfurt provided me with a translator to interview four heads of departments who helped craft that city's red-light district compromise. The willingness of organizations to provide translation assistance to an unknown researcher is evidence of their desire to publicize their viewpoint and philosophy. When I suspected that translators were being directed to edit the statements, I reviewed the tapes afterward with translators of my own.

I posed neutral questions about organizational goals and local events to elicit my interviewees' commonsense understanding of prostitution. I then mirrored interviewees' definition of the situation back to them, avoiding characterizations they opposed. These general conversations about organizational conceptualization strategies provided the manifest content about justifications to regulate prostitution. But these conversations also provided the material from which to draw inferences about participants' conception of persons, citizenship, women, and autonomy, and the proper role for the state and civil society in each. Perceived as an outsider by virtue of my sex, my relative youth, and my nationality, I often played the role of American naif in which I was cast, which invariably led to rich monologues that began with, "what you have to understand about us is . . ." For more on my interviewing methods, see Chapter 9.

I did not set out to interview primarily women, but the day-to-day business of prostitution control and human trafficking prevention is overwhelmingly a woman's realm. Be they civil servants or chiefs of police, prostitutes or politicians, social workers or religious Sisters, it is women who work with, or advocate on behalf of, prostitutes and victims of trafficking. There are many places in which a trafficking victim who decides to prosecute might find herself confronting women at every level, from prosecutor to judge and at every step in between. In Sweden, Finland, Holland, and Germany, prostitution reform is a process that has been driven by women at all levels—the grassroots, the city, the nation, and the transnational organization.

Though academic accounts of human trafficking and migration often invoke "flows" though "space," their programs take place largely in these offices in cities, the coordinating nodes of the movement of capital, goods, people, and ideas.[52] In the two pioneer countries that first rationalized prostitution, the Netherlands and Sweden, I conducted interviews with key actors from the capital cities—Amsterdam and Stockholm. I also drew upon the large existing literature about prostitution policy in these countries. From the wave of countries debating national prostitution reform in early 2001, I selected the two that first sent proposals to parliament, Finland and Germany. In the end, only these two EU countries passed new prostitution legislation by 2013 of the nine that debated them.

The shared milieu of prostitution regulation is reflected in their workplaces. Because NGOs and downsized state agencies depend upon uncertain funding, they live on shoestring budgets that composed the background soundtrack to my interviews: the buzz of fluorescent lights, the scraping of tinny teaspoons in shared IKEA coffee mugs, the raps of routine intrusions into shared office space, the murmur of neighboring conversations through gypsum walls, and the whirring of overworked printers and photocopiers. Thus it is incorrect to say that one or another policy is enacted "on the ground" or "in the international sphere." These groups share parallel territories in physical places, albeit ones with different notions of the good society that must be defended.

Finland and Germany are important cases because their reforms were neither so sweeping nor ideologically pure as their more well-known predecessors. In Finland, I conducted interviews primarily in Helsinki and Turku (Åbo), but also in Tampere and Rovaniemi. As a small country, I was able to interview not only city councillors and parliamentarians, but also government ministers alongside NGO leaders and community activists. Berlin is unique in Germany for licensing brothels almost anywhere within the city, the country's largest. Its policies featured an important détente between social workers and police that was heralded as a national model to address human trafficking.[53] Frankfurt follows the typical German pattern of restricting brothels to "tolerance" zones, though as home to Europe's largest conference center it is also believed to house the highest number of clandestine escorts. It provoked national headlines when a political crisis over the city's red-light district led to a high-stakes roundtable on prostitution. In Germany, I conducted ethnographic observations and interviews primarily in Frankfurt-am-Main and Berlin, but also in Hamburg and Cologne. Focusing on these case studies allowed me to see how two political compromises worked in contrast to the more famous—and ideologically less complicated—cases of Sweden and the Netherlands.

The Chapters That Follow

Chapter 2 describes how prostitution proved a contentious issue just as EU cooperation seemed poised to build on stunning achievements in economic, territorial, and legal unification with unanimity on such social issues as abortion, age of consent, and gay rights.[54] The EU discord over prostitution is a measure of its success at funding a wide range of ideological projects. Groups working to abolish prostitution received EU funds targeted for developing a European transnational civil society, while transnational public health funding has inadvertently bolstered NGOs favoring sex workers' rights. The rise of the EU's so-called third pillar of security and justice that was inaugurated by the 1992 Treaty of Amsterdam highlighted the difficulties of harmonizing criminal law, welfare policies, and immigration. Under these conditions the migrant prostitute emerged as a symbol of vulnerability demanding state protections, a way for national populations to distinguish themselves and their ways of life from their most intransigent opponents: their friends and neighbors. The striking endurance of national ways of doing things despite explicit attempts to harmonize them, embedded in state definitions of vulnerability, distinguishes the consolidation and reinforcement of national identity in the face of European integration. These national identities derailed European unification in 2005 as the proposed constitution was torpedoed; national prostitution reforms also ceased, suggesting that unification was the context for national differentiation.

Chapters 3 through 6 present case studies of prostitution rationalization from the Netherlands, Sweden, Germany, and Finland. Each illustrates the compromises and ambiguities of national prostitution reforms on the ground. In Chapter 3, I talk about how prostitution is one of the issues on which the Dutch are proud that their country is a *gidsland*, an international policy pioneer on issues such as euthanasia, gay rights, and soft drugs. Although tourists could be forgiven for thinking that Dutch brothels had always been legal, it was only 1999 that the Dutch made sex work a legal occupation and permitted working contracts between buyers, sellers, and businesses. Though the Dutch present these reforms as part of an internal process of measured debate, the problems the reforms were designed to address had been identified in the early 1980s, but not acted upon until the late 1990s. Chapter 3 shows that only in the context of mooted EU harmonization for crime, welfare, and migration policies did action occur, framed in the virtuous terms of pragmatism. It is in praise of this national virtue that the Dutch justify their legislation in contentious international meetings, highlighting others' unrealistic ideologies. Pragmatism and consensus are, not coincidentally, enshrined in national welfare law, especially the role of the state in mediating between employers and workers, a model that now applies to sex work as well.

As Chapter 4 notes, when Sweden became the first nation to criminalize the purchase of sex while permitting its sale, it had very little prostitution compared to its neighbors. For Swedes, the law seemed a natural outgrowth of decades of gender equality debates and measures to protect the vulnerable from violence. Yet this law only became relevant when public support for the European project stalled and the Continent seemed particularly deficient in the Swedish virtue of gender equality. Swedes are happy to promote their policy even in the face of fierce criticism because they view their nation as a pioneer in human rights policies that other nations will recognize . . . eventually. Central to their sense of moral leadership is a cradle-to-grave welfare state with comprehensive provisions for gender equality, protections that were finally extended to cover victims of male sexuality as well.

Germany legalized prostitution at the end of 2001, but unlike the Netherlands or Sweden, it did so only after regional court cases rendered old laws untenable. Germans describe their system as the product of virtuous compromise, without reference to the external events that put prostitution on the legislative agenda. Chapter 5 shows that the German system shares with the Dutch the recognition of sex as work, just as their shared corporatist welfare philosophy provides benefits and protections through employment. The German prostitution reform differs from the Dutch in retaining prohibitions against contracts between corporate employers and sex workers, for their own protection. While this distinction between sex as a trade and as a business causes endless headaches for the officials who must implement it, supporters describe it as a necessary virtue of German political consensus.

Though the Finnish Parliament has entertained four bills that criminalize the purchase of sex, Chapter 6 explains why it only criminalized the purchase of sex from victims of exploitation and human trafficking. This compromise with the Swedish model reflects their shared state guarantees of comprehensive gender equality, but foregrounds Finnish national concerns with Russian migrants. Finnish feminists successfully banned prostitution from public spaces, giving police the powers to remove sex workers from street corners and pressuring newspapers to stop carrying sex contact ads. The compromise between feminist idealism was tempered by the realism of a small nation caught between powerful international forces, and for whom the sight of vulnerable Russian prostitutes provoked many emotional reactions, but solidarity was not one of them.

Chapter 7 introduces the metaphor of seeing as a welfare state to make sense of the patterns of similarity and difference among my four case studies. This metaphor tweaks James Scott's well-known phrase by considering the variety of states and the different ways they see. Welfare state scholars, already accustomed to thinking of three "worlds" of states, already think about their guarantees of financial transfers, job protections, and educational policies. I argue that these policies also institutionalize national common sense about the good life and its threats, which is particularly potent regarding proper gender roles or sexual lives. This chapter articulates the book's primary contribution to theories of the state, building on feminist welfare state scholarship, cultural sociology, and political science. I argue that each nation's prostitution debate was consistent with a general cultural repertoire embedded in welfare state *policies* and citizen *expectations*. These form the cultural tools by which citizens make sense of threats that demand state solutions. When citizens see as the state, they are making a necessary virtue out of the tools at hand. That those citizenship tools of welfare policy are not unique to their own countries helps explain patterns of similarity.

Chapter 8 applies the theoretical and empirical insights of the book to contemporary debates about globalization and the state. The international consensus over the problem of human trafficking is surprising given domestic disagreements over its relationship to prostitution. In each of the case studies, officials depict their legislative solution as the natural extension of domestic debates to deal with problems imposed from outside by *neoliberalism* or *globalization*. In fact, problems stemmed in practice from the principled opposition of EU neighbors and other allies. The EU is itself almost a perfect embodiment of the anxieties attributed to globalization: the erosion of the state, the homogenization of national cultures, lost control over domestic politics, and subjugation to a distant, uncaring corporation. Abject stories of transnational victimization are an allegory for domestic anxieties about globalization that bolsters the nation-state's mandate to bind and protect all its citizens from becoming "loose."

2

States of Anxiety: Prostitution Reform as a Symptom of European Integration

Figure 2.0 Fortress Europe: Welcome to Entropy Prostitution reforms only became national issues after the EU began harmonizing immigration, justice and welfare, raising anxieties that integration might lead to isolation and stagnation. Brussels 2005.

Source: author photo

Until 1998, most European countries shared a *de jure* legal frame for prostitution, even if *de facto* regulation on the ground varied from city to city within a country. Prostitution was broadly decriminalized, but laws against the exploitation of prostitutes meant brothels and formal sex businesses were banned.[1] Beginning in 1998, a number of national parliaments took up the issue of prostitution but along divergent policy paths. Some parliaments favored abolishing prostitution, others legalization, and others debated both proposals, including Belgium and the United Kingdom, and policies in between, like Germany and Finland. Why did prostitution become a burning political issue in Europe? Why did so many join the debate about new national prostitution reforms from 1998 to 2004? And why, in the end, did the Netherlands and Germany enact full legalization, while Sweden and Finland enacted abolitionist policies toward prostitution?

The countries that adopted legislation are extremely similar: Northern European countries with secular populations and robust welfare states that prioritize government consultations with all stakeholders to preserve a just and orderly economy. They enacted these policies at a time when they were reaching concord on a host of other contentious issues. As EU members, they had just completed sweeping reforms that harmonized tariffs, abolished internal border controls, and brought their economies into alignment, creating a European single market.[2]

In this chapter, I show that the harmonizing policies of the European Union created a field for conflict over prostitution policy by bringing national elites into closer contact.[3] The 1997 Treaty of Amsterdam, after five years of negotiation, opened EU negotiations for common policies on criminal justice, immigration, and social policy. Until that time, the European project was successfully framed in terms of four freedoms of movement—goods, capital, services, and people. After the euphoria that marked the debut of the Euro currency in 1999, the EU was the object of triumphant books proclaiming "Why Europe Will Run the 21st Century," "The European Dream: How Europe's Vision of the Future Is Quietly Eclipsing the American Dream," and "The United States of Europe: The New Superpower and the End of American Supremacy."[4]

Unnoticed in Brussels during this time was the way the EU came to be seen not as a source of freedom but constraint for national parliaments and, increasingly, their citizens. The prospect of harmonized social welfare and criminal justice provisions added to the sense that nation-states were being eroded, while a "European citizenship" became less desirable and even openly questioned. After the disastrous failure of the European Constitution in 2005, a new spate of books punctuated Europe's deflated optimism: "Euroclash: The EU, European Identity, and the Future of Europe," "The Last Days of Europe: Epitaph for an Old Continent," "What's Wrong with the European Union and How to Fix It," and "After the Fall: The End of the European Dream and the Decline of a Continent."[5] Anxiety and disenchantment, indeed.

It was in this context that EU countries with similar de jure legislation but different de facto norms on prostitution moved to sharply distinguish their policies from their neighbors, lest future EU agreements force them into an unwelcome compromise. The potential expansion of European authority added to the anxieties that Member States were already facing with the fall of the Soviet Bloc, the dramatic influx of migrants from formerly Communist countries, and the sovereignty already transferred to the Union over such key domestic issues as currency control and borders. This coincided with an increase in international attention to human trafficking from the International Labor Organization (ILO) in 1998, the United Nations (UN) in 2000, the Organization for Security and Cooperation in Europe (OSCE) in 2003, and the United States through its State Department's "name and shame" Annual Trafficking in Persons (TIP) Reports starting in 2001.

The EU launched an ambitious new program to harmonize criminal justice and social policies in 1997 that exposed divisions among even the most similar allies. The Treaty of Amsterdam, signed in that year, proposed new common policy areas "freedom, security and justice" to parallel the existing freedoms of currency, customs, and movement. This was to build a "third pillar" of Police and Judicial Cooperation for the Union in addition to the existing two pillars of the European Communities and a Common Foreign and Security Policy, a goal that had been authorized by the 1992 Maastricht Treaty. This third pillar marked a grand attempt to move the EU beyond its economic foundations toward a unified European polity with shared norms of citizenship, with an explicit focus on matters of terrorism, organized crime, and human trafficking. As such, the Treaty of Amsterdam attempted to formalize a kind of supranational citizenship. This included explicit debates about the rights that EU citizens should enjoy, the shared values between European countries, and common ways to define social problems.

One year after the Treaty of Amsterdam was signed, the rush to establish national standards for prostitution began (see Table 2.1). By the time the Treaty came into force in 1999, the Dutch and Swedish parliaments were well on their way to approving their national prostitution reforms. In all, 9 of 15 Member State parliaments debated proposals to create national prostitution regulations by mid-2004.

The consolidation of opposing prostitution policies stymied the EU's movement into any of the areas of social concern it represented—citizenship,

Table 2.1   The European Union Creates the Field for Prostitution Conflict, 1990–2006[1]

1990	The Germanies reunite, the Soviet Union dissolves.
1991	Western European countries experience the beginning of a wave of migration from Eastern Europe and the former Soviet Union.
1993	**The Maastricht Treaty creates the European Union and ambitious new plans for common European border controls, tariff policies, and a European currency.**
	TAMPEP launched to provide health services to migrant prostitutes by the predecessor institution of the EU DG for Health and Consumer Protection.
1995	Sweden, Finland, and Austria join the Union.
	The EU's Schengen Convention takes effect, enacting a common visa policy and eliminating internal border controls within most of the EU.
	The EU launches its "third pillar" program, opening discussions to harmonize social policies, including immigration, justice, and social welfare policies.
1997	**The Treaty of Amsterdam signed, making substantial changes to the organization of the EU including granting the European Parliament increased powers, opening negotiations on a common foreign and security policy, and establishing a common European area of freedom, security, and justice.**
	The EU launches the DAPHNE project to combat violence against women and children, funding anti–human trafficking programs for the first time.
1998	Portugal reforms its prostitution regulations.
	Denmark decriminalizes prostitution.
	The EU STOP project studies Europe-wide coordination on antitrafficking activities.
	The UN's International Labor Organization recognizes sex work.
1999	**The Treaty of Amsterdam comes into force.**
	The Netherlands lifts the ban on brothels, legalizing prostitution as a profession.
	Sweden criminalizes the purchase of sex, defining prostitution as akin to rape.
	Athens passes a municipal brothel ordinance, prompting debates in Greek parliament.
2000	German court rules prostitution "not immoral."
	Helsinki classifies prostitution a public nuisance, along with public urination and allowing the snow to slide off your roof and block public thoroughfares.
	The Euro currency launched in the 11 "Eurozone" members.
2001	Germany legalizes prostitution.
	Finland classifies prostitution a public nuisance.
	Finland stresses antitrafficking during its tenure in the rotating EU presidency.
	US State Department creates the Office to Monitor and Combat Trafficking in Persons, begins publishing its Trafficking in Persons reports (TIPs).

UN's antitrafficking Palermo Protocol adopted, a compromise between EU countries who view it as a vehicle to define all prostitution as human trafficking, and those with legalized prostitution who view it as a tool to fight human trafficking.

2002   Italy proposes legalizing brothels.

Belgian Parliament considers two bills: one to abolish prostitution, the other to legalize it.

2003   France strengthens its antisolicitation ordinances; French prostitutes protest outside the Justice Ministry.

Norway passes a new human trafficking law that includes previous laws against pimping that curtail prostitution business arrangements.

Czech Republic debates legalizing brothels.

The OSCE creates a Special Representative and Coordinator for Combating Trafficking in Human Beings; its first director is Finnish, the second Swedish.

Athens is the target of prostitution protests by the Nordic Council, led by Swedish deputy prime minister.

2004   EU-15 joined by 10 new members, mainly from Central and Eastern Europe

The Nordic Council criticizes Athens for its legal brothels in the run-up to the Olympic games.

Greece debates reforming its prostitution laws.

Scottish Parliament debates prostitution tolerance zones.

British Parliament considers revising its prostitution policies.

Spanish Parliament debates legalization.

Italian Parliament drops abolitionist proposal.

Finland adds criminal trafficking offenses and fines for selling sex in public.

Luxembourg reforms its visa laws, deporting non-EU women working on artists licenses and issuing no new artist visas to non-EU women.

The European Parliament holds hearings on allegations that the international sex industry has improperly influenced members.

Italian Parliament drops prostitution reform.

2005   *EU constitution fails referenda in the Netherlands and France, stalling the Union's expansion into the areas of immigration, justice, and social policy.*

Norwegian Parliament rejects abolitionist bill.

Estonian Parliament drops legalization proposal.

Spanish legalization proposal dropped.

2006   German cities receive international criticism for planning temporary brothels during the World Cup; Swedish Equality Minister demands his nation boycott the World Cup; Germany joins the EU in preparing for an increase in human trafficking that never materializes.

---

[1] Compiled from press sources including the DW, AP, APF, HSIE, and Reuters wire services, the Europa Gateway to the European Union (http://europa.eu/), and (TAMPEP 2005).

law enforcement, gender norms, immigration, and future social policy harmonization. When the EU's Treaty of Amsterdam opened negotiations for a common European citizenship, immigration policy, justice system, and social policy, Member States reacted by bolstering their policies on prostitution. The prostitute distilled all of these concerns: law and order, criminality, the protection of vulnerable citizens, and fears that the lack of internal movement controls would mean an influx of desperate migrants from Eastern Europe. The prostitution debates motivated European states to defend their borders, territorially, socially, and morally. Member States were, in effect, strengthening themselves at the same time the EU was trying to coordinate them and, potentially, assume these powers for itself.

When the Schengen Agreements of 1990 eliminated internal border controls, there were fears that lax enforcement by one Member State would allow an influx of migrants into "blameless" countries with exemplary enforcement. The looming accession of ten new Eastern European members in 2004 only heightened the twin fears that these mostly Central and Eastern European countries would be unable to manage migrants from non-EU countries even as these new EU citizens would use their new freedom of movement to flood into more prosperous labor markets in the old west of Europe.

Popular anxiety over the accession of the new Member States galvanized fears that the EU was overreaching its original economic mandate, these anxieties shifted out of the tacit realm of policy and into the explicit realm, embodied by growing popular dissatisfaction with the proposed constitution for Europe. This stalemate between abolitionist and legalizing nations foreshadowed the breakdown of the European Union's ambitious third pillar expansion that culminated in the spectacular defeat of the proposed European Constitution in 2005. France and the Netherlands decisively rejected it in the spring of 2005. This was a stunning defeat and rejection of the EU's centralization by two of the original six members of the embryonic EU. This marked the end of the EU's dramatic growth—but also a marked decline in pan-European debates on prostitution.

In this chapter, I provide a framework for understanding the role the EU played in Member State prostitution politics. The EU's attempt to consolidate its third pillar exposed the difficulty of promoting a freedom of security. Out of a diversity of ways to talk about prostitution, three main stories emerged: prostitution can be voluntary "sex work"; all prostitutes are victims of "violence against women"; and a story about "trafficked women" that coexists uneasily with the other two. Increased international alarm over human trafficking brings these conflicting national definitions of prostitution into direct conflict. It was precisely the universal agreement that something must be done to help victims of human trafficking, but staunch disagreement about its relationship to prostitution, that upset EU attempts to harmonize policies on migrantion, social welfare, or criminal justice.

Europe: A Field of Social Policy Conflict

The EU, one of the grandest ideas of the twentieth century, is in practice a cumbersome bureaucracy that would give Franz Kafka pause. There is an expansive political-scientific literature on the EU, most of it unremittingly technical and dry. My research draws upon the small number of anthropological and sociological works that focus on the interaction between EU and Member State meanings and institutions.[6]

I think about the EU as a field of social policy, drawing upon the concept of field developed by Pierre Bourdieu.[7] I use his well-articulated theory of social action as the theoretical skeleton on which to assemble the fleshy story of my data. Bourdieu's theoretical framework is less a theory *about* culture than a set of building blocks for understanding and modeling the interrelationship of culture, structure, and action. Bourdieu uses the many meanings of field to elaborate this: a playing field, as of soccer, where conflict and creativity are structured by rules; or a magnetic field, by which participants unconsciously orient themselves toward achieving socially defined goals. It is a forum that brings together policy stakeholders from various Member States, but also from various policy realms, academics, bureaucrats, NGO activists, local officials, European specialists, and lawyers of every stripe. The EU draws these players into a game where it articulates rules for consensus, conflict, and collaboration.

It is productive to think of the EU field of social policy along both of these lines. It is like a playing field where individuals choose sides and then follow the informal but mutually understood rules of international diplomacy to craft consensus and compromise. Though participants draw upon formal skills in this work, just as soccer players have developed ball skills, they are also motivated by internal dispositions. These dispositions are those ingrained habits that motivate players to be risk-takers or not, to their preference for an offensive or defensive stance, or their temperament toward teamwork. These dispositions may feel like instincts or seem to be personality traits, but they are the product of the social environment and thus not as immutable or inherent as those concepts suggest.

For this discussion of the EU social field, it is only necessary to understand that the EU's move into social policy after 1995 created a forum for those national players to deal with each other, as friends or opponents. Individuals brought with them not only their skills and dispositions that were relevant to EU competition, but also the cultures of their respective countries and their everyday occupations—policing, social work, social activism, or bureaucratic administration.

EU programs thus reflect compromises between national positions and the demands of the specific groups who had input into the policy process. Programs contain budgets and rules for their dispersal. These programs can end up directly funding particular policy positions when they give money to researchers to promote their existing expertise— akin to American Congressional earmarks (or "pork"). For example, the responsible minister directed funds for antitrafficking in to STAKES, the Finnish research organization on health and social welfare, to a unit that already had an abolitionist bent. This guaranteed that the Finnish contributions to the European reports would reflect the abolitionist position and gave that research group a higher profile within Finland and Europe. Meanwhile, funds that promoted the health of workers were available from other arms of the European Commission, promoting the sex work perspective in societies where such a view was anathema, supporting as it did the policy of legalizing sex work. For example, Estonia's debates to legalize prostitution were shelved after objections from Sweden, one of the country's largest trading partners and largest sources of individual-country development funds.

EU programs often create semiautonomous bureaucracies that distribute funds at their own discretion, checked only by periodic reauthorization from the EU authority that created them. These are akin to the relationships between the American Congress and the Corporation for Public Broadcasting, the National Endowment for the Arts, or the National Institutes of Health. These institutions acquire offices and administrators of their own, but if they offend policy stakeholders they can find themselves in the middle of contentious politics that seek to curtail their missions or starve them of funds.

The EU funds such a huge array of programs, however, that it is inevitable that some of them are ideologically incompatible or violate one or another Member State's sensibilities. These programs often end up funding contrarian organizations within Member States. This is key because the EU, a forum for conflict and compromise, tacitly funds local-level conflicts within its own Member States. It is also important because most theories about EU civil society focus solely on cooperation without considering how the success of the EU might also be measured by conflict.[8] The next section shows how the unintended consequences of EU antitrafficking and public health programs have been to fund a wide array of NGOs that conflict with each other *and* their own countries' new national prostitution reforms.

The EU: Funding the (Dis)loyal Opposition

The EU is *such* a decentralized collection of authorities and governs *such* a huge diversity of interests that it is remarkable it makes any forward progress at all. Chief among its entities are the legislative body of the European Parliament; the executive body of the European Commission with one representative per member; and the European Council, composed of the prime ministers of each state. The commissioners, one for each Member State, lead ministerial authorities such as "Fisheries," "Justice and Home Affairs," or "Trade." The commissioners are supposed to be loyal solely to the EU, but they are also the sole representatives of their country in the most exclusive and powerful EU body. These cabinet-type bureaucracies, known as "Directorates General" (DGs), each fund their own short- and long-term projects. Given the divided loyalties of the commissioners—to their Member State, their DG area of authority, and the EU itself—it is unavoidable that projects receive funds that are opposed by individual Member States, just as some projects are regaled as a particular triumph for a single country or a couple of close allies that are not to other states' liking.

In particular, the DGs fund a wide range of NGOs to foster international dialogue and build linkages for a Europe-wide civil society. The diametrically opposed philosophical camps in prostitution policy are reflected in the two different NGO factions that both received EC funding. NGOs with an abolitionist ideology were often funded by the then-named DGs of "Employment and Social Affairs" and "Justice and Home Affairs" under the aegis of programs to promote gender equality and human rights. Abolitionist NGOs used this money to lobby against state-recognized prostitution in favor of programs that link prostitution to violence against women and human trafficking.

NGOs that worked directly with prostitutes, on the other hand, are staffed by activists who support decriminalization and were almost always antiabolitionist. These NGOs receive money from the DGs for Employment and Social Affairs, but also from "Health and Consumer Affairs." These DGs also fund projects for public health outreach, AIDS education, legal advice centers for migrants, and projects that worked directly with prostitutes themselves and reflect the antiabolitionist sentiment of their staffers.

The complexity of the EU's nested authorities and funding caused monies to be dispersed to organizations that dissent from the Member States' new prostitution reforms. But even projects that receive universal acclaim, such as those that fight human trafficking, are not immune from controversy. The appearance of international consensus over the evils of human trafficking are belied by the range of projects to combat it, ranging from those that help non-EU migrant prostitutes to those that beef up border controls to keep them from entering in the first place. Three projects support the existence of an EU field of social policy and its ability to create both consensus and conflict over the issue of prostitution: DAPHNE, STOP, and TAMPEP. I also profile the European Women's Lobby and its support for the work of one member of the European Parliament (MEP), Marianne Eriksson of the Swedish Left Party, to highlight the conflict between EU funding, NGOs, and national interests.

The STOP Program

The STOP program, one of the legacies of Sweden's first EU Commissioner Anita Gradin, was launched in 1995 by the DG of Justice and Home Affairs as the EU's first program to specifically target human trafficking, building upon the work of DAPHNE. It funded projects in seven EU countries to create networks of helping organizations in both sending and receiving countries. Both NGOs and government agencies were eligible for the funds. STOP is a good example of how the concept of human trafficking is so broad that it encompasses opposing definitions of prostitution and funds organizations who are ideologically opposed to each other.

In Finland, STAKES and Pro-tukipiste are two organizations that frequently clashed over Finnish prostitution policy; both received STOP funds. STAKES is the acronym of the Finnish National Research Institute for Health and Welfare, a large government agency that is roughly the equivalent of both the United States' National Institutes of Health and National Institutes of Mental Health. Pro-tukipiste is the City of Helsinki's Prostitutes' Help Center and one of the only openly antiabolitionist organizations in Finland. Although they are ideological opposites, both used STOP monies in similar ways: to fund research and build networks across borders, especially with neighboring countries.

The Finnish minister who held the portfolios for Women and Health and Social Welfare, Eva Biaudet, directed STAKES to create the "Programme" for the Prevention of Prostitution and Violence against Women, a project that signaled its definition of prostitution quite clearly in the tite. The program received STOP funds, as did research by the Ministry of the Interior to assess the amount of trafficking in and through Finland.[9] Minister Biaudet went on to advocate for DAPHNE reauthorization, citing the Programme as a model project for other European countries, and approved and promoted as exemplary European projects Finland's first woman president, Tarja Halonen.[10]

While the Ministry of the Interior project was relatively independent, the STAKES Programme was headed by self-described radical feminists whose activities were criticized by another official as "not really research, just pure ideology." The researchers from the Programme were prominent in advocacy on behalf of Swedish-style abolition in Finland, with close ties to leading feminist organizations in both countries. STAKES funded an international conference to problematize the role of the clients in prostitution, attracting primarily researchers from other Nordic countries.[11] This group helped prepare materials used by Finnish government officials to raise human trafficking concerns during their six-month tenure in the rotating EU presidency.

As part of the Finnish presidency of the EU, STAKES convened the EU Experts Meeting on Violence against Women, which specifically linked prostitution to violence against women and human trafficking. In her opening remarks of the conference, Minister Biaudet was unequivocal in her desire to build a Nordic consensus along Swedish abolitionist lines:

> According to Nordic thinking, prostitution and trafficking in women form an essential but many times neglected manifestation of violence against women . . . in order to prevent prostitution, it is vital to understand and rearrange the social and cultural patterns and structures that perpetuate the sex/trade. Clients, procurers and indirect profiteers need to be targeted. Preventive actions and control have to be directed to this "invisible" side of the sex industry.[12]

Like much of the Programme's work, Minister Biaudet's language uses the same ideological framework as the Swedish legislation. It blames the invisibility of prostitution on an invisible sex industry. It places the blame for prostitution upon the demand on men because women are victims. And it equates all prostitution with violence against women and human trafficking.

When the Organization for Security and Cooperation in Europe (OSCE) created an antitrafficking post in 2003, Eva Biaudet was recognized for her European leadership on the issue with her appointment to be its first special representative. The second was Kajsa Wahlberg, deputy director of Sweden's National Bureau of Investigation, whose work is profiled in Chapter 4.

Their ideological opposite was the NGO Pro-tukipiste, Helsinki's Prostitutes' Help Center. As of the only openly antiabolition organizations in the country, its director was frequently interviewed in the media and represents a contrarian view to the government proposals to curtail prostitution. Pro-Tukipiste received its initial funding and start-up expertise from the Deaconess Institute, the social service arm of the Finnish

Lutheran Church. It later branched out to become an independent NGO, though still enjoying a closer relationship to its religious sister organization in social work.

Pro-tukipiste also received funds from the STOP project as part of its leadership of the Meritähti (Starfish) project. It crafted this project in coordination with other Prostitutes' Help Centers in Tallinn, Estonia, and St. Petersburg, Russia. These three cities, linked for centuries, also constituted basic building blocks of migration between Estonia. As the only EU-15 Member State with a border with Russia, Finland's Pro-tukipiste was granted STOP project funding for Meritähti to gain information about migrant prostitution and create awareness programs to prevent exploitation in the migration process. By forging a network with sister organizations in the other two cities from which most Helsinki migrant prostitutes depart, Pro-Tukipiste was able to gain valuable insights and credibility for its claims that it understood the migrant sex networks better than organizations or individuals that did not have a presence "on the ground" in the Baltic. When conflicting with the STAKES researchers and Finland's senior politicians, Pro-tukipiste and Meritähti framed its experience as a necessary corrective to the ideological purity of politicians.

The DAPHNE Program

Founded at the behest of Sweden's first EU commissioner, Anita Gradin, the DAPHNE project began disbursing funds in 1997 for "research and action in favor of Europe's most vulnerable citizens" (DG for Freedom, Security, and Justice 2007). DAPHNE funds research on domestic violence, reducing bullying in schools, and awareness campaigns on the sexual exploitation of women and children. Some of this research goes to academic researchers, but some is conducted by NGOs and government organizations. DAPHNE also funds the general operations of some of these NGOs.

Men are not targets of any DAPHNE programs unless they are children or otherwise dependent, reflecting the particular gendered perspective on violence that the program institutionalizes (see Figure 2.1). In the posters, exploitation is connected to the social isolation of women, the cure for which is consciousness-raising. About one-third of DAPHNE's initial activities were dedicated to prostitution and human trafficking.

DAPHNE's roots in social democratic values of gender equality can be seen in the story of its founding. This incompatibility of prostitution with gender equality can be seen in the work of a woman who helped put prostitution on the EU agenda. Anita Gradin is a formidable grande dame of Swedish Social Democratic Party politics and a key player in European

Figure 2.1   DAPHNE Project Poster Portraying Women as Victims

Source: http://ec.europa.eu/anti-trafficking, accessed May 1, 2008

politics for both women and Sweden. Of her time in the pan-European human rights body, she described pride in being a feminist path breaker:

> When I was in the Council of Europe I was told there was this whispering in the halls, warnings that you must be careful around these Nordic women because some of them may come back as Ministers. And I did! <nodding *just so*>.

After holding many party and Ministerial posts, she was appointed Sweden's first EU commissioner when it acceded in 1995, assuming the prestigious portfolio of Justice and Home Affairs. There she showed herself to be a consummate statecrafter, mobilizing the EU machinery, NGOs, and INGOs to create programs for trafficked women while simultaneously inspiring domestic politics back home. Even in retirement, she still consulted informally on political matters and served on the board of directors for Kvinnoforum, a prominent feminist think tank that receives most of its funds from the state.

When we sat down she launched into a helpful, well-rehearsed sketch of her background in "equality issues" that lasted for 20 minutes. My first question was about her role putting human trafficking on the European Agenda as an EU commissioner. She explained:

> Now, back when I joined the commission in 1995 was when the third pillar of justice and home affairs and these questions of migration and harmonization were just being taken up, and I pressed to "put trafficking on the agenda" then, and of course it was a struggle. Many of my colleagues, especially my male colleagues I must say, said that there are no problems, this is not a problem, we do not have these problems. And my law department said that I have no legal basis for considering this, it is not in my purview. But I said this is ridiculous. If the EU is taking up cross-border issues like crime—if this international slave trade, as I call it, is not cross border crime I don't know what is! <looking severely over the rims of her glasses>.

She frames her struggle both in gendered terms—men do not recognize the existence of an international slave trade—and institutional ones—the government's EU legal advisors did not think she had the authority to act on this matter.

Commissioner Gradin described the difficulties of establishing a coordinated EU migration policy as preventing a real solution to human trafficking. She interrupted her account with a digression about voluntary prostitutes who she characterized as unworldly and naive:

> *AG:* Of course there are women who knew what they would be doing, that knew they were coming to work here in prostitution, but they told me that they didn't know this was going to be a question of life or death! Or they thought they would be paid when they got here, yes, they thought they would be paid! Not to end up like slaves with their papers taken and put in a flat and locked tight. No, they thought this was going to be working like in their own country. And the ones I talked to, most of them want to go home. And the IOM [International Organization for Migration] has experience with these return programs to make it so the pimps are not able to reach them again. <pauses thoughtfully>
> You know, then I was in Amsterdam, this must have been in the late 80s or so, I talked to some prostitutes there and I have to tell you I did not find them convincing, no, not convincing at all.
> *GM:* Convincing?

AG: That they were happy to sell themselves to men for money. And what, now can you earn enough money before you are 35 to have a pension that is going to support you for the rest of your life? That you are not going to be put in danger of violence or turn to drugs or alcohol to deal with all of this violence? No, they did not convince me that this is a happy life at all.

For Commissioner Gradin, women are naive to think that prostitution can lead to independence. Prostitution is inherently violent and unfair, ruled by pimps and slaveholders. If women who believe prostitution can provide autonomy are a bit "mad," women who remain in prostitution voluntarily are "sad," living unhappy lives of addiction and victimization. Sex work is an oxymoron in such grave conditions. The European commissioner responsible for the very un-Swedish separation of prostitution from human trafficking did so out of political necessity, not some conviction of their distinctiveness.

Ms. Gradin's work exemplifies the social democratic disposition advocating gender equality and solidarity and Sweden's push to "Swedify Europe" through its EU membership. Faced by a row of "faceless men in gray suits" at the EU, she used her lifetime of professional equality expertise in Sweden to make the EU work for the most vulnerable women in its borders. She brought together political agencies at all levels to support the creation of her two programs that adhered to key Swedish policy goals of gender-targeted programs to rescue victims of prostitution. That this required a compromise with "pro-prostitution" forces within the EU was a regrettable but necessary political act that advanced the larger goal of cultivating Swedish values within the bureaucracies of Europe. No politician before or since had done as much to place human trafficking on the international political agenda. Her creation of the DAPHNE program benefited not only victims of human trafficking, European gender egalitarianisms, but also the Swedish way of seeing the world that generated it. After its first one-year run, it was extended to a full four-year term as DAPHNE II. In 2005, it relaunched as DAPHNE III, a semipermanent program within the DG of Justice and Home Affairs. This ceremonial milestone was marked by its first logo so that DAPHNE recipients around Europe could identify themselves to each other and to their constituencies as part of a successful EU program (see Figure 2.2). The DAPHNE project is permeated with abolitionist sentiment, not least by generally ignoring men as part of its definition of vulnerability. The project received its name, the website explained,

> Because in ancient Greek mythology, DAPHNE was a pure, innocent young woman pursued by the god Apollo who had fallen in love with her. Desperate to fend off Apollo's sexual advances, DAPHNE called upon her father, the river god Peneus, to help her. As Apollo touched her, the god turned DAPHNE into a laurel bush, *DAPHNE* in Greek.[13]

Figure 2.2　Logo of the DAPHNE Project, 2005　The DAPHNE project received an official logo when the program was relaunched in 2005.

Source: http://ec.europa.eu/anti-trafficking, accessed Nov 20, 2005

This statement, by the then-named directorate general for freedom (which included criminal justice), recalls the projects name as one in which a woman in distress is given protection and literal roots.

The logo's use of the EU colors were intended to "recall the colors of the European emblem and, with the stars of the European emblem, remind us that DAPHNE projects are European projects, working across national borders to identify common problems and common solutions facing the region." And the "d" resembling a ball of wool or string is meant to evoke how its "projects are organized around making links, prompting networking across countries, across sectors and between people, but also suggesting that problems can be unraveled and a way out can be found."[14]

The DAPHNE project's name symbolizes its good intentions, but they do not live up to expectations when it comes to helping victims of human trafficking. Non-EU citizens who are helped by DAPHNE-funded programs are often repatriated to their country of origin, not given roots within the EU as the Greek legend suggests. Indeed, one of the perennial complaints of NGOs who work with victims of trafficking is the lack of EU or Member State residency permits that would allow victims to stay in the EU. This concern was not addressed when the European Parliament renewed DAPHNE in 2007 through 2013.

TAMPEP

While STOP and DAPHNE were programs that came out of the EU power over justice and security, TAMPEP is a program created by the EC Health and Consumer Affairs DG. Founded in 1997 as the "Transnational AIDS/STI Prevention among Migrant Prostitutes in Europe Project," it is currently the largest project that serves prostitutes' welfare that receives EU funding.

TAMPEP strives to be accessible to prostitutes from diverse ethnic and racial nbackgrounds with programs that engage prostitutes as more than just organizational clients, but as research and goal-setting partners. This made them increasingly controversial as abolitionist forces within the EU began to question its existence. Licia Brussa has been the head of the TAMPEP foundation since its incorporation and is a widely published expert on European migrant prostitution.[15]

TAMPEP funded the creation of a network of prostitutes' help centers across Europe to share information and best practices. TAMPEP also specifically focused on the plight of migrant prostitutes, highlighting their difficulties with both advocacy and an active network of academic researchers.[16] Their advocacy was criticized by abolitionist researchers as exacerbating and facilitating human trafficking.[17] Many of these projects were loosely associated with prostitutes' rights organizations, whether formally or informally, and reflected a pro-sex work and antiabolitionist bias of workers who were directly involved with the practical concerns of prostitutes. This included Helsinki's Pro-Tukipiste, which eventually joined the network and received funds from the project, helping sustain its mission— and a voice of dissent within Finland against the criminalization of male clients of female prostitutes.

In the Netherlands, Bonded Labor in the Netherlands (BlinN) was the TAMPEP representative, headed by Sandra Claasen. As she explains, this provides the Netherlands with information about how and why migrant prostitutes are coming to the country:

> As TAMPEP is an international network, they are doing some monitoring. They have been following 200 women who have been working in sex work in Bulgaria: how many have been working abroad, how many would like to be . . . But they come and go and come and go.

Such information is important for understanding what services migrants need:

> If they want to return to their country of origin for us what is very difficult is we don't know what happens to them if they go because we lose contact. We are starting a project . . . to see what happens when women get from Western Europe back to their home countries so we can see what we can do in terms of education, vocational training that provides more possibilities for them when they return. For the Netherlands the difficult thing is that they have to return, in Spain there are more possibilities to stay as a labor migrant.

When working with a migrant population, having ties to an EU-funded network provides local service providers important information.

The work BLinN does, in part with TAMPEP funds, addresses European-wide concerns about human trafficking but also poses a challenge to Dutch law and policy. This "internal dissent" is one of the ways that EU funding causes conflict within countries. As Claasen explains BlinN's critiques of Dutch antitrafficking legislation:

> We did some research on foreign intervention centers on human trafficking there are some that should not be there but there are others that might be victims but they don't want to press charges and then Dutch legislation doesn't offer them any more possibilities. But for us because they are already in detention for deportation doesn't mean that we can't anymore do anything to help her upon her return or if she gets out. It's difficult, because you don't want to be part of some machinery of deportation but you also have to face reality and help these women who are part and inform them and inform staff of deportation centers about issues of human trafficking.

In other words, the tension between state funding and its priorities for border control can conflict with EU priorities of serving vulnerable populations.

BlinN's work stands in stark contrast to the goals of the DAPHNE program, from which it received no funds, focused as it was on the exploitation of labor migrants in general and not women in particular. As I show in Chapter 3, this focus on labor is a hallmark of Dutch society. Indeed, BlinN changed its name in 2011 to FairWork, "dedicated to a slavery-free Netherlands."

The European Network for Male Prostitution was the first EU-funded project to focus specifically on male prostitutes and their health needs. It was founded by a male sex worker help project in the Netherlands and, with funding from a Dutch AIDS Foundation and the DG for Health and Consumer Protection, expanded to network male sex worker projects in 24 countries. In 2004 the project was merged with TAMPEP, in part because of Swedish objections to the project's goals, its funding, and the participation of a Swedish NGO in the network.

When subsequent controversies overcame other EU AIDS prevention projects for male prostitutes and marginal citizens, they were folded into TAMPEP. These included the European Network for Male Prostitutes (ENMP) and the European Project for AIDS Prevention (EUROPAP). TAMPEP's advocacy networks were strong enough to resist calls for its elimination, as it absorbed the staff and missions of the other projects.

The European Women's Lobby

The European Women's Lobby (EWL) is the umbrella feminist organization funded by the European Union, with national chapters in 28

European countries and 19 Europe-wide organizations. It receives 80 percent of its funds from the DG for Employment, Social Affairs, and Equal Opportunities. Although it is meant to be an umbrella for all feminist organizations in Europe, in practice it serves as a clearinghouse for radical feminists who equate prostitution with human trafficking (see Figure 2.3).

The EWL is closely allied with the US-based Coalition Against Trafficking in Women (CATW), a self-described radical feminist organization that was involved in drafting the United Nations Palermo Protocol and helped the Bush administration draft the 2005 Trafficking Victims Protection Act. The EWL provides a European ally for American efforts to oppose the legalization of prostitution and promote a definition of human trafficking that equates it to prostitution. CATW's main international antagonist is the Global Alliance Against Trafficking in Women (GAATW) based in Bangkok; Sanda Claasen of BlinN is a member of its governing board.

The EWL is a frequent voice in debates across a range of European institutions in support of abolitionist prostitution policies and definitions that link prostitution to violence against women, gender inequality, and human trafficking. It supports organizations that dissent from the legalization regulations in the Netherlands and Germany, including Catholic organizations with whom it shares few other sympathies except the protection of women from prostitution. In addition, it cooperates with international organizations to provide a European face for abolitionism at international organizations including OSCE, the ILO, and the UN. Through its support of the European Women's Lobby, the EU ensures that abolitionists have a strong voice, both in Brussels and in each Member State

Figure 2.3   European Women's Lobby Campaign against Prostitution The European Women's Lobby (EWL) supports an abolitionist stance toward prostitution

Source: http://www.womenlobby.org, Accessed Dec 30, 2012

In 2002, Swedish Member of the European Parliament (MEP) Marianne Eriksson convened hearings in conjunction with the EWL to discuss a report that investigated "what influence the advocates of the sex industry exert through lobbying on the institutions of the EU, whether as individuals or in the form of organizations, businesses, projects or other groups."[18] This followed her 1997 proposal to criminalize the clients of prostitutes throughout the EU, which earned her scorn in the European Parliament (EP) but plaudits at home, coming as it did two years before the Swedish law against sex purchasing. As she made clear, Sweden's view is diametrically opposed to that of countries that legalize prostitution:

> "What differentiates us from the Netherlands and Germany, for example, is that we link this 'slave trade' with prostitution, and even pornography," says Marianne Eriksson. "Everyone in the EU is against human trafficking, of course, but we make the assumption that prostitution is never 'voluntary.'"[19]

This explicit contrast between Sweden and its EU partners highlights the stark contrast between their policies once human trafficking programs brought them into conflict.

Eriksson's report followed years of debate within the EP's Committee on Women's Rights and Equal Opportunities, which had previously refused to commission such a report. Eriksson's report criticized many of the projects funded by the EC, including TAMPEP. It concluded that while "legislation on prostitution is a matter for the national governments," because it "affects the fight against trafficking . . . it is therefore crucially important to take up the question of prostitution for discussion at the European level too."[20]

In 2004, Eriksson convened hearings "on the consequences of the sex industry in the European Union." Her initial Draft Report included a motion for a European Parliament Resolution that claimed Member States had "capitulated" to the market:

> In recent years, several of the EU Member States have capitulated and, instead of fighting against such exploitation of human beings, have accepted the prevailing situation and, through legalization and regulation of prostitution, have helped to make what was previously a criminal activity part of the legal economic sector. **The Member State then becomes part of the sex industry** [emphasis in original], yet another profiteer on the market. (2004)

Further dramatizing European dissent over prostitution, Eriksson's Draft Report explicitly blames Germany and the Netherlands for the exploitation they say they are ameliorating, implicating them as legal pimps profiteering from the exploitation of human beings

Testimony presented at the hearings echoed this view. Janice Raymond, the American Co-Executive Director of the Coalition against Trafficking in Women, whose work is frequently cited by the US State Department, averred:

> The normalization of sexual exploitation has been greatly enhanced by the legalization/decriminalization of the sex industry in various countries in Europe. Legalization has been a gift to traffickers and pimps who, overnight, become legitimate businessmen. Prostitution becomes a public good and governments derive enormous revenues from its legal legitimation. Legalization, or what we call State-sponsored prostitution, has become . . . normalized in [the] E.U.[21]

If the speakers linked globalization and the legalization of prostitution to rape, sexual addiction, and human trafficking, they blame states for exacerbating the problems by supporting them.

The hearings also stimulated a vigorous defense of the EU programs under attack. TAMPEP researchers, in particular, converged on Brussels to testify on behalf of migrant prostitutes and from the position of social workers with actual knowledge of prostitutes' needs, as distinguished from utopian or ideological politics that were just not practical. One research recast Finland and Sweden's abolitionist approach to prostitution as migration restriction. These restrictions do not protect women, she argued, but put them at increased risk while providing no programs for their support:

> Restrictive migration legislation means that women need so-called "third parties" in order to enter, or to participate in, the migration process. This makes them an easy target for dependency and exploitation, and—the worst-case scenario—for trafficking . . . the debate on trafficking in women should, in fact, be a debate about labor migration and human rights. States should investigate violations and punish the perpetrators, but / should also provide effective assistance to trafficked persons.[22]

Her view was echoed by other researchers who called for funds to help victims, not punish them with delusions of the ability to control prostitution by controlling migrant prostitutes.

The one-sided nature of the hearing's purpose, with its calculated insults to Member States that had legalized prostitution, was ill-designed to craft any sort of consensus on the relationship between prostitution and human trafficking. The response that it generated, with counteraccusations that abolition is the cause of harm to the most vulnerable women, was similarly ill-suited to compromise. The result was a media sensation that received wide coverage within the EU and back in Member States, where political posturing was widely interpreted as defending domestic "reason" against "unreasonable" allies and a fractious EU. The most measurable impact of the hearings was the promotion of the Swedish model as the gold standard of abolitionist legislation, and the consolidation of Marianne Eriksson's status as the premier champion of women's rights in the EP, at least among abolitionists in favor of the criminalization of male clients.

The EU: A Field of National Distinction

If the EU is conventionally seen as a forum for transnational cooperation, it is also a field of competition where states distinguish themselves from their neighbors. The next four chapters are case studies of the first four countries to enact these national prostitution reforms. My interviewees describe how their state has implemented a commonsense reform based on modest improvements, common sense that nevertheless diverges wildly from its neighbors. But by creating a forum where Member State policies are debated, the EU also created a forum for national distinction. When stakeholders describe their country's prostitution policy or best practice in combating trafficking, they are simultaneously criticizing competing systems of social control. For the Dutch, Germany's system is hopeful but unorganized; Sweden's an unmitigated disaster. For the Germans, the Netherlands system of legalization tolerates too much criminality while Sweden's actually creates criminality by driving prostitution underground. For Finnish abolitionists, the Swedish system is an ideal that they cannot attain, even though they set the terms of the debate so effectively that prostitution legalization was hardly thinkable. For many Germans unhappy with their compromise, the Dutch model is also an unattainable ideal, even as the supporters of Dutch sex workers declined to support legalization because of its lack of support for migrant sex workers.

The shared symbol of the pan-European debate about prostitution reform was thus ambivalent: Was she a migrant or a citizen? Poor or rich? A slave or free? This debate was solved by a bifurcation in the discourse about prostitution itself. Stories of prostitution, which had been many-voiced before, increasingly became one of three tropes: sex work by choice, prostitution as inherent violence against women, and a tacit truce over the exploitation of human trafficking.

The articulation of sexual exploitation to women's migration figured in national debates by separating prostitution from migration. Migrant prostitution, which does not assume the degree of freedom or exploitation in a given case, thus lost out to human trafficking, by which all migrant prostitution became an inherent evil to be combated domestically and internationally. This human trafficking discourse served several purposes.

It provided a humanitarian reason to deport sex workers—those migrant prostitutes who insisted upon their desire to sell sex in EU countries whether they legalized or abolished prostitutes. They could easily be redefined as victims of human trafficking and "repatriated" to countries of origin. Most important, it redefined women's migration as inherently connected with danger and sexual exploitation.

The 1995, EU focus on common border security was demonized by European social justice groups as "Fortress Europe." As the photograph on the title page of this chapter suggests, immigration advocates believed that hard borders to Europe would cause lost flexibility, innovation, and dynamism. Human trafficking researchers assembled evidence that restrictive border policies cause harm to migrants by making the process more expensive, more dangerous, and less transparent.[23] It is unclear, then, whether the increased demand for smuggling and trafficking into the EU is due to an increased rate of migration or a hardening of the European frontier due to the Schengen Accords.[24] This debate paralleled the American debate over the source of harm on the United States–Mexico border: exploitative smugglers, or the hardened border itself.

At the time there was also little concrete evidence that trafficking conduits differ in substantive ways than ordinary circuits of transnational migration. Ethnographic and legal researchers who tried to locate "victims of trafficking" in its early days concluded that while terrible human rights abuses occur elsewhere, it was not occuring among women migrating to or through countries ranging from Turkey, Finland, Indonesia, the Netherlands, the Dominican Republic, Israel, Germany, or between the Philippines and Belgium.[25]

What is interesting about this research is the degree to which it parallels the White Slavery debates of 100 years ago. Researchers today find little evidence that White Slavery occurred on anything like the scale envisioned by fin de siècle Progressives. One legal sociologist dismisses white slavery as a "myth," while a social historian concludes from archival records that less than 10 percent of prostitutes were drawn from white slavery, conclusions that have been echoed in more recent studies.[26]

Research on contemporary human trafficking in Europe is similarly unreliable. Estimates of the number of trafficking victims into the EU as of May 2004 ranged from 50,000 to 700,000 per year. Scant evidence exists that trafficking is any way different from ordinary chain migration, by which migrants follow their fellow community members based on personal ties. Nor is there systematic evidence that migration for prostitution is monopolized by organized crime. This lack of evidence in specific cases does little to call the very concept of human trafficking into question, however. Descriptions of contemporary migration as "feminized" merely describe a parity in global migration between women and men. Human trafficking discussions in Europe rarely mention the possibility of male victims in the migration process, focusing on female exploitation in domestic labor and "the sex industry."[27]

As a concept, human trafficking is useful for both abolitionists and prostitution legalizers, a point to which I return in Chapter 8. It provides a site of agreement for opposing definitions of prostitution. It allows states to strengthen their borders in a stated attempt to rescue trafficking victims before they enter their countries, with the added side benefit of being able to monitor migration and crime in general. And it is a potentially unlimited source of public motivation because there is always the fear that pervasive trafficking rings have not been detected because they are too wily, too far "underground," or too powerful to be captured. This anxiety justifies increased powers for the state[28]—and the EU—just as it did 100 years ago.

How the "Social Problem" Sabotaged the "Social Dimension"

Prostitution, which became such a charged issue in the nineteenth century that it was euphemistically defined as "*the* social problem," thus sabotaged the EU's expansion into the "social dimension" of policies on welfare, migration and criminal law. Anxiety over external threats to the nation became articulated to disenchantment with the EU. The divergence in Member State prostitution policies was a powerful challenge to the European Commission's (EC) goal to coordinate Member State social policies or craft a coherent antitrafficking strategy. The problem is that the trafficking construct, which combines migration policy over which the EU has competency, and social policy over which it does not, may threaten the Common Market at the core of the Union. A report warned:

> The risk of compartmentalizing the internal market could justify the use of [an article to impose trade sanctions against a Member State] in such a situation . . . this example is not pure fantasy given the increasingly different approaches adopted by Member States as regards prostitution. (E. U. Network of Independent Experts in Fundamental Rights 2003, 14–15)

These "excessively different levels of protection for fundamental rights" further jeopardize "the mutual trust States have for each other" (28). What the EC approach misses is that it is not different *levels* of protections for fundamental rights that undermines mutual understanding, but different *conceptions* of those rights and the proper way to protect them.

3

Dutch Pragmatism and the Difficulties of Professionalizing Prostitution

Figure 3.0   Red Light Districts Are for Everyone Amsterdam's red light district is proudly featured on souvenirs and official tourist information.

Source: author photo

The Dutch explain their prostitution policies as the virtue of the cultural values they prize: a pragmatic regulated tolerance and the sense of being a *gidsland*, a global moral leader. These explanations are insightful because they dramatize the cultural values prized by Dutch citizens, but they miss some taken-for-granted ways in which Dutch citizenship helps explain the particular policy choice of legalized prostitution. This chapter shows the ways in which Dutch stakeholders explain prostitution legalization as the product of *gedogen* and a *gidsland* in the context of competing ways of doing things within Europe. I highlight, however, the ways in which labor is a core value of Dutch citizenship that makes professionalizing prostitution make sense as a method of controlling, and its abolition naive (see Table 3.1).

Seeing Transparency in Amsterdam

Visitors to Amsterdam in the decades before the 1999 legalization of brothels could be forgiven for thinking that prostitution had always been legal in the Netherlands. The *De Wallen* red-light zone is in the heart of the city, encircling the medieval cathedral *Oude Kerk* and steps from one of Europe's busiest train stations.[1] Scantily clad women of all sizes, ages, and races aggressively beckoned from red-lit windows, confounding assumptions that stationary women were passive, or that only men could be sexual hunters.[2] Though foreigners had long interpreted De Wallen's brazenness

Table 3.1 Dutch Prostitution Reform Timeline

1981	Government begins funding the Foundation against Trafficking in Women (STV —*Stichting tegen Vrouwenhandel*); the first country to do so.
1988	STV convinces the Justice Ministry to issue visas to victims of human trafficking, the first nation to do so.
1992	Parliament passes legislation against human trafficking; first country to do so.
1994	Dutch Association of Municipalities (VNG) issues model bylaws for municipal prostitution regulation.
1999	Legislation lifts the ban on brothels, permitting contracts between sex workers and sex business operators (*exploitants*).
2001	European Court of Justice rules that the Netherlands cannot restrict EU nationals from the prostitution market because legal work is open to all EU citizens.
2007	Dutch government issues a largely critical assessment of the law.
	Statue installed in the Amsterdam red-light district to commemorate sex workers.
2008	Amsterdam mayor's office proposes shuttering brothel windows to reduce their concentration in the historic red-light district.
2009	Dutch Justice Ministry orders 320 window brothels closed to eliminate criminality.

and prominent police patrols as legalization, the window brothels existed in a gray area of the law. Officially forbidden, they were municipally tolerated, first informally through police practices and later through city ordinances that were technically in violation of national legislation against pimping.

Tourist agencies funneled busloads of American, German, and Japanese retirees into the narrow alleys where the spectators become part of the street show, pointing and laughing at each others' facial expressions that betrayed disgust, surprise, or shock. Packs of young men tumbled out of the plentiful bars, sex shops, and marijuana-vending "brown cafes," while gay men alone or in duos strolled between gay bars, some catering to the rough leather scene. Festive hurrahs from strangers greeted an embarrassed man who slid out of a window brothel still tucking in his shirt. A group of Spanish nuns attracted more attention than the prostitutes as they slowed for their Sister in a wheelchair, a beatific smile lighting her face. This festival atmosphere makes it the kind of place you could take your mother—as I have.

Indeed, until 2008—a year that is a key inflection point in the implementation of Dutch prostitution legalization—the red-light district was promoted on national and city tourist sites as one of the places that tourists must experience to understand the Dutch way of life. Where other cities might be content to let the sleeping dogs of vice lie, Amsterdam groomed them for show. De Wallen was featured on the National Bureau of Tourism and Conventions (NBTC) website as one of the city's "quaint districts" that is a safe and historic part of the city, urging visitors to go "to a place you wouldn't normally want to be seen" to appreciate "some of the most beautiful buildings in Amsterdam."[3] Indeed, above the scarlet neon windows are the seventeenth-century plaques that, before mass literacy, served as addresses and sometimes clues to the family names or occupation of the original inhabitants: "house of the black swan" or "house of the red schooner." The NBTC site directed tourists to the neighborhoods' "unusual shops and interesting pubs," blithely noting that these are located alongside the infamous

> *Deutsche Brucke* (German Bridge). This bridge owes its name to the many German heroin prostitutes who work here. Some advice: if you visit the red light district do not bring your camera. Taking photos is not prohibited, however, it is far from appreciated.

This tourist site has made Amsterdam synonymous with prostitution for generations of tourists, international businessmen, bachelor party planners, and tour guides.

Yet the tourist who strolled beyond the Disney-like city center[4] into the streets where everyday Amsterdammers lived was rewarded with other sights unique to people-watching in the Netherlands. Eye-level apartment windows are bare of curtains, blinds, or shades, providing endless glimpses into the low-grade dramas of everyday life: a skinny young man in lime-green underpants frying an egg in his daylight studio flat, a man and woman snuggling on their IKEA sofa watching "Friends" with Dutch subtitles, a harried mother trying to keep her toddlers from smearing dinner through their hair. As a Dutch friend and colleague rebutted what I perceived as the "shamelessness" of Amsterdammers, "Only people with something to hide cover their windows." Bemused at my voyeuristic interest, she continued, "but only people without manners look!"

As with their everyday lives, so too in social policy do the Dutch operate from a moral position of transparency. The vicissitudes of their policies on soft drugs, euthanasia, and prostitution are wide open for the world to see, but to criticize them is the moral equivalent of gawking: admitting that you're an ill-mannered person who looked. In this vein, Dutch prostitution policy is an object of global curiosity that government sources readily strive to satisfy. Agencies ranging from the Foreign Ministry and Amsterdam City Hall to Radio Netherlands Worldwide post information sheets about Dutch law on their websites in English for international audiences.[5]

This metaphor of looking is present in the statements by the Netherlands' longest-serving National Rapporteur on Trafficking in Human Beings, Corinne Dettmeijer-Vermeulen. The Netherlands was the first country to appoint a National Rapporteur, a position she described as important because "if you don't want to see trafficking around the corner, it's not there. Only if you proactively search for it, will you find it . . . victims do not always come forward, so you have to have eyes in the community."[6] The National Rapporteur is there to look where others look away. As Ms. Dettmeijer explained, "Exploitation partly occurs in hidden sectors such as the (unlicensed) sex industry, the informal economy and behind closed doors in private households, making it difficult to detect—victims of sexual and labor exploitation are reluctant to come forward."[7]

Her office is also there to encourage state agencies and each elected government to critically examine their internal policies toward human trafficking, "After all, as we all know, trafficking is easily overlooked if you do not want to see it . . . In general, authorities in the Netherlands have wanted to see."[8] This "in general" is the product of her office's independence, a factor she stressed repeatedly. Unlike Sweden's National Rapporteur, which is based in the National Police Board, the Dutch National Rapporteur on Trafficking in Human Beings is its own office, allowing her the ability to criticize elected governments and state agencies alike: "The Rapporteur has held a mirror up to the agencies and other organizations engaged in the fight against human trafficking in the Netherlands. They have looked in that mirror."[9]

This independence also allows for nonideological, evidence-based recommendations, which she also likens to a mirror: "Monitoring the effectiveness of this fight is a way of holding up a mirror. I do so by collecting information and reporting to the Dutch government. Making recommendations based on scientific research is an important part of that, and allows for the development of research-based policy."[10] Visibility is the key: Her office is also an investigative force that brings hidden processes into the light through annual reports, such as one that exposed human trafficking in smaller cities:

> The first objective in an effective fight against human trafficking is to make the phenomenon visible. That was the key message of my last report: Human trafficking that is hidden must be revealed—and once brought to light, it must be better recorded . . . My research showed that many of the smaller local authorities still are not sufficiently aware of the problem, or turn a blind eye. Thinking that trafficking is limited to prostitution areas, many smaller municipalities fail to see that this crime affects them too.[11]

This focus on smaller cities was echoed by Amsterdam's chief public prosecutor Martin Bolhaar, in part because of a misunderstanding about the trafficking in work other than sex:

> Unfortunately, we find that many municipal officials have a very different perspective to look at applicants for a brothel license. It is important to ensure that officials are going to ask the right questions . . . Unfortunately there are still local officials who say "exploitation doesn't come to us in the countryside." They are wrong, according to our research. We see a lot of exploitation, from bakers and *au pairs* to abuses in agriculture and horticulture.[12]

Trafficking affects everybody in the Netherlands, Ms. Dettmeijer stresses, and it's her job to marshal state, civil society, and ordinary citizens to actively look at that which is deliberately hidden.

Unlike other countries' Rapporteurs, the Dutch office has long stressed the importance of human trafficking in other labor sectors. She was the first Rapporteur to identify labor unions as potential partners in the fight against human trafficking, not just in identifying exploitation but also by offering support to migrant workers:

> I have emphasized the need for the involvement of NGOs. I have highlighted two relatively new partners: the academic world and the judiciary. But we must look beyond and seek new bedfellows. Trade unions for example, who up till now have not really embraced the migrant worker as they should.

This is a tall order in a country that has been roiled by nativist and populist parties that have targeted immigrants, especially Muslims.

The Dutch derive tangible pride from the attention they receive about their social policies because it reinforces and validates their sense of being a *gidsland* ("guiding nation"), a country that takes the lead in difficult policy issues.[13] In a striking parallel to the "Swedish model" of criminalizing prostitution clients, the "Dutch model" of an independent, well-funded, and aggressive National Rapporteur's office has been widely praised, including by Finland's Eva Biaudet.[14] Sociologist Frank Lechner has described the muted contemporary manifestations of Dutch *gidsland* as a "form of cosmopolitan nationalism [that] may itself become a model for potential global nice guys to follow." These qualifications denote a sense of pragmatism—"may become" for "potential" nice guys—that reflects the turmoil in Dutch politics from the 2000s: the rise of a nationalist populism, political assassinations, and concerns over Islamic immigrants. This social order is often dramatized as uniquely Dutch but, as I show in the next chapter, the Swedes, too, have a sense as a moral beacon to the world that brings the two countries into muted conflict.

The Dutch dramatize these virtues as the product of necessity: to fight back the sea. This is often described as the *polder* model, after the Dutch word that describes the farmland reclaimed from the sea through an ingenious system of dykes, berms, locks, and pumps. As explained by Eelco Tasma, a senior policy advisor for the Dutch National Trade Union Confederation:

> Some support the theory that in order to fight the sea successfully it was necessary to cooperate and not fight each other . . . whether or not this is true this idea of having a common goal between classes and also between employers and workers was certainly dominant when the country tried to get back to its feet after the Second World War. Then the government made the choice to seek cooperation because rebuilding the country asked for joint efforts of all parties concerned.[15]

The polder story as told from the workers' perspective thus has a muted criticism of a myth useful for suppressing conflict, yet dramatizes the circumstances of a small country easily overrun by the sea or more powerful neighbors: France in the nineteenth century, Germany in the twentieth. The Dutch have thus made a virtue out of the pragmatism necessary to survive, a virtue political scientist Joyce Outshoorn cites when she analyzed Dutch prostitution policy as the product of "pragmatism in the polder."[16] Similarly, Dutch Supreme Court Justice Ybo Buruma had described the polder system as underpinning "Dutch tolerance:" "ordinary people's wish to deal with danger rationally by suspending moral judgments."[17] Tolerance of prostitution is thus not quite the celebration of window brothels, but a transparency that keeps "dangers" in the open.

Though the Dutch often describe this polder model of social dialogue of mutual consultation and cooperation as unique to the Netherlands, they are in fact common to all four countries profiled in this book. Each of the four countries in this study also refer to their policies as rational and pragmatic, just as all four have political systems that feature government consultations with industry and unions to reduce strikes and promote an orderly economy. If social dialogue, pragmatism, and rationality cannot explain the difference between the Dutch prostitution reform and the other countries' policies, what can?

A Moral Leader in Labor Protections

In its welfare state, the Netherlands shares with Germany the allocation of social benefits on the basis of employment status, producing both high rates of social coverage and low rates of women's full-time employment.[18] In both countries, extending protections to prostitutes by professionalizing them merely extended the existing inclusion roadmap to cover new territory: the vulnerable workers in the red-light districts. Prostitution legalization thus proceeded according to the Netherlands' corporatist welfare state. As political scientist Joyce Outshoorn summarizes Dutch political culture, "the orderly scene of corporatism in process stands in stark contrast to the reputation that prostitution in The Netherlands has abroad."[19] Dutch experts are at great pains to stress that legalized prostitution does not mean libertarianism or a laissez-faire attitude, but strict regulations and a clear specification of when and where prostitution is legal—and where it is not.[20] Legalization meant a municipal licensing system, whereby mayors have the power to restrict brothels to specific areas, but also meant the banning of streetwalking.

Unlike Germany, however, the Netherlands' sense of itself as a moral leader set its policy on a conflict with other countries with an equally evangelical foreign policy regarding prostitution and human trafficking— namely Sweden and the United States. Neither Germany nor the Netherlands features gender as a core category for politics, making the prostitution abolitionism of Sweden and Finland less likely options.

Part of the reason the Dutch and Swedes are such perfect foils for each other are misunderstandings of one Dutch word sometimes translated merely as tolerance. *Gedogen* implies regulation and not a laissez-faire tolerance of anything-goes. This misunderstanding was present in a widely quoted journalistic account of the bureaucratic hurdles imposed by the law: "The Dutch, as it turns out, are far less tolerant than expected."[21]

Such an assessment misses the regulatory aspect of *gedogen*. For example, a social worker described Dutch prostitution policy as consistent with Dutch policy on marijuana:

> *MvH*: Yeah, it's like we call it *gedogen*, it's like when drugs were not legal but who cares, the police know where the brown cafes are, they know where the dealers are. As long as there's no crime around it, in the sense that they are stealing things from other people who have nothing to do with it.
> *GM*: If you don't disturb the neighbors?
> *MvH*: Yeah, if you don't disturb, just do your thing.

Gedogen is about reducing social conflict, not the laissez-faire tolerance of individuals' choices made under conditions of personal liberty, as it might be in the United States, or the tolerance of a dirty house, as the word implies for Swedes.

Other international confusion arises around the Dutch word *exploitant*. In Dutch it simply means an operator, as of machinery or a business. Pimping is defined, in almost every country and in the Dutch statute repealed in 1999, as the exploitation of a prostitute's earnings. Early on, the office of the Dutch National Rapporteur realized this and wrote into their first annual report—translated into English for an international audience—the following explanation:

> The Dutch term for the wording "running of prostitution" is the term "exploitatie," which has a neutral meaning. Because literal translation of this term into English ("exploitation") could easily lead to confusion with the forbidden forms of organizing prostitution, for the purpose of this report is chosen for a more descriptive translation.[22]

Miscommunication regarding this "false friend" between the Dutch and English definitions of *exploit* were common among interviewees and government reports alike. As the 2007 government report assessing the law's impact states, "the exploitation of a sex establishment without the needed license is punishable by law."[23] Similarly, the director[24] of Amsterdam's Prostitution and Health Center described how their services are required to be posted in places where "exploitants" employ prostitutes:

> Because we are GGD and from the city of Amsterdam, the exploitants need to have this information in their office as well. It's not completely official but they should give the women that come in and sign for a window, when they're new, they have to inform them about our existence: "We have a center for you where you can get yourself tested and where you can go when you have any problems." So all the window exploitants have our cards and most of the clubs as well.

This blurring between the Dutch use of exploit to mean operate and the English meaning "to take advantage of" is strangely apt, as the legalization of brothels repealed the crime of pimping, formerly defined as the exploitation of prostitutes. As a *gidsland* and first nation in Europe to legalize prostitution at the turn of the new millennium, the Netherlands attracted considerable international attention that struggled to understand the regulated part of *gedogen*'s tolerance, and the wisdom of enlisting "exploitants" as partners in stopping human trafficking.

Professionalizing the Sex Industry

The Netherlands passed a bill to legalize prostitution in 1999, which took effect in 2000. The bill recognized prostitution as a profession for the purposes of health and social benefits, revoked the ban on brothels and pimping from the penal code, and introduced new penalties for exploitation connected to minors and human trafficking. The key part of the Netherlands' reform was the repeal of the Penal Code section prohibiting pimping, or the exploitation of the earnings of a prostitute. According to the government, the legislation had six goals:

1. "Control and regulation of the exploitation of voluntary prostitution," primarily through municipal licensing,
2. Combating coerced prostitution,
3. Protecting minors from sexual abuse,
4. Protecting "the position of prostitutes,"
5. Disentangling prostitution from criminal networks, and
6. Reducing "prostitution by illegal foreign nationals."[25]

As is clear from this list, the primary purposes were control and protection, with only one of the six goals aimed vaguely at protecting "the position" of prostitutes. Popularly the bill was known as the repeal of the brothel ban,[26] and involved permitting the long-established "relax businesses" (*Relaxbedrijven*) to legally employ sex workers and thus receive earnings from prostitution—what formerly had been prohibited as pimping.

The Netherlands was not the first jurisdiction to permit legalized prostitution—provinces and states in other countries already permitted legal sex work, including in Australia, Austria, and the United States.[27] Furthermore, many countries had legalized and regulated prostitution back in the nineteenth century, starting with France in the 1830s.[28] This first wave of legalization was upended by the first wave of feminism, in which the Netherlands also took part when it criminalized brothels and solicitation with its 1911 Morality Acts.[29] These same groups established a network of institutions to protect young women migrating to the city for work, ranging from railway-station Travelers' Aid patrols, YWCA hostels and chaperoned dances and parties.[30] Even in the 1950s the Netherlands was a staunchly conservative country in family patterns, in its free market policies, and in its conformity to the international norms regarding the separation of sexuality from the public sphere.[31] This changed during the 1960s.

With the sexual revolution the Netherlands reinvented itself, enacting a comprehensive welfare state and adapting its old national virtue of tolerance toward religions (Calvinism, Catholicism, Judaism) to modern lifestyles including single motherhood, homosexuality, soft drug use, and prostitution. It was at this time that prostitution became one of the tolerated lifestyle practices by which the Netherlands draws moral boundaries between itself and outsiders, with today's red-light windows becoming public and publicly accepted.

Legalizing prostitution had been on the political agenda in the 1970s when a center-left government had proposed it. The spread of a more "exhibitionist" and "aggressive" sex industry in the 1980s led the influential Association of Dutch Municipalities to lobby for the repeal of the brothel ban to better regulate what was no longer discreet.[32] This was tabled after the subsequent election of a center-right government that remained in power until 1996. For supporters, this was a mere interregnum before a broad "rainbow coalition" government was elected that did not include the domestic opponents to legalization, the religious parties. Thus little regret was expressed by proponents of legalization over the 18-year delay from first proposal to eventual enactment because this ensured its acceptance among the public.[33]

The 1999 reforms provided a legal basis for the sex businesses that had operated since the 1960s, but did so in keeping with the Dutch corporatist welfare state by professionalizing them, with all the standard enforcement and red tape such a process entails. Although selling sex was legal before, the use of the word "profession" was significant because it recognized sex work as labor under the law, clearing the way for prostitutes to access business financing and services, to unionize, and to qualify for national health insurance and pensions as self-employed persons. The legalization of brothels made labor laws applicable to both brothels and their employees, incorporating prostitutes within workplace health and safety criteria. With social order and social welfare governed largely through employment, the legalization of prostitution made sense, and could be put into place by existing state agencies, unions, and nonprofits.

The bill also gave local governments the ability to license brothels under their own standards. Theoretically this gave towns with no prostitution the right to maintain the status quo, but it also gave brothel entrepreneurs a legal process to appeal summary rejections and mechanisms to force towns to specify which parts of the community could, in theory at least, be designated for prostitution. As Professor Outshoorn explained, "It emerged that local councils 'froze' the number of brothels in their precincts, not allowing new competitors to the market. Some orthodox Protestant councils refused to license any sex business." (CITE 2012). The bill thus nationalized prostitution, opening up processes whereby towns that had traditionally restricted brothels could be challenged, causing consternation in the more conservative rural and religious areas of the country, which had never had the city-center red-light districts favored by the richer western port cities. As Outshoorn continued, "the secular parties, who invoked constitution law, [pointed] out that the Penal Code is binding for the whole territory of the Netherlands." [CITE 2012] Criminal law against illegal sex work not only protected victims—including domestic prostitutes—but also imposed a centralized policy upon the nation.

Critics charge that the Dutch reform made prostitution a job like any other, but this isn't exactly true. The bill explicitly notes that prostitutes have the right to refuse any client or any act, under constitutional guarantees for their right to the integrity of the human being. As a government report explains, "prostitutes should always have the possibility to refuse clients and/or sexual acts due to section 11 of the Constitution."[34] Thus although prostitutes may be employees, they have special rights to control their conditions of work that other employees do not share. While a sex worker may have an employment contract, her employer nevertheless has less control over his employees' work process than in other sectors. Yet this focus on employers and employment was important for the Dutch because it promised to normalize an industry, bring it out of the gray area of criminality and money laundering, and into the bright light where there would be nothing to hide. Far from a laissez-faire, anything-goes atmosphere, orderly regulation brings social peace.

Dutch Openness and Regulated Tolerance

Such regulated tolerance was on display when I visited the primary interface between the red-light district and the Dutch tourist industry, the Prostitution Information Center (PIC). It is a nonprofit foundation founded in 1994 by former sex worker Mariska Majoor. The small establishment is a shop, mini museum, and art gallery where Majoor fields media inquiries, answers the questions of passersby, and leads tours of the district. Many of her publications are for sale, including a pamphlet that answers frequently asked questions and her book "When Sex

Becomes Work."[35] In practice, however, it is also a resource promoted by government and nonprofits alike that reflects the ability of a former sex worker to both set up a business and leave the profession.

Our chat was twice interrupted: by an Italian news crew that arrived to schedule an interview and a brisk businesslike woman in her 60s with a small boy in tow. While the older woman talked to Ms. Majoor, the boy wandered among the shelves in the shop, trailing his fingers along bags of penis pasta and vagina-shaped lollypops before selecting small plastic penises that he made into cars, creating a car chase on the wooden floors. After several minutes, the woman left some papers with Majoor, told the boy to put up his toys, and left. As Majoor explained, "She was from the Salvation Army here in the District. They are organizing some self-defense classes for prostitutes. Of course they want them to leave the profession, but they are good classes and so I will post these flyers and let the girls know." When I asked if there was ever a conflict with the Salvation Army's methods of rescuing prostitutes, Majoor laughed, "No, no, they are realistic. They do not push too hard and we respect them for that, we can both tolerate each other here in the district, because after all they were here first!" This object lesson in tolerance illustrated the pragmatism of regulated tolerance. The Salvation Army may be there to save souls, but they do so not through fire and brimstone but through practical offerings of classes useful to sex workers. The PIC may reject the motives of the Salvation Army, but that does not mean denying sex workers information about their practical offerings.

Despite the attention given the publicly visible brothels and prostitutes in street windows, the majority of the trade had no public face. The most optimistic estimates put half of Dutch prostitutes working in the red-light districts, with the rest working in upscale private brothels or escort services, or the downmarket automobile zones where something like streetwalking was permitted. They were essentially a parking lot with stalls to shield cars from one another, sex taking place in the cars. Located in industrial districts or parking lots, they feature health centers, surveillance for prostitute protection, and a sort of "living room" with social service information, coffee, and hot showers for women.[36] The area was well-lit and under camera surveillance for everyone's safety, and an on-site social service center provided information, hot showers, and safer-sex information and materials. Though such zones are sometimes criticized by policy experts for facilitating prostitution, such criticism is received amicably by the Dutch. After all, such narrow-minded definitions of social service and safety only reinforce Dutch mores of tolerance and pragmatism.

The 1999 brothel ban repeal had little effect on these other forms of prostitution. Dutch prostitutes note that much of the domestic trade can be profitably carried out through escort services, freelancing through private advertising in newspapers or the Internet, reaching men who do not wish to be seen going to and from the red-light districts, and carried out by women who don't wish to stand in a window where any mother's friend can wander past. Indeed, one of the boons of the old system was anonymity. As Christy ten Broeke, a board member of De Rode Draad, complained of expectations of transparency, "They have children who are in school. Their parents, sometimes their husbands, don't know what they do. They don't want it written down anywhere."[37] If the new municipal controls were unpopular with some sex workers, they barely touched others in prostitution from more desperate circumstances. These included undocumented migrants who were victims of human trafficking cartels, private rings exploiting developmentally disabled adults or the drug-addicted, or the girlfriends of abusive and controlling men who required them to sell sex.

The international attention paid to the flashy De Wallen district, ignoring the majority of prostitution elsewhere in the Netherlands, parallels the attention paid to the Dutch prostitution experience over that of other nations, including Germany and Austria. Shared by all of these corporatist welfare states are a division between free and forced prostitution, a focus on citizenship through labor market status, and the use of state social services as points of regulation.

Social Services as Points of Regulation

The operation of the brothel ban's repeal in practice illustrates the corporatist principles of Dutch social welfare, with its pragmatic regulation and mutual consultations that make social services points of regulation and discipline. Mariska van Huissteden was the director of Amsterdam Prostitution and Health Center known by its acronym and house number as P&G292 (*Prostitutie en Gezondheidscentrum 292*). P&G292 is a comprehensive health clinic with medical and social work services for sex workers funded by the Amsterdam Public Health Service, GGD (*Geneeskundige en Gezondheidsdienst*), in collaboration with an NGO partner. It offers services by appointment in an old building in a fine street in the city center. Our wide-ranging interview covered the intents of the law, challenges to its implementation, and the Dutch principles that put it into conflict with other prostitution regimes. Neighbors first opposed the center, but they were won over when the city, NGO, and staff sat down with them to hear their concerns about noise, loitering, and potential violence. As Director van Huissteden explained:

> We formed a neighborhood committee and told them what's going to happen and listened very carefully to what they had to say, and embedded

that in our house rules, for example. I think the committee fell apart about, not even a year after we started here. There were two or three more get-togethers with the people in the neighborhood and that was it. And we hear nothing anymore. Everybody's very happy with us. We're good neighbors and there's no problems.

Thus even in a nice street, a Prostitution and Health Center could be integrated with social dialogue and a tolerance that included incorporating neighbors' concerns into the institutions rules.

P&G292's extensive outreach is evidenced by the fact that by 2010, nearly a quarter of De Wallen's workers had been clients despite the regular turnover.[38] Director van Huissteden stressed that they are always reaching out to establish how their services are different from other groups that canvas the red-light district:

> We go into the Red Light District, we always have this card in our hands. We go to window sites, we give the card, and we make contact with them, point at it: "do you know us?" Sometimes they're a little skeptical but that's mainly because there's a lot of religious groups walking around there that want to talk to them. "No, no, not the Church again."

De Wallen is the target not only of P&G292's free government services, but also an impressive infrastructure of domestic and international religious outreach, ranging from mission tour groups to established missions like the Salvation Army. When I told Director van Huissteden that I was to meet with some of these religious groups, she suggested two that, like P&G292, are invested in long-term work: "Yeah, they're good organizations which are already very much embedded in the Dutch culture, but you also have others, American-based, that get a lot of funding from America, and they're not so helpful." Collaboration with local partners means even those organizations that opposed prostitution's legalization, so long as they are "embedded in Dutch culture."

Working in concert with relax-business operators is also part of the way the reforms were implemented. As Director Huissteden describes the facilities offered by brothel managers to her staff:

> *MvH*: In the Red Light District, we have one exploitant where we can have a room on the second floor. He has a special chair for us as well . . . it's great to have a place there where you can do your STD checkups right there. We try to get the women to come to the center for the next visit.
> *GM*: Why does he do this?
> *MvH*: Because of course it's good for him and his business too. He offers the women a place to get checked and can get a checkup right after work. You

don't have to come first to get acquainted with us. And that way, he can be sure that these women who are working are checked as well. So it's a win-win situation.

Such close partnerships with brothel managers are not confined to the central red-light area that is the focus of so much international attention, but to peripheral areas as well. In these areas, the "exploitants" who legally run prostitution businesses also cooperate in line with *gedogen*'s regulated tolerance:

> *MvH*: In the south of Amsterdam, there's a window area as well, we have one of the exploitants, a woman who always offers us a room when we call, so we go there next week again. We just get one of the working rooms and use its bed and bathroom to do the examinations. Now most of them do, and yeah, again it's because we're with the [Amsterdam Public Health Services] GGD, we're public health, there's sort of an urge that you cannot say no to us when we want to come in and do checkup. So we can also come into clubs very easily this way.
>
> *GM*: So it sounds like there's just a lot of cooperation.
>
> *MvH*: Yeah. Yeah. We're very happy with that. Yeah.

Cooperation between government, employers, and workers, as prescribed by Dutch law and culture for all industries, is likewise the norm for prostitution reforms.

Although most international discussions of Dutch prostitution law focus on its impact on the women who may now sell sex as professionals, its impact has been no less dramatic on the professionalization of brothel managers. Professionalization was the theme of Director van Huissteden's response to my question as to whether brothel managers cooperated to curry favor with the government:

> *GM*: So it looks good for them to tell the government, "And we did this, we did this, and we had GGD come in and they will provide our services?"
>
> *MvH*: "And how do you take care of your women? How do you take care of your business so it is healthy and good?" Well, you can show that by showing that you have the information from the GGD or from [us], the prostitution health center, that you have a regular line with them, that you call in yourself when your information needs to be updated, that you're open for us when we come once every three months for a check-up of the location. So it's a good cooperation in that way. And they need to be professional as well.
>
> *GM*: Right.
>
> *MvH*: So it's not only prostitution that is legal, but it's the profession and everyone around it has to cooperate in that system to make it better.

Serving prostitutes' health, for the Director of Amsterdam's Prostitution and Health Center, thus involves not only clinical work with sex workers, but the professional socialization of brothel managers to care for their employees.

The Dutch focus on sex workers is evident in the way the professionalization of brothel managers occurs: by treating the women in the sex industry as professionals. In response to my question about the professionalization of brothel managers, Director van Huissteden's cited the importance of teaching them to treat sex workers as professionals, because this supports womens' ability to make informed decisions about the risks involved in their work:

> GM: You're training the exploitants and club owners to be professionals in their work?
> MvH: Yeah, or what does it mean to have professionals working—
> GM: —for you—
> MvH: —for you, yeah. You should also treat them as professionals. For the women it means that they all have the right to say yes or no to things that they do or don't want to do. It's their body. It's their rights as a prostitute to say "I only work with condoms" or if you don't want to do that, okay, it's your own risk. But you take that risk, not because your club owner or your exploitant says to take that risk. And this gives empowerment to the women themselves, but it's a process that we're still in. It doesn't change overnight. Especially because you still get new women every time. It's an ongoing process.

This stress on the *process* of *cooperation* permeated government documents and my conversations, stressing the role of government support in helping vulnerable workers make informed decisions about their individual circumstances. This contrasts with the resistance to individualized risk in Sweden and Finland where solidarity is the answer to the risks posed to the individual. But in a situation where there are always new women, or women are coming and going, such solidarity is hard to come by. The Dutch way is to enlist the exploitants as partners, something antithetical to the Swedish or Finnish way.

Director van Huissteden's description of the law comes from this on-the-ground work with her clients as helping them gain this empowerment. As she describes, the original bill was really insufficient for accomplishing the professionalization of sex work:

> It doesn't mean that they have to get out of prostitution but have to get out of the underdog position. What does it mean to have a legal profession? I think after legalization they started to recognize, oh it means more than that. If it's

a profession, you should be taught what your rights are, how to conduct a proper business, how to pay taxes, how to budget, all the rules, all things that are with a legal profession came afterwards.

This "afterwards" work of empowerment, of course, is the kind of work done by her organization, funded for health work but interpreted broadly in a way that supports occupational health, including by training exploitant "bosses" to care for employees in a professional manner.

The individual-worker based system of the Dutch system is stressed also in this "after" and ongoing work of empowerment:

> *MvH*: And that's the way to get to the men or sometimes women behind it. To slowly gain the confidence of those women that's part of our work, to slowly gain their confidence, empower them and let them know that what they're doing is not wrong but the system that they're in is corrupt. And that the money that they earn should be their money and not some man's who says who's protecting you. Police are here to protect you. The system is here to protect you. You are protected.
>
> *GM*: Society is here to protect?
>
> *MvH*: And if you want a pimp to pay the money to, pay it to the taxes! [Laughs.] The official pimp as I call it, huh. Because that's also where one third of your money is going to.

For Director van Huissteden, the system of which she is a part is designed to replace pimps by making the state, and the taxman, the pimps. But if this sounds horrific to prostitution abolitionists, it is only part of the pragmatic compromises that have made pimps part of the Dutch system already. Indeed, part of the error of the reforms, she says, is by not organizing this system and enlisting them sooner:

> Well we still work to improve because the service you get from paying taxes should be a bit better. Should be more services out of it than you can get now. Now you pay, and yeah, you can get some back. But what you got from it is not much. So that's what I said. If we legalize and then we have "Oh my god it's legal. Now we have to organize these services!" when they should have organized before it was legalized.

For the Dutch, cooperation between local and national government agencies, police and social workers, brothel owners, managers, and sex workers can make even industrial sex "healthy and good." Yet the challenges to organizing the system—and its late start—were revealed in stark form in the government's 2007 evaluation.

The Challenges of Professionalizing Prostitution

From its passage mayors and government administrators have tweaked the reform's implementation, in part because the government's own 2007 evaluation report admitted that little had changed on the ground: "the labor relations in the licensed sector have barely changed . . . the legal position of prostitutes is bad."[39] The report blamed this on a misunderstanding: "prostitutes and sex business owners now feel that the regulations have become stricter, whereas in practice it is a matter of a stricter enforcement, which has replaced the former policy of tolerance." If those involved in the sex industry see few benefits to the law, it may be because the law's most controversial aspects and primary benefit—employer/employee relationships—has not yet been implemented. Despite the fact that the Dutch prostitution reform granted prostitutes the right to form employee relationships with business owners, few have done so. Relax-business operators claim that they are business service providers for clients who are self-employed.[40] In the first six years of the law, the government brought several lawsuits against exploitants to show that they are in fact employers, winning most of them. Despite this, even as late as 2007, "business owners still use the argument, by now superseded by jurisprudence, that it is impossible for employer-employee relations to exist in the prostitution sector."[41] What was clear to the government is that this employment relationship confers the benefits of the law, but the fact that exploitants still refused to recognize their responsibilities indicated that the government's clarity was not shared.

Aditionally, Sex workers were also refusing their "rights" as complicated and invasive rules. This revealed several barriers to enforcing employment rights on the ostensible beneficiaries of prostitution legalization. As Red Thread spokesperson Metje Blaak complained, "We're going back to 1900, when men behind in the cigar shop could meet a woman. It's because of all the rules that apply there for the prostitution sector . . . It is a serious matter, because many women are exploited in such cases. They blackmail, there is no control. If the police discover an illegal brothel, they move so to another building." The results, she says, are a shift from window brothels where women might be bound by employment rules and taxes and toward less regulated places where they can be more independent: "Women are creative and find other places than legal clubs. I see soliciting more women, but also with friends from home, in hotels and in caravans along the highway." [CITES] In its comprehensive survey of sex workers, the government found that "by their own account, approximately 95% of the prostitutes in the licensed sector should be regarded as a self-employed person."[42] Prostitutes refuse salaried employment, for example, because "they presume they will then have to give up what attracted them to self-employment in the first place: freedom, independence, temporariness and flexibility, and earning a lot of money."[43]

Stigma is one aspect of the sex industry that cannot be legislated away, and a desire for anonymity prevents some sex workers from registering. Becoming a licensed sex worker means giving up anonymity, ranked the most important aspect for their work. It is useful to evade the authorities, but especially intimate acquaintances. As the 2007 government report sympathetically explained:

> Because the women want to keep their work a secret for their family and acquaintances, for fear of their incomprehension. For many of the women, their anonymity is a matter of extreme importance, on account of which they are extra reticent when asked to give their private address, for instance for registering at the Chamber of Commerce.[44]

Incomprehension seems a mild way to describe the stigma of sex work, long recognized by sex workers' rights activists as one of the biggest barriers to reframing sex as labor, and is the biggest rebuke to any claim that prostitution is work like any other.[45]

Some of sex workers' refusal to become employees comes from an unwillingness to pay taxes. Most participants in the sex industry do not pay taxes: more than 60 percent of licensed prostitutes working in relax businesses and 75 percent of escorts surveyed by the government in 2007 had never paid taxes. Yet while some of these refusals were structural, such as the desire to maintain anonymity, some of them are cultural, related to the outlaw status of the sex trade. The report summarized:

> The main argument for tax evasion is that prostitutes think they already earn very little. Related to this, some consider their work not to be a steady profession, or think they cannot work enough hours. For some prostitutes, tax evasion is a matter of principle; they think that paying tax does not agree with working in the prostitution sector. In this context, the quotation "this involves my body; I will not pay tax over it" is telling.

In other words, sex workers themselves do not believe that prostitution is a profession like any other.

A final challenge to the state in getting prostitutes to pay tax, and thus pay into the social system, is that some are currently drawing support from it: The government report claimed that "a large part of the prostitutes receives social security; they do not want their extra income to become known to the Social Services or the Employee Insurance Implementing Body."[46] If part of the wages of sex work is stigma, many feel justified in drawing social benefit to top up their compensation.

The 2007 government report described this persistent inability to convince prostitutes that they were employees and brothel operators that they were bosses as a "cultural barrier." Sex workers report that "having no administrative bother" was one of the top three most important aspect of their work as independent operators. You can almost feel the frustration when the report notes, "The importance of not having a lot of administrative bother, however, does in fact contrast with the wish to work as a self-employed person. After all, someone who is self-employed generally has to keep up with more administration than an employee."[47] If this argument strikes the government as irrational, so too does the insistence that "the system" was designed to help prostitutes when it is found so wanting by those in charge of implementing it.

In keeping with P&G292's van Huissteden's criticism, the government found that the legislation had failed to provide support for sex workers who want to leave the trade. Despite government mandates, as late as 2007 "only 6% of the municipalities indicate they pay attention to the possibilities for prostitutes of leaving the prostitution sector."[48] Between 2008 and 2012, the government funded 13 projects for prostitutes who wanted to leave the sex industry, but no further government funds have become available.

According to P&G292's Mariska van Huissteden, there are still some brothel managers who weren't fully cooperating as expected by the city of Amsterdam. Yet she still has faith in cooperation and professionalization as the way forward because P&G292 still gains information even about these ostensibly closed clubs:

> GM: Do you have exploitants who discourage you from coming around ever?
> MvH: Well, there's still a few. But there's still a few clubs that do not respond when we call, when we want to come present ourselves to the women that work there or can we do, is there any interest in doing the checkup on location. There's still clubs we cannot come into, some of them are only high end and have their own doctors or have a special line with the hospital in the neighborhood where the women can go, which is also very good if they have it very well organized, nothing wrong with that. We also have clubs that we question a lot whether they are legal, or that the things that are conducted there are not the way we would like to see prostitution working. The women are urged to do things still without condoms, so we cannot easily get in there. But we keep an eye on them through the women that come to us anyhow, and they tell us stories about what happens in the place. It's a difficult area to get into. But most of the time the exploitants, the club owners, also escort services, they're very willing to help us and get the information to the women.

By "keeping an eye" on these clubs through the eyes of women whose trust they have gained, the social workers and clinicians of P&G292 can provide information not only to the city, but also to the police, their government partners.

The metaphor cited by government and nonprofit was a chain of partners. I asked Director van Huissteden how P&G292 dealt with club owners who were not cooperating.

> GM: When you find out, or if you start hearing information about one of these clubs that you find disturbing, how does your organization deal with that?
>
> MvH: Well, we have a chain of partners, as we call it, and we work in a chain of all sorts of organizations and government, the police, and the fire quad to try to eliminate things like human trafficking ... And there where clubs are not behaving in the way we would like them to, we try to find a way to get them convicted, or to get their license revoked, but that's a tough way. It's difficult to get it revoked once they have a license, so it's a process.

The chain of partners is there to ensure the process of cooperation, ranging from making contact with individual sex workers, to inspections of their working places, all the way to convictions of criminals.

After the 2001 amendments to the prostitution legislation, the government began withdrawing funds from civil society organizations it had previously funded to create the corporatist partners whose advice had helped craft the law. The PIC lost government funding, as did the world's most famous prostitutes rights' organization, *De Rode Draad* (The Red Thread). Formed in 1985, the group advocated for better legal rights, and provided support services, receiving government funds for HIV prevention. With legalization in 2000, they advised the union Dutch Labor Movement Federation (*Federatie Nederlandse Vakbeweging*, FNV), which began accepting sex workers as members. When the government withdrew funding from De Rode Draad in 2005, the organization limped along before declaring bankruptcy in 2012. It exists now only in archives and the services provided by that of the portion incorporated into the FNV, the *Vakbond Vakwerk*. The organization's name reads as "union for trade work," yet *vak* ("box") is also slang for the window brothels, yielding a name that also cleverly implies the Union for Window Brothel Work.

Also defunded was the Mr. A de Graaf Foundation (*Stichting Mr. A. de Graaf*). It was started in 1960 as a shelter for women who wanted to leave prostitution, but became an independent but government-funded institute for prostitution policy in the 1980s.[49] The mission of its founder was thus turned 180 degrees when it was repurposed to provide research on incorporating prostitutes in society and began advocating for the legalization of prostitution. For over 30 years the foundation conducted research for government and third parties, facilitated consultations between sex workers' rights organizations and government, and published newsletters and magazines by and for sex workers and relax-business operators. Its government funding withdrawn in 2004, the closure of the Mr. A. de Graaf Foundation signaled the end of the government's need for a third-party NGO to conduct research and foster civil society among sex workers now that the police, tax, and health agencies were fully capable of obtaining that information themselves.[50] It was independence from these very interests that had made the Mr. A. de Graaf reports so influential in the debates that brought legalization. Now that prostitution was legal, the institute that helped draft the boilerplate language and provided parliamentary advice regarding prostitution had helped eliminate itself.

In 2007 the Amsterdam mayor's office launched a campaign Platform 1012, named after De Wallen's postcode, reimagining the neighborhood as calling for a diversification of businesses, in part by buying out brothel windows and renting them to fashion and art businesses. Criticisms of the government tourist office's promotion of de Wallen resulted in the removal of those sections of the national tourist website, and in 2008 the Amsterdam mayor's office promised to remove the brothel windows surrounding the *Oude Kerk* cathedral and Mariska Majoor's Prostitution Information center. Further legislation was proposed in 2014 to require all sex businesses to have a license, closing loopholes whereby some escort services were operating in the Netherlands from outside the country or from municipalities without licensing regimes, "owners of commercial sex businesses will be screened more rigorously," and sex work will be forbidden to those under 21 years of age. These innovations continue, demonstrating clearly that legalization is not libertinism, and that the main intents of the law—e.g., control—continue to be refined and extended.

Transnational Comparisons and Conflict

Despite ample evidence that prostitution's legalization in the Netherlands has been implemented in ways to restrict and control the industry, and is openly acknowledged as a work in progress, it is still misunderstood abroad. As Deputy Chief of the National Police Ruud Bik explained, "Sixty percent of the women in window prostitution are forced or exploited [but] in countries like Sweden, where prostitution is illegal, they stabbing their heads in the sand. Previously, there was misery in the Netherlands, but that was less visible to the outside world."[51] Director van Huissteden too remains optimistic about the law's possibilities despite her critiques, implicitly evoking the Netherlands' status as *gidsland*, while explicitly rejecting Sweden's moral leadership.

> *MvH*: In the long haul we showed a lot of countries that the way to do it, or the way we do it, might just have the effect we want it to have, that they said we would never have. Because they have the problem. We don't have the problem. We eliminated the problem by not making it a problem anymore. And it's not a problem if it's not so exciting anymore. So people won't, or maybe they will smoke weed, smoke even heroin too. It's less harmful than being an alcoholic.
>
> *GM*: Yeah?
>
> *MvH*: And it's the same way with prostitution. You can deny it. You can say it's not there. But if [here in the Netherlands] you have a customer and he goes to a prostitute and he in negotiating or in the contacting, finds out that she is a potential victim of human trafficking, that makes him going in as a crime and going out as a rapist . . . but that does not mean that all prostitution and all the clients are rapists. In Sweden, you get convicted if you go to a prostitute. Why!? Why!?

The link Ms. van Huissteden drew between prostitution policy and alcohol and drugs was a frequent one in my interviews. Political scientist Joyce Outshoorn draws an explicit contrast between the superior Dutch corporatism and Sweden's moralistic social democracy. "Sweden, with its long-standing social-democratic tradition of the attempted reform of human nature, resulting in punitive laws ranging from the regulation of alcohol to work fare for the unemployed" is contrasted with "the Netherlands, with its traditionally more cosmopolitan and pragmatic society."[52] Sweden may *attempt* to reform human nature by being punitive, but it sacrifices pragmatism and cosmopolitanism, two principles valued by the Dutch experience of progress.[53] Prostitution, like alcohol and drugs, are sensitive issues that readily evoke concerns about self-control and the relationship between personal choices and social problems. Yet in Europe, it was not drugs policy or alcohol regulation that prompted transnational conflict, but prostitution.

I continued by posing the negative connotation the word tolerance had for my Swedish interviewees:

> *GM*: It's funny because in Sweden, when I've done interviews there, they say "yes, the Dutch *tolerate*. We could tolerate a dirty house but we don't."
>
> *MvH*: Yeah [laughs].
>
> *GM*: And they use this as negative.
>
> *MvH*: Yeah, but they don't tolerate very much. And Sweden, they're not very tolerant. They don't like the Dutch very tolerant way. Theirs also it's very expensive, to be intolerant against drugs so they have a lot of underground

crime. They really have underground systems there. There's a network of things that are really underground . . . it's really unnerving. Lots of things happening there are not on the streets. It's like rats. I'm amazed that they think it's okay to be so clean and not accept something in your house, and then to just throw it underground. <laughs>

For van Huissteden, intolerance cannot be a virtue, as it can be for Swedes in the next chapter. Yet this perception that tolerance led to transparency is challenged by the 2007 government report that noted the policy's lack of effect, and the movement of prostitution out of the licensed regulated sector and into the less-regulated escort sector. To be intolerant is merely to draw blinds over the problems that go underground.

Similarly, the Dutch government explicitly refuted Swedish claims that the brothel repeal had caused exploitation. As the 2007 reform evaluation defiantly asserted:

> Internationally, the Netherlands is viewed by some countries as a country where there are no limits with regard to prostitution and where trafficking in human beings is facilitated. However, it is likely trafficking in human beings has become more difficult, because the enforcement of the regulations has increased in comparison to the former situation, when all exploitation of prostitution was prohibited.[54]

This assertion by the government's 2007 assessment of the brothel ban's repeal was translated into English and widely dispersed. It was not bombastic—reductions in trafficking are likely—an exceedingly realistic and pragmatic way to evaluate policy, one with rhetorical power in the Netherlands but an ambiguity that does not satisfy Swedish and other abolitionist critics. Indeed, the 2014 assessment of two Dutch criminologists is that:

> the screening of brothel owners and the monitoring of the compliance of licensing conditions do not create levels of transparency that enable sex trafficking to be exposed. The prostitution business retains many characteristics of an illegitimate market and the legalization and regulation of the prostitution sector has not driven out organized crime. On the contrary, fighting sex trafficking using the criminal justice system may even be harder in the legalized prostitution sector.[55]

After a string of such critical assessments, religious parties have called for revising the laws, some even proposing Swedish-style criminalization of clients of prostitution. Yet the Dutch *exploitation* of prostitution, like its tolerance, are both carefully regulated and constantly assessed, actions that only became nationally important when other social controls frayed under reductions in the social safety net during the 1990s

Extending the Protections of a Frayed Social Safety Net

Although the Dutch are proud of extending citizenship rights to prostitutes, they only did so after the corporatist welfare state had already become frayed. Rising medical co-pays and reduced benefits accompanied economic recessions in the early 1990s and 2000s, prompting populist parties to call for restricting immigration and restoring benefits. As the Mr. A de Graaf Foundation's Marieke van Doorninck critiqued the implementation of the law, "What we saw over time is that the Ministry of Social Services faded into the background and the Ministry of Justice took on a bigger and bigger role in putting forward the legislation. The emphasis today has been to get legal control over a workplace that was a great cover for all sorts of illegal activity. The emphasis has not been on decent labor conditions."[56] It was thus a threadbare and moth-eaten blanket that was offered to sex workers. Which, I argue, was an implicit function of the legislation, to remind all Dutch citizens of their social protections.

P&G292 Director Mariska van Huissteden described the changes in social security. Our conversation about her organization's work connecting sex workers to social services quickly turned to their inadequacy for everyone.

> *MvH*: Our insurance plans used to have a guarantee . . . But then we got into a new system that you have a basic security system that everybody has to pay. All the Dutch people . . . I now pay about 125 per month and I'm still not completely insured. If you have health problems, you still get a lot of bills that the insurance company doesn't pay.
>
> *GM*: Is this because of state finances?
>
> *MvH*: Yeah, I think so. They said that it's the market system y'know and it's more expensive. I don't think it's good. Before, the state paid. The state gave you the insurance and everybody was just happy with that. But it's the same with all sorts of things. It's also the postal service who used to be from the state or the train system who used to be state-organized but it's all free market economy now . . . It's not very socialist, but of course we are, for Americans, those scary socialists!

To American eyes, the Dutch guarantees of housing and social benefits seem socialist, but the Dutch experience them as part of a free market economy "where nobody controls anymore" that commentators link to a rising tide of neoliberal government policies around the globe.

This neoliberalism, associated with European expansion and blamed for rising numbers of immigrants and an eroded safety net, formed part of the globalization anxiety that formed a backdrop to the timing of the Dutch prostitution reforms. Controls were imposed on prostitution not only to support prostitutes—which was only one of six points justifying the 1999 brothel ban repeal—but to control criminality, immigration, and other anxieties linked to globalization. From the 1980s onward, "prostitution was linked to the fear of mafia practices and 'floods' of illegal sex workers entering the country."[57] Yet it was not until the late 1990s, in the midst of European Union optimism over harmonized immigration and social welfare rights, and conflicts in the United Nations and the International Labor Organization over prostitution, that these long-standing anxieties resulted in policy change.

A pragmatic approach to prostitution is a key part of the Netherlands' national identity. The Netherlands' pride in their tolerance and pragmatism has long kept prostitution as a significant touchstone that differentiates them from their neighbors, alongside such issues as gay and lesbian rights, euthanasia, and the decriminalization of soft drugs possession.[58] Regulated tolerance To outsiders, the Dutch public's bland tolerance of these issues is as shocking as the equanimity with which any respectable matron is willing to explain—in English or German or French or Spanish—that it is better to have such things out in the open where they can be better controlled. To Dutch citizens, this regulated tolerance provides a source of national identity and pride that bolsters a national history of compromise among religions, social classes, and geographical regions.[59] The frequency about which it is spoken—on government websites, at the red-light district's information center, in academic circles—is evidence of the frequency with which citizens can "feel Dutch" as they engage with the new prostitution politics, advocating for their eminently pragmatic common sense in the face of international skepticism. That Dutch prostitution reforms founder at the level of the bureaucracy of sex is almost beside the point: seeing prostitution as the Dutch state is part of its social citizenship. It also reminds the Dutch of their virtues at a time when such virtues were being eroded domestically by rising economic inequality and government retrenchment.

4

Legislating Peace for Women: Sweden's Sex Purchase Act

Figure 4.0 Vulnerable Women as Object Lesson Vulnerable women form an essential purpose for Sweden governance, both in reinforcing Swedish women's autonomy and instructing men in gender equality. Statuary at the Swedish National Museum (*Nordiska Museet*), Stockholm.

Source: author photo

"Model nation, world conscience, the country that protects its citizens from the cradle to the grave."[1] So a glossy book published by an arm of the Foreign Ministry describes Sweden, a member of one of the world's smallest, self-nominated clubs: nations that are moral beacons to the world. The United States is a member, of course, and so is France. But among these three countries, only Sweden has fewer than 9 million inhabitants and has not had colonies since the eighteenth century nor fought a war since the early nineteenth. With the construction of their social democratic welfare state in the years of the Cold War, Swedes have trumpeted their "third way" between capitalism and socialism to justify their moral leadership in the world. This leadership is an obligation to share successes, especially in the sexual realm, and especially regarding its successes in curtailing prostitution (see Table 4.1). As the Swedish Association for Sexuality Education (RFSU) modestly explains, "There is a major demand for the results of the Swedish experience in other parts of the world."[2]

By Dutch standards, Sweden barely had a commercial sex industry before it passed legislation to abolish it. Stockholm featured only two strip clubs for a population of 1.6 million and brothels were already illegal and clandestine. As one interviewee wryly noted, "If you [come] to Stockholm to get a lot of sex, you will be disappointed because of the reason if women can choose, they can also choose to say no there." Two streets at the edge of gentrifying working-class neighborhoods featured streetwalking, but the first complaints about prostitution came not from residents but from Swedish prostitutes themselves. Their complaints that Eastern European women were undercutting prices were made not to the police, but to the municipal social work units whose role was to connect women to city services, condoms, and lubricant and report crimes on behalf of women

Table 4.1   Swedish Prostitution Reform Timeline

1999	Sweden passes its *sexköpslag* as part of a broader bill on women's peace.
2001	Government declares that there is no need to study the law.
2003	Deputy Prime Minister Margareta Winberg leads Nordic Council protests against brothels in Athens in the run up to the Olympics.
2004	Estonian proposal to legalize sex work fails after fierce Swedish criticism.
2005	Sex Reform Act renews the *sexköpslag*.
2007	First government review of the law lauds its successes but chides lack of prosecutions.
2009	Norway and Iceland adopt "Swedish-style" prostitution ban with public support from Swedish government officials.
2010	Swedish Institute publishes a full-color 55-page book "Targeting the Sex Buyer: The Swedish Example."

unwilling to make official reports themselves. This was significant because what brought the police's attention to vulnerable migrants was not the crime of prostitution, but the concerns of Swedish prostitutes.

Prostitution in Sweden was made public not by visible prostitution, but by the public debates themselves. Screaming headlines in the nation's newspapers and documentaries and debates on television and radio brought prostitution into every home: "Sold as a Slave to Sweden," "Lily Sues Her Landlord for Pimping: 'They Raised the Rent Because I Am a Prostitute,'" "Tanning Salon Had a Brothel in the Basement," "No One Will Say Which Politicians Bought Sex from Underage Children," and "Medical Student and Mother Anna, 27, Sells Sex to Support Her Family."[3]

This chapter presents interviews with Swedish officials charged with implementing the new law in government and civil society. It allows proponents of the law to describe their conflicts with non-Swedes in international meetings, and domestic critics of the law to describe their conflicts with government officials who often hold the purse strings to their nonprofit organizations. These views are rarely aired in public or outside of Sweden. I show that these conflicts are less about the sale of sex itself than about broader issues of the best ways to protect vulnerable women and to protect national values in the face of global pressures, and the purpose of law itself. I will describe the institutional infrastructure for Swedish culture, including the role of the welfare state and feminism in making the Swedish policy plausible—and "sex work" an oxymoron.

Guaranteeing Peace for Women through the Sex-Purchase Law

Swedish prostitution reforms were passed as part of a 1999 bill to prevent violence against women titled the *kvinnofrid*, literally "women's peace." Part of this bill was what is formally known as the Law That Prohibits the Purchase of Sexual Services but became known as the *sexköpslag*, or "sex-purchase law." Sweden became the first country to prohibit the purchase of sex while leaving its sale decriminalized. Or, as an arm of the Swedish foreign ministry described in a 52-page full-color booklet,

> Even if the law was preceded by extensive debate and is still called into question in many parts of the world, it has received considerable support from the Swedish population. The practice of focusing on the sex buyers and neutralizing the demand for sexual services in order to combat prostitution and human trafficking for sexual purposes is often referred to as "the Swedish example."[4]

This was done to prevent the punishment of the weaker party in the prostitution transaction—women—while punishing the stronger—men. In the words of its author, "The ultimate goal of the Law is to protect the women in prostitution by, among other measures, addressing the root cause of prostitution and trafficking: the men who assume the right to purchase female human beings and sexually exploit them."[5] The penalties for a first offense were 3,000 Swedish crowns (about US$600 in 2000) with increased fines and the possibility of up to six months of jail time for second or third offenses.

Sweden's National Rapporteur on human trafficking and detective-inspector of the National Bureau of Investigation (RKP, or *Rikskriminal-polisen*) noted that incarceration was not a main purpose of the law: "Jail time is not the point. It is understood that the publicity surrounding the arrest and fine is a punishment of its own." Though a 2007 report chided that "traffickers rarely get convicted in court,"[6] one of the law's authors, Professor Madeleine Leijonhufvud, described convictions as only one of the law's effects. Prostitution, she writes, is "definitely was not about marginalized men otherwise unable to find sexual contact. The clientele in question had a social status to lose. Therefore, the law could work as a scare tactic."[7] This emphasis that men of all social classes used prostitutes—not just low-class men—meant that the law could reimpose Swedish values on an area that had been slipping in recent years. As I will show, the causes of these threats were external: globalization and the European Union.

A Natural Outgrowth of Long-Standing Debates

While outsiders treat the *sexköpslag* as a sudden rash of moralistic high-mindedness, Swedes emphasize it as the outgrowth of long-standing debates about social solidarity and gender equality since the 1950s. I spoke to Eva Zillén and Åsa Carlman from *Kvinna till Kvinna* (Woman to Woman—KtK), a nonprofit that "supports networks between women's organizations in conflict zones." KtK became involved in Stockholm-area roundtables on prostitution due to their work with Bosnian women and their NGOs for postwar reconstruction. KtK was upheld as a model of Swedish transnational work against human trafficking in the 2010 Swedish Institute book on the Swedish Example.[8]

Both Zillén and Carlman emphasized the law is an outgrowth of long-standing debates that have empowered Swedish women and slowly transformed gender relations in the country:

> ÅC: You have to look a really long way back, a 25-years long debate on prostitution, and then you have to get it together with the gender equality debate.
>
> EZ: The big difference between Sweden and a lot of other European countries, I find, is that I know no male friend of mine would ever tell me that he had gone to a prostitute—

ÅC: —because it implies your view on women. It says that you have this view on women that they are objects, which is not accepted.

EZ: And also because, for quite a long time, Swedish women have had the right to have a sexuality, and have sex. So it's also actually together with that debate.

In other words, the *sexköpslag* is more the result of decades of work on gender equality that has created a positive view of women and a public sphere where prostitution is unacceptable.

These decades of discussion have shaped an understanding of gender equality in which women's labor is important but sex work is an oxymoron. As Eva Zillén explained:

> This is in many ways a very political law and it will take time. We could not have had it without these past five years of discussions, and I think that is sometimes forgotten now. We have that discussion; we have a certain amount of gender equality. We have had the right to our own bodies, women in Sweden. We have had this that it is really bad for men to go to see prostitutes for as long as I have been growing up.

Thus the *sexköpslag* did not spring fully formed upon an unsuspecting populace, but is the outcome of long discussions and emergent consensus. Indeed, just after the law was passed a newspaper touted "strong support for the controversial prostitution law," noting that "4 of 10 Swedes want to forbid the sale of sexual services." A year and a half later, support was even stronger: "8 of 10 Swedes want prostitution to stay illegal."[9] Zillén's description of the law as "political" thus reflects the active work in shaping that consensus, work that is rarely acknowledged domestically by the law's supporters or externally by the law's critics.

Sweden enshrined gender equality as a key component first of the Social Democratic Party that ruled Sweden for 60 years, but has since become an accepted facet of Swedish society. Kajsa Wahlberg is the National Rapporteur on Trafficking and the deputy director of the National Bureau of Investigation (RKP—*Rikskriminalpolisen*), the part of the National Police Board that leads Sweden's international efforts to combat crime. As Director Wahlberg describes Swedish cultural values, it doesn't matter in which party they originated, there is a Swedish consensus about social solidarity that forms the basis of *kvinnofrid*:

> Whether you are a Social Democrat or not, you are being affected that everyone should be cared for somehow. We can't accept that people are sleeping in the streets, and we can't accept that children don't have food for the day, and that families suffer, and that you don't have a job so you have to be supported. And we care so much about the individual that [we reject] the attitude that you help yourself if you have problems.

Thus supporting the criminalization of purchasing sex is an act of solidarity with vulnerable individuals and a social good for everyone.

On Morality, Moralism, and the Law

Where critics see the *sexköpslag* as an example of sanctimonious Swedish moralism, its supporters explicitly reject morality as a purpose of the law. In the following exchange, Director Wahlberg relates her experiences explaining the law at international law enforcement meetings and the difficulty in conveying that the law is not about morality but about helping the victims of violence and maintaining equality between the sexes:

> *KW*: I get comments, "God, you Swedes are known for being so tall, long and sex-oriented, pornography. How can you suddenly be so moral and strict?" But it's not about morality, I think.
> *GM*: What's it about?
> *KW*: It's about the individual that you hurt. When you look at prostitution as violence against women, it's not a moral thing, it's more about that you hurt women in prostitution, and you use power when you buy someone else, when you take the right to buy someone else. And abuse this person's body. And the risks in prostitution for violence and diseases, and we have had young foreign women who have caught HIV because they have been sold and used as play tools for men. I think this is very, very serious.
> *GM*: So if this law, if it's not a moral thing, is it fixing a power imbalance? Is it a caring thing?
> *KW*: Yes it is a caring thing, and also a matter of equality between men and women. And equality between men and women is very high on the political agenda. And it threatens the equality between men and women too, if there is constantly a group of women that can be bought in prostitution.

In this exchange, Director Wahlberg explicitly places women's peace outside the realm of morality and in the realm of equality, a good in itself that is outside politics. She notes that the sex buyer uses not only power in the purchase, but is also exercising a right that has been eliminated in Sweden. The *kvinnofrid* encompasses two self-evident public goods: protection of individuals from harm, even self-harm, and maintaining gender equality. The outsiders who do not recognize these public goods misinterpret *kvinnofrid* as finger-wagging moralism, when for Swedes it is one plank among many supporting Swedish society, a collective decision to put a thumb on the scales of justice to correct gendered power imbalance.

Solidarity, or How Prostitution Is Like Alcohol or Spanking

Swedes drew upon two metaphors to explain precedents for the *sexköpslag*: the 1979 legislation to outlaw the corporal punishment of children and the 1955 National Alcohol Monopoly that imposed state control on all beverage sales (*Systembolaget*). Sweden was the first country to outlaw corporal punishment, and the social affairs minister described it as an act of international leadership at the law's 30-year celebration in 2009: "Many countries have followed our model but we still have a way to go."[10] Director Wahlberg also drew upon this previous legislation to explain *kvinnofrid* but described it in more explicit terms: "In the 50's Sweden also brought up the discussion about not to beat up your children in order to raise them. So that was hotly debated too. It was so strange, 'of course we have to beat up the children to raise them.'" In other words, *kvinnofrid* was an example of a long-standing debate in Sweden that change domestic culture that became a model for the world. An individual may enjoy prostitution or drugs, but the social problems these cause require their curtailment.

For domestic supporters of the *sexköpslag*, women can hardly consent to prostitution. Even if a Swedish woman believed she had chosen prostitution, social solidarity requires society to intervene. As Director Wahlberg explains,

> We have in Sweden, our system has affected us in that we care if an individual hurts him or herself, if you see what I mean. We don't think it's ok if you take drugs. OK, it's fine with you [Americans] if you wish to drug yourself to death, if you wish to fuck yourself to death, fine. But we [Swedes] think that women in prostitution, if we talk about *them*, they hurt themselves, they hurt their loved ones, their families, their children, their parents they worry about them. And as a parent the last thing you want is for your kid to end up in drugs and in prostitution. Those are some of the worst things that can happen . . . We don't live as isolated islands here. What I say and what I do affects other people. But in other countries it's more up to the individual: "I grow up and I can decide for myself and I can do whatever I want, and no one else cares about it."

Two themes justify *kvinnofrid* as an issue beyond morality: individual actions must be curtailed when they affect other people, and solidarity requires that individuals not be allowed to hurt themselves.

This logic underpins the state alcohol monopoly, which supporters of the *sexköpslag* cite as another example of Swedish solidarity. As the *Systembolaget* explains on its website, "*Systembolaget* exists for one reason: to minimize alcohol-related problems by selling alcohol in a responsible way, without profit motive."[11] As Åsa Carlman from *Kvinna till Kvinna* (KtK) explained,

> We in Sweden think that it's a solidarity thing that we are not having a prob-
> lem with the alcohol. It's ok for us to go to this special store to buy alcohol
> because we know from research and from the past that it actually prevents
> women from being beaten, and people from being over-drunk and having
> huge livers. And I would say [*kvinnofrid*] is a little bit the same thing, that a
> solidarity with women who have bad self-esteem. And it's a solidarity with
> men having bad self-esteem and [feeling they must] buy sex.

In Sweden, everyone can express small acts of solidarity with victims in society. Buying alcohol during the restricted hours of the state liquor stores and giving up the right to buy it in the evenings or on weekends shows solidarity with the victims of domestic violence and those suffering the health problems of alcohol addiction. Supporters of the *sexköpslag* are showing solidarity with those who are hurt in systems of prostitution.

The *sexköpslag*'s opponents use the metaphor of the *Systembolaget* as well. Although Sweden's Center Party officially supports the law, its youth wing (*Centerns ungdomsförbund*) voted in 2009 to scrap the law and decriminalize the purchase of sexual services. This platform was subsequently endorsed by the youth wing of Prime Minister Fredrik Reinfeldt's Liberal Party as well. As one of the supporters of decriminalization stated: "When we can buy alcohol, we ought to be able to buy sexual services."[12]

Even if Swedes wanted to sell sex, their rights may be overridden because the presence of prostitution within Sweden affects *all* women. In other words, the legislation was necessary to protect the rights of all women to walk the streets, a good that supersedes the right of individual women to sell sex. In fact, in the first years after the law was passed, the government often promoted a figure that street prostitution had declined by 80 percent. Critics noted that the police often cruised streets with prostitutes to try to arrest clients, driving sex workers and their clients indoors. Critics of the law dismissed this tangible outcome.

One of the most high-profile critics of the law was the Swedish Association for Sexuality Education (RFSU). As their spokesperson Karin Nilsson told me,

> What we say and others say and claim as a victory is that we don't have any
> prostitution in the streets now. Of course we don't. We could have told you
> that. But is that the same as saying that we don't have prostitution anymore?
> It's a transition period. It's going underground, it's going into buildings or
> wherever.

Increased enforcement didn't reduce prostitution, just moved it around. Supporters of the law cite the transition to the Internet as unrelated to the law, while opponents described it as "tightening the thumbscrews" on vulnerable women.[13]

Despite these explicit discussions of prostitution and place, there seems to be one tangible benefit of the law that has escaped public discussion. As Zillén and Carlman of *Kvinna till Kvinna* noted, moving prostitution off the streets was a tangible success of the law for all women by freeing them from men's public judgment and making the streets safe:

> GM: What about the women, like Rosea, the Swedish Prostitute's Association, who say that they are able to make the decision on their own not to sell?
>
> EZ: I can say that it affects me. It affects the way that men look at me. And it does.
>
> ÅC: It has had an effect, the law, that it has taken away a lot of the prostitution from the streets, has had the effect that I can walk on the streets in this town, I have the right to the streets at all time.
>
> GM: Was it uncomfortable before?
>
> ÅC: It was. Some places you wouldn't want to go, because you were [seen as] a prostitute. And now I have the right to walk on the streets, and I'm happy for that. I think that's good. And I think, no matter if there's a small group of women who thinks that they have been deprived the right [to sell sex], I think there are plenty more women who think they have the right to the streets. And we don't talk about that because that's [considered] so egoistic.
>
> GM: Why would it be egoistic though, because with all laws you talk about costs and benefits—
>
> EZ: —but I have rarely heard it as a benefit of the law.
>
> GM: I hear them saying a lot of that prostitution is going off of the streets. Prostitution is going off of the streets—
>
> ÅC: —like a mantra—
>
> GM: —yes, and then I don't hear anyone say . . . it has had this one concrete win that you both recognize as freeing yourselves.
>
> ÅC: But that's the definite win so far, is that we have a better mental climate for women, because we have this thing that we say: Women are not objects. In this very concrete way, so that's the first win.

Thus for domestic supporters of *kvinnofrid*, the removal of prostitution from the streets is a tangible step in creating a "better mental climate for women," free of being sexualized in public and giving them the freedom to the city's streets.

This freedom of Swedish women to experience *kvinnofrid*—women's peace—is dramatized by contrast with the dangers women face in other countries. As Åsa Carlman notes, "The problem in the countries where the girls and women come from is this—that they are so hidden away and kept away and locked up, so they get desperate, and the provisions for getting a real job sort of tend to get smaller, because they should be so protected. So it actually makes it easier for the traffickers." As Eva Zillén continues about Iraq and Kosovo where women are kidnapped from the streets: "Women and girls cannot be involved in any political work because they have to be protected every day, every second, and they cannot walk freely in the society." So for an NGO that supports the law and the Swedish approach to human trafficking, there are concrete situations to contrast with Swedish values and realities.

The dangers to the public sphere are not confined to prostitution on the streets. As many interviewees noted, the debates around *kvinnofrid* paralleled other conversations about sex in public. These included the use of women's bodies in advertisements, the sexualization of young girls through adult underwear styles, and the proliferation of pornography that makes it difficult for girls to say no. Eva Zillén drew the following connections:

> Quite a lot of boys shout "whore" to their fellow students of the other gender. The backlash is that a lot of girls know that you have to shave everywhere . . . a lot of young girls more now [feel] that they need to say yes to a lot of sex things that is not ordinary sex, but they [must] experiment as well.

These incursions of sexuality into the public sphere are evidence of the lack of full gender equality and the everyday assaults on women's ability to form healthy selves. This need to manage the public sphere to benefit all women ultimately justifies the law. Such attention to the public sphere was also demonstrated by a cartoon poster campaign against such whore-shaming. In two other Swedish offices where I interviewed, I saw the image of a boy calling a girl "Whore!" followed by a panel of the girl turning him into a frog with the caption, "No, a witch!"

Although the *sexköpslag* was widely popular in the early 2000s—newspapers frequently cited support approaching 80 percent—it nevertheless attracted broad if muted criticism from unlikely places within Sweden: among the government officials and nonprofit organizations charged with implementing it. While criticisms from outside Sweden focused on the spirit of the law, internal criticism was as frequently about failures in its definition and implementation.

Internal Conflict: One Policy, One Feminism

External critiques of the *sexköpslag* miss the robust internal debate on the legislation. Where supporters and critics of *kvinnofrid* agree is that there is not enough support for women in prostitution. For the RFSU, it is practical concerns about people's daily lives that led to their opposition to the *sexköpslag*: "If you look at the behavior of men, and women of course I guess, who actually go out there and buy sex, I don't think it will have this impact if you just focus first of all on the men and don't put the resources needed for the women." As KtK's Eva Zillén noted, "If you compare the Balkan region and Sweden, the Balkan region has much better methods of taking care of the women than Sweden has, because we don't have any . . . It's always deportation, because no one wants to take them. Not many countries will see [being trafficked] as a possibility for people to stay in their countries."

For these critics, the focus is too much on punishing male clients of prostitution rather than on helping the women, in part due to lack of funds. As Åsa Carlman averred, "The focus in Sweden and elsewhere I would say really is on prosecuting and fining the criminals. And not really caring about the women because they are sort of lost human beings or something, since they've been through what they have." RKP Director Kajsa Wahlberg concurred, "One of the most frequents complaints I have made is that the resources promised in the debates have never been made available, it all comes down to money." These arguments echoed larger political disputes over welfare state retrenchment that began in the 1990s.

Whether domestic nonprofits supported or opposed *kvinnofrid*, all justified their opinions with reference to their clinical practice and day-to-day contact with female victims. They contrasted this practical experience with the concerns of politicians, who lacked experience and were tainted either by ideological rigidity or political compromise. Interviewees from NGOs made this strong distinction between the one-policy-fits-all approach of the *sexköpslag* supporters and their nuanced understanding based on practical experience through individual caseworking, work that has costs. As RFSU's Karin Nilsson explained:

> You need to put more money into social programs, into programs focusing on different groups within prostitution, and also to acknowledge that there *are* different groups. Groups that will say that they actually enjoy what they are doing. And then you need to have a dialogue with them on their terms as well.

This is a similarity to KtK, the nonprofit that supports the law. But KtK's Eva Zillén also noted that individual differences among victims made it difficult to provide support:

> EZ: We have difficulties dealing with women who actually went away [from their home country] thinking that they would work as prostitutes, but also

> thinking that they would also get paid for it, and ending up in trafficking circles because they are not the good ones. They were not lured into the business.
>
> ÅC: Yeah, and that is the saying, "*real* trafficking victims." No, they weren't just prostitutes—
>
> EZ: —when they got the exact same treatment! And they might just have been less naive, and knew that maybe that was the only way to get out and get money from a country like Columbia.

Government officials interpret this assertion of differences among women involved in prostitution as an implicit critique of the *sexköpslag*. As the RFSU's Karin Nilsson explained, "We do find ourselves being misunderstood. Especially by the [government Division] for Equality. We are simply trying to say that there is no easy way out. We don't think of this legislation as the answer."

Nilsson stressed that this diversity of opinion was present internally within the RFSU itself: "You need to know this discussion within our office is of course not one voice. There are people in favor of the law . . . there are very many perspectives and voices within this organization. I find this very interesting, that there are many different opinions." And yet, RFSU's diversity of opinions and attention to multiple experiences does not translate easily into being heard. As another NGO official described her colleagues in other organizations,

> They approve of the law, but they still want a more comprehensive discussion and debate, where more perspectives can be allowed, and we can actually have a dialogue. I think that's actually the problem with Sweden right now. It's like we're stuck, there's one position there [in the government] but there's really not a clear position here [among NGOs]. And there are other positions, at least other voices, trying to get through

If RFSU was unique in taking a public position against the law, in spite of its internal dissent, other NGOs in favor of the *sexköpslag* still felt themselves silenced in their discussions about the law.

The forceful, unambiguous government position was identified as a problem by many organizations. As another NGO leader stated flatly: "we have identified this Unit of Equality as one of the problems . . . Because they decided the system is how you're supposed to perceive things. And if you don't, you're not invited to a meeting, you're not invited to speak. Which is very strange . . . if they actually wanted to listen to the NGOs in Sweden who actually work on these issues, and were prepared to be criticized, and see that as something good, then that would be so much easier for us." The government policy—one broadly supported by Swedish NGOs—was presented so uniformly that these same NGOs felt it could not be criticized even to improve it.

The focus on *gendered* violence narrows the definition of prostitution to women as victims, a point that even proponents of broader meanings often forget. The RFSU official related her experience at an EU meeting on HIV/AIDS:

> We had a lot of comments on the draft of the declaration. And we were traveling to the [Swedish] Ministry of Social Affairs, and there was this discussion—the first thing actually that she said to me was "No, we don't want to talk about sex workers. The Swedish position is that we talk about prostituted women." It was not prostitutes, but prostituted women, which was interesting because again only women, right?

Such diverse opinions are more possible when dealing in transnational environments, but the domestic focus on gendered violence focuses Swedish attention exclusively upon women in prostitution to the exclusion of men. If the state is the thumb upon the scales of justice to correct gender imbalance, in Sweden it can only weigh in favor of female victims against male perpetrators.

It also reflects the official state view of gender that has become institutionalized both in the policies of the welfare state and the installation of a univocal state feminism in Sweden.[14] As RFSU described the government, "There's only one way to be a good feminist, and if you're not, then you need to be corrected." Rather than a spectrum of feminisms, as is common in the United States or the United Kingdom, when the state gets involved in feminism, it gets to pick winners and losers.

Conflict between Swedes and Other Europeans

If *kvinnofrid* brings Swedes into conflict with their European colleagues, it is a conflict that emphasizes Swedish virtues and reinforces common values, such as the impossibility of sex being work. Even domestic critics of the *sexköpslag* rarely want to see prostitution legalized. As Åsa Carlman of KtK explains, "To legalize prostitution as a good way of dealing with prostitution would be to go the patriarchal way, so the men could continue to buy women's bodies." The legalization of prostitution in the Netherlands is criticized for representing a laissez-faire attitude toward morality. As special advisor to the Division of Gender Equality that drafted the *kvinnofrid*, Gunilla Ekberg writes, "Prostitution has been normalized by neoliberals as a form of sexual entertainment . . . what previously was viewed as a severe form of sexual exploitation is now a woman's right to do what she wants with her body and a way to sexual liberation and self-determination"[15]. In contrast to this "stagnant repressive political agenda," she describes Sweden's recognition that prostitution is "a form of male sexual violence against women and children" is "an essential part of efforts to create a contemporary and democratic society where full gender equality is the norm" (ibid.).

International conferences on women's health and especially human trafficking become standoffs over prostitution policy. As KtK's Eva Zillén described the misunderstandings she has experienced,

> *EZ*: When leaving Sweden you get attacked over the Swedish law, it's so . . . <shakes head in frustration> And quite many haven't really understood what it is about. It's still insisting on thinking we are after the women, that we are somehow going to punish the women, and of course it's somehow punishing the women [because they aren't] getting to choose their own way of finding an income.

This denial of an individual right to sell sex is the source of this misunderstanding and leads to charges of moralism and naiveté. But it also leads Ms. Zillén to grant the criticism that saving prostitutes from sex buyers does not help them earn money some other way.

While outsiders misunderstand Swedish values, Zillén lays some of the blame on the internal political climate within Sweden, especially the way the government promotes the *sexköpslag* in other countries. Foreign critics tell her:

> *EZ*: That we are naive, that we are just taking a higher moral [ground that can] not be reached . . . we always get that. Most of the time you get attacked, and I think that it's partly because there is not a good discussion around here [in Sweden]. With great political wills, to say that a lot of countries are very very interested in our law. <sarcastically> Yeah, a lot of countries are, but most of them are in the way like, "how could you possibly have such a law?"

Most foreign interest in the *sexköpslag* is not positive, at least in KtK's international encounters. Director Wahlberg casts this skepticism in an optimistic light when she reports an early interaction:

> *KW*: I have a German colleague within this task force against organized crime, and he was the first one in '99 to decide "You are crazy in Sweden! Prohibiting men from buying sexual services! You can't do that!" But on the other side, if you can prevent trafficking with your legislation, I wish you very good luck. He was the first one to see that possibility.

It is this confidence that other nations will eventually come around to Swedish thinking, and that Swedes will not change their mind, that she brings to her presentations at international law enforcement conferences:

> KW: I will get flashbacks and think, God, how far away we are from each other, how far away we are from how we think. And how we view prostitution. But I think this will not affect us [here in Sweden]. We are so clear about our standpoint here that we will not change and go the German or Dutch way, no.

Just as the "Swedish model" serves as a foil against which the Dutch and Germans articulate their national virtues, so does legalized prostitution exemplify Sweden's. Sweden's role as a beacon to Europe was part of the motivation for joining the EU in the first place, with the continent sometimes cast unflatteringly as "Brothel Europe."

Brothel Europe

The experts I interviewed did not see the *sexköpslag*'s as a response to EU politics and stressed it as the careful achievement of long-term internal debates within Sweden. A historical perspective on the timing of policy changes suggests otherwise. We see this (1) with the timing of the mainstream adoption of a Swedish-style radical feminism, (2) with the discourse that links prostitution to European integration, and (3) with the persistent linking of prostitution and EU politics, especially when it comes to migrant labor.

One common story of the *kvinnofrid* legislation explains its timing as a response to complaints from domestic Swedish prostitutes in the late 1990s. But prostitution and human trafficking had featured in debates years earlier during the controversial referendum that approved Sweden's 1995 accession to the European Union. Although the yes vote was approved by the prime minister and his ruling Social Democratic Party, it passed with difficulty because of high-profile Social Democratic defectors and the united opposition of the far left and far right. Sweden's first EU Commissioner Anita Gradin made human trafficking a European issue starting in 1995, which brought it to the fore of domestic politics as well. In 2004, the weakened Social Democratic–led government again put forward a national resolution to join the Euro currency, a measure that was soundly defeated, leading to the fall of the government and only the second time in 60 years that the Social Democratic Party was not in power.

As part of his doomed campaign to stay in power, in 2004 the (male) prime minister Gøran Persson declared the ruling Social Democratic

Party to be a feminist party. The move was roundly criticized. On the right, it was seen as pandering political correctness. On the left, it was seen as stating something that was not true given the persistent gender inequalities in Sweden. At the same time, a new radical feminist political party (*Feministisk Initiativ*—FI) formed to advocate more forceful gender policies outside the traditional political parties. The emergence of an explicitly feminist party on the heels of the Social Democratic Party's official feminist designation was a rebuke. In criticism of the Social Democrats' tepid *sexköpslag* FI proposed monetary reparations for prostitutes, a proposition supported by American radical feminist legal theorist Catherine Mackinnon.[16]

EU opponents argued that Sweden's progressive morality and social democracy would be diluted if it lost control of its borders and internal affairs. In 1994, in the midst of the bruising Swedish debates about joining the EU, a pamphlet appeared with the same title opposing the Swedish bid for membership. "30,000 women were perched on the borders ready to flood Sweden with prostitution" it proclaimed, taking advantage of lax European border enforcement and Sweden's generous welfare benefits. One of its authors was Sven-Axel Månsson, a graduate student of social work just beginning the research that would make him one of Sweden's leading researchers on prostitution and, later, a vocal supporter of the *sexköpslag*. While it is unclear how wide a readership this pamphlet received, it spoke to widespread anxieties about the EU being a Trojan horse that would smuggle into Sweden foreign ideas like sex work along with Eastern European women. Such ideas spread beyond the pamphlet and into the public sphere: a January newspaper editorial warned "with the widening of the EU, we will be flooded with prostitutes from Eastern Europe," a claim repeated often in follow-up articles and debates.[17]

Sweden did ultimately join the EU, supported by the then-dominant Social Democratic Party, and Persson's extremely popular heir-apparent Anna Lindh. She was the deputy prime minister and the literal face of the government's effort to ratify the referendum, a role that included many media appearances and her image on billboards all over the country. The government's argument was that Sweden's sovereignty would be protected by EU rules, but that its influence would be increased by the opportunity to participate in the debates that were shaping the continent in the European Commission and Parliament. Though many feared that Sweden would be swamped by *Bordel Europa*, having a popular and experienced politician like Anna Lindh as the face of the EU campaign was meant to convince voters that Sweden—and she—could inject Swedish values into the continent, including Swedish gender equality. The government slogan was the EU membership could "Swedify Europe," a campaign that boosted polls to a toss-up. The murder of Anna Lindh by a mentally ill asylum-seeker only three days before the referendum may have contributed to its narrow passage out of sympathy to her wishes. Ultimately successful, this campaign tapped into the Swedish desire to be a moral innovator and beacon of human rights, long a part of Swedish national self-image.[18]

Prostitution policies still feature in Swedish criticisms of Europe. The "People's Movement No to the EU" (*Foldrörelsen Nej till EU*) regularly publishes newsletter items criticizing the legalization of prostitution or the lack of European Parliament support for measures to stop "prostitution and human trafficking." For example, the EU is described as "almost misogynist" for considering "prostitution as a profession."[19] Germany was criticized for legalizing prostitution in 2001. Now selling sex in Germany is "about the same thing as selling candy, in the legal sense." The news item continues, "The Act purports to improve the situation of prostitutes and try to free the sex trade from organized crime." [20] Hungary is criticized for making prostitutes pay tax, because "critics believe that the policy is more about increasing income tax revenues than making prostitutes feel better."[21] Headlines such as these regularly appeared in mainstream papers as well, equating Europe with prostitution.

The fear that migrants were swamping Sweden was a concern expressed by the nonprofits in favor of *kvinnofrid*. KtK's Eva Zillén notes that outside Sweden, organizations like theirs are open to accusations:

Of being against migration, accused of being against the rights of women from the Eastern countries to come to Sweden and Western Europe, because it's saying that the only way to stop this is by closing the borders. And sometimes there is this extreme [suggestion based on our work]: "don't let any women of this-and-this age enter the country."

Indeed, the fact that such proposals were occasionally discussed in Swedish papers justified this criticism from abroad.

The women from KtK mocked the smug Swedish view that their country was the best in the world and a natural magnet for foreigners,

FV1: We [in this office] don't think that Sweden is the only country in the EU, [most Swedes] live on this strange assumption that everybody wants to come here. Everybody wants to come to Sweden and live in this country where it's incredibly cold until the end of March. They don't go to some incredibly warm country, no, they choose to go up North so they don't see the sun for months. I mean, no not everybody wants to come to Sweden, but we really think that we have to have legislation that works because everyone wants to come to us.

> *FV2*: Yeah, and we have unemployment, and they are going to steal our jobs, and if they're not going to steal our jobs, they're going to steal our wealth and healthcare.
> *FV1*: <sarcastically> Well they're just coming here to get on our welfare system, you didn't know that.

For NGO workers with broad international experience, there was a disappointing provincialism in Swedish skepticism about migration and asylum seekers.

A criticism of Swedish xenophobia or chauvinism also enters KtK's discussion of the domestic Swedish view of prostitution-sending countries:

> *FV*: You'd also think that everybody living in Eastern Europe are more or less criminals. Not only criminals by overusing the welfare system, but also in organized crime.

In other words, all the countries on the verge of entering the EU in 2004 seemed full of criminals, some destined to commit crimes in Sweden by virtue of robbing the public purse, and others by being involved in illicit trafficking.

A Moral Leader in Gender Equality

In her oft-cited piece for international audiences describing why she helped author the *sexköpslag*, Gunilla Ekberg describes its conception at the Swedish Women's Lobby congress of 1998:

> Ebon Kram, former chairperson of ROKS (the National Organization for Women's Shelters in Sweden), recommended that prostitution be put on the agenda. Her proposal was ignored in favor of other matters perceived to be more important. This angered Marinne Kekonius, member of the battered women's shelter in Enköping, Sweden, who rose to deliver these words, reminding women of the importance of supporting prostituted women: "Remember, all women can become prostituted. What if our country is invaded, do you really think that the women in Yugoslavia were imagining a future in prostitution before the war started?" After this speech, the proposal passed unanimously.[22]

This birth story captures the importance of gender solidarity for the Swedish nation-state project and the empathy it elicits for women made vulnerable through war and prostitution. It also highlights the qualities that propel conflict between Swedes and non-Swedes in international forums: not the sale of sex itself, but differences in ways to protect vulnerable women, and how these strategies form a potent part of national identity that must be defended in the face of threats.

The prostitutes imagined by Swedes are women forced into prostitution by violence, so society must be made a better place for them. This is a reasonable proposition within Sweden, given its robust welfare state that guarantees its citizens housing, education, public transportation, parental leave, childcare, old-age support, and paid vacations. Seeing as a Swedish state means restricting practices known to provide the structural foundations for violence, including the sale of alcohol, the use of women's bodies in advertising, and representations of violence in the media. Given this cultural and institutional context, it is reasonable for Swedes to assume that prostitution can be overcome. These policy contexts are lacking in international critiques of the law's morality.

I have also shown that the international context in which prostitution reform became necessary in Sweden revolved around the perception of pressures from outside, especially around European Union timetables. It is common that the law is understood in a cultural context of Swedishness. Both supporters and critics of the law see it as the outcome of Swedish values, whether virtuous or sanctimonious. Using cultural values alone to explain the importance and timing of the law thus founders on the teleology that Sweden did a Swedish thing because it was Sweden. Instead, the Swedish bureaucracy of sex is part of a social citizenship that emphasizes worker protections alongside a nation-state project that strenuously acts to equalize gender relations.

The Swedish *kvinnofrid* emphasizes a basic conflict over the relationship of law to morality. Advocates of the *sexköpslag* emphasize that it is not a moralistic law but the outcome of a hard-won consensus about protecting gender equality. To its domestic critics, however, the law is moralistic in asserting a truth about women's experiences in prostitution that does not apply to everyone. Sociologists have shown that this is a common strategy during contentious politics to draw symbolic boundaries around permissible topics in a way that excludes opposing viewpoints—seeing as a state means some things are difficult to see. Here Sweden is being framed as a "haven in a heartless [European] world" where the *sexköpslag* is framed as being so natural as being beyond critique, relegating its critics among supporters of sexual violence and slavery—and prostitution legalizers. The distinction that the *sexköpslag*'s opponents make between moralism and morality is between acceptable politics and unacceptable compromise: one woman's moral imperative is another's finger-wagging moralism.

What I have emphasized in this section is the institutional contexts of Swedishness that underpin the law. The relative strength of Sweden's welfare state makes credible Swedish claims to value gender equality in practice and not theory. Ironically it is this very muscularity that renders unintelligible the claims of Swedish sex workers that they can consent and choose individual clients, much less their profession or lifestyle. Indeed sex workers in Sweden feel that they are understood as crazy, so unintelligible are their arguments about consent. In a country where everyone gives up the right to purchase alcohol at certain times out of solidarity with its victims, it is easy to understand how the rhetoric of sex workers' rights falls on deaf ears.

In this context, it is not ridiculous for Swedish feminists to imagine being forced into prostitution, though it has not had foreign troops on its soil since the early nineteenth century. The privilege of being a Swede means the moral necessity of imagining what it is like to be from a less fortunate nation, and the obligation to show solidarity with the vulnerable even when this means giving up individual rights. In a country where gender equality is such a strong virtue, the vulnerable are always women. And being Swedish means knowing that other nations will eventually come around to seeing the right way of seeing social problems, as they have with child abuse, marital rape, armed neutrality, and international peacekeeping.

As the women of KtK, who both criticize the law's implementation and support its principles, summarized, "We think that the law is very good, and the problem is, as I said before, for us to have it actually functioning." In time, these imperfections will be fixed and other societies will see the wisdom of the Swedish model. But in the meantime, she concedes, "quite a lot of countries are not ready for it," adding optimistically, "yet."

5

German Consensus for Sex Work, Compromise over Sex Business

Figure 5.0   Frankfurt Brothel Germany's legalization of prostitution was explicitly designed not to enhance the status of prostitution, such as that conducted at this Frankfurt brothel.

Source: author photo

Given its outsized importance in European affairs, surprisingly little has been written about German prostitution regulation.[1] Yet the contradictions of the German experience say more about the ambiguities of governing prostitution than the flashier and more-publicized case of the Netherlands. Germany legalized prostitution at the end of 2001, ostensibly giving prostitutes access to the same benefits as other occupations, especially health care, unemployment insurance, and pensions. As described by a government report, parliament intended "neither to abolish prostitution nor to enhance its status. Rather, the emphasis was placed on improving conditions under which prostitutes work so as to benefit those women and men who voluntarily earn their living by prostitution."[2] This fine line between abolition and legalization—enhancing prostitutes' labor status, but not enhancing prostitution—marks a difference from the Dutch model and describes many of the difficulties of regulating prostitution in Germany (see Table 5.1.).

Sex Workers without Bosses, Entrepreneurs without Businesses

Before legalization, however, there were many indications that the old system by which prostitution had been managed was already crumbling in cities all over the country. National news stories at the end of the millennium highlighted the difficulties faced by Hamburg officials in controlling mafia networks,[3] a botched prosecution of Hells Angels for human trafficking in Stuttgart,[4] Munich's largest-ever police raid to

Table 5.1   German Prostitution Reform Timeline

1998	Berlin State Senate establishes the Joint Working Group on Prostitution Policy.
2000	State Court of Hesse declares prostitution "employment" under German law.
	Frankfurt Foreigners' Department conduct document controls/raids on the railway station red-light district.
	Frankfurt City Council establishes the Roundtable on Prostitution.
	Berlin State Court defines prostitution a profession under German law.
2001	In December, German Parliament passes bill legalizing prostitution and strengthening punishments for pimping and human trafficking.
2002	Frankfurt Roundtable on Prostitution presents conclusions to City Parliament (*Römer*).
2004	Frankfurt *Römer* approves Roundtable on Prostitution report.
	Berlin State Parliament approves procedural "treaty" between the police and NGOs on antitrafficking cooperation.

Note: Actions with national implications in bold.

"smash a brothel cartel,"[5] and Berlin restaurant licensing agents struggling to close restaurants used to facilitate prostitution.[6]

The first move toward national prostitution reforms in Germany came not from national legislation, as in Sweden or the Netherlands, or municipal reforms, as in Finland, but from two court cases. The first one occurred in 2000 when the State Court of Hesse ruled that brothel prostitutes were employees for the purposes of a compensation case.[7] The decision clarified prostitution as an occupation requiring work permission for Frankfurt's migration authority. In Germany, immigration is controlled at the municipal level. Concern had been building throughout the 1990s over the apparent rise in illegal migrants in Frankfurt's brothels and a spate of spectacular crimes perpetrated by organized crime networks from other countries.[8]

The second ruling, in Berlin, ruled that prostitution was not immoral (*sittenwidrigkeit*) in 2001, removing the Christian jurisprudential basis by which prostitution had been prohibited.[9] The ruling allowed Café Pssst, a hotel and bar established for prostitutes and their clients to meet, to retain its restaurant and liquor licenses.[10] If prostitution in the Nordic countries was defined as gender inequality, and in the Netherlands as work, the German ruling was a compromise between important cultural principles of workers' rights and protections for the vulnerable encoded in its welfare state.

On the basis of the court rulings, the Green Party reintroduced its 1990 proposal to legalize prostitution, giving *sex workers* access to the health benefits, pension schemes, and unemployment benefits accorded to self-employed workers.[11] In line with the law's strengthened prohibitions against sexual exploitation, however, the prohibition on employment contracts between businesses and sex workers was maintained.[12] The new law created a seeming paradox under German employment legislation by defining prostitution as a trade (*Gewerbe*) but not a business (*Betrieb*).[13] In other words, sex work was legalized only in the context of self-employment, and sex workers could not sign contracts with an employer. This compromise marked a stark distinction with the Dutch legislation with which it is often lumped, and institutionalized a state classification that was neither purely rational, nor one with precedent in German law.

The German compromise on sex work does resemble its solution to abortion, however, in the way that the state reconciles important individual and social concerns. The German Constitutional Court ruled that fetal life is protected from conception onward, but ruled permissible a law that permits abortion through the first trimester if accompanied by counseling to persuade the woman to bear the child *and* a government guarantee of day care for all children three to four years of age. As scholars summarize, "In the German context, the right to life of the fetus and the right of a woman to self-determination are reconcilable. The welfare state is what reconciles them."[14] Policy frames women as the best guarantors of fetal life, allowing them to make a decision under conditions of state support for raising children *and* a reminder of societal interests in their choice to bear the child. Similarly, prostitutes are enabled as decision makers, but protected from employer relations—compromising a general principle of corporatist social citizenship but still defining the prostitution in terms of employment.

The two court rulings, which prompted national legislators to take up the issue, reflected the fact that Germany's large cities and their state courts had already been dealing with a breakdown in the "immorality" clause that had prohibited prostitution at the federal level. Germany's legalization was *decentralized*, reflecting Germany's federal structure, giving municipalities the zoning authority to permit or prohibit brothels: "There is no single 'German model' . . . each jurisdiction has developed its own policies, and [organized] prostitution remains illegal in many parts of the country."[15] Its legalization was also *limited*, reflecting a particularly German reconciliation between a woman's ability to decide what is best for her in difficult circumstances *and* societal interests in reducing exploitation.

Frankfurt's response resembled the Dutch way: inviting all the stakeholders to meetings to work out some common framework. In Germany, sex workers' rights organizations were explicitly invited to the policy table and a compromise was reached where sex work was permitted as a limited business to maintain protections for women workers. This contrasted starkly with the Nordic countries, where sex workers were silenced and the debate was about how to restrict prostitution from the public sphere and whether the criminalization of clients was the best response. As the German federal government's 2007 assessment of the law described its purpose, the act "defines prostitution as an autonomous decision that is to be respected by the law but which is typically associated with considerable dangers and risks . . . [which are] primarily determined by the conditions under which the prostitutes are working."[16] If this allowed prostitution access to the public sphere of business, it did so by privatizing the intimate transaction for prostitutes' own protection, insisting that prostitution is a relationship between two people without other ties, such as landlords, accountants, or housecleaners, but also by denying sex buyers any guarantees over the services they were purchasing.

This focus on consensus to protect workers reflects the domestic context of the German welfare state that prioritizes security for worker families and minimal benefits for unmarried dependents. Pensions and other benefits accrue from employment, as they do in the Netherlands. Though Germans, like Swedes, refer to their system as an exceptional middle way (*Sonderweg*) between capitalism and socialism, the German system does not share the essential principle of gender equality because unlike the Swedish focus on individual autonomy, the German model privileges the family as a unit of citizenship.[17] This privileges a liberal feminism within the state, in which women have the choice between full-time motherhood and part- or full-time work (the fact that there is a severe lack of state childcare means that these principles, like those of prostitution, are important in ways that transcend their practice as I describe below).[18]

By limiting prostitution to a self-employed trade, German legalization thus allowed prostitutes to become workers by recognizing their *Gewerbe*, the way by which workers and their dependents gain benefits. Sex workers participated in the consultations to craft local processes or legislation. Preventing them from having a place of business (*Betrieb*), however, *protected* them from unscrupulous employers. As the federal government's assessment of the law emphasized:

> Prostitution was not to become a "job like any other." The employer's right to issue instructions was largely restricted in favor of prostitutes' right to sexual self-determination. No prostitute is to be obliged to serve a particular client or to engage in certain sexual practices against her will.[19]

German policy confirmed prostitutes' status as dependents of a sort— female dependents at that—representing a "middle way" between the full-scale legalization of the Netherlands where employer contracts with prostitutes are legal, and the prohibition of sex buying in Sweden because all prostitutes are abused dependents. The German model, so often lumped in with the Dutch, thus directly addresses one of the abolitionist critiques of regulating prostitution—that it becomes a "job like any other."

This chapter presents a case study of Frankfurt-am-Main because it had all the characteristics of German process: court actions undermining its pre-2001 prostitution laws, extensive consultations at the municipal and state levels all over the country for how to respond, consultations that were collated into legislation at the national level. I show how German codetermination was managed in Frankfurt in ways consistent with the subsequent national extension of citizenship to prostitutes according to the principles of corporatist welfare states, but which protected prostitutes by denying them employment contracts. This compromise was a sort of enforced, limited autonomy, according sex workers citizenship but protecting them from the full might of the market according to the inclusion roadmap of the German welfare state.

Public Tolerance for Private Transactions

Frankfurt has three red-light zones, two small and one large central one, reflecting municipal compromises. The history of prostitution in German cities is more varied than many other countries, reflecting the diversity and late-unification of the country.[20] This is reflected in the wide variance in local prostitution practices. Prostitution was regulated quite differently in different regions, mirroring the federal structure that guaranteed state autonomies and diversity in German ways of doing things. Germany had a long fame of prostitution related to its occupation by foreign forces after the two World Wars, culminating in the image of the St. Pauli girl of Hamburg's *Reeperbahn* that still adorns a popular American beer brand. Prostitution is prosaic to German cities provided it is confined to a small red-light district or "tolerance zone," common to almost any medium to small city.

German cities vary in the location of their tolerance zones. Frankfurt's are right in the center of the city, and they tend to be located in the very center of larger or more Protestant cities, or in industrial areas or just outside city limits in Catholic or more conservative areas.[21] The exception to this politico-religious rule of thumb is Berlin, a city-state within the German federal system and continental Europe's largest metropolitan area. Berlin has long permitted brothels in any area not too near schools or churches provided they do not become a public nuisance. The prewar apartment building in which I lived was just off the swank shopping district of Schlossstrasse. The first floor of the building along my block contained a wine boutique, an internet café, a travel agency, and a brothel called Netti's that was so quiet as to seem deserted save for its electric-pink sign that turned on every evening and off by daybreak. Brothels and sex businesses are not restricted to specific zones in Berlin, in ways that would never be permitted in Sweden, Finland, or even the Netherlands (see Figure 5.1).

Advertisements in Berlin's tabloid evening papers' "discreet" section listed hundreds of phone numbers with addresses scattered all over the city, in every borough, often near on- and off-ramps to the motorways, and only occasionally grouping in particular streets.

Brothels were technically illegal under German laws before and after the reform. Running a brothel was associated with pimping and coercion—and an employment contract. Three institutional arrangements skirted this prohibition. One was for women to work a bar and to take clients to a nearby hotel or rented room that was not associated with the bar—the strategy that Café Pssst violated because its owner also owned the hotel used for assignations.[22] Another was for women to work out of their apartment

Figure 5.1   Berlin Brothel In discreet contrast to the Eros Centers, this brothel in a well-to-do Berlin neighborhood advertises in newspapers but is visible only at night. Metal window shades are raised to reveal the string of red heart lights; the door buzzer is marked only by a red nametag.

Source: author photo

using listings in newspapers or Internet sites to attract clients as independent entrepreneurs, the only way to legally conduct prostitution in most countries where it is decriminalized.

The third was the most visible and easily misunderstood. "Eros Centers" are essentially large motels in which prostitutes rent rooms to sell sex. They were tolerated in many cities even when prostitution was still immoral under German law, demonstrating how the German reforms made *de jure* what had been *de facto* in many cities. The insecurity under which Eros Centers operated did not render them discreet. They featured illuminated red hearts, flashing signs, and multilingual touts urging single male passersby to enter. They arouse little attention despite their comic ornamentation and central locations (see Figure 5.2).

The entrance of this brothel in one of Frankfurt's tolerance zones requires one to walk under the outstretched fiberglass legs of a woman wearing panties and red high heels. These legs are directly opposite the city's Employment Office that administers welfare benefits and job retraining programs. Such a juxtaposition would be unthinkable in Sweden where the thought that women in economic difficulties might turn to prostitution is abhorrent. On the other side of the building, illuminated red hearts beam

Figure 5.2   Frankfurt Brothel This Eros Center in one of Frankfurt's smaller tolerance zones features illuminated red hearts in its windows visible to the downtown skyscrapers across the river. The entrance features a pair of larger-than-life woman's legs to attract passersby.

Source: author photo

the brothels' location to the skyscrapers of Europe's financial district across the river Main.

Eros Centers rent rooms to women for 24-hour periods at rates similar to deluxe hotels. Men enter the center and walk down each hallway and up the stairs to the next floor, peering into open doors. The overwhelming smell is of bleach. Whatever sacrifices this makes for romance and eroticism it makes up for in its reinforcement that the business is *clean*. Closed doors denote someone who is with a client or not at home, while open doors invariably feature a beckoning woman wearing lingerie, surrounded by photos of family and friends taped to a mirror, fake flowers, colored lamps, and the Afrobeat or *cumbia* of her native country. Municipal officials were right in their assumption that the women were foreign: a brothel manager of a 30-room Eros Center reports, "we have so many different people in the house. We have people from the US, we have Russian people, we have Germans, we have Turks, we are very international in fact. Not only the clients, the girls as well. We house international girls, from Thailand to Latino girls."

Although these Eros Centers appear to be brothels, the lack of a direct employer–employee relationship between prostitute and manager renders them permissible under the German system in which it is legal to sell sex as long as it is a private transaction. Juppe Bunsen manages one of the largest centers in Frankfurt's *Bahnhofsviertel*, after a brief career as a police officer. He says that the high rents for the rooms are justified because of the scrupulous records they keep to ensure that the on-site transactions are legal, their advertising and visible location that draws clients, the security that staff provides for women workers, and the pleasant and supportive conditions they provide for the women. In an economic slump, these services are essential to retaining the workers who pay rent to the center:

> When our house is so busy, it is because we provide good service to the girls. They come in the morning; they like to eat when they are hungry. We make them a breakfast or whatever. In these times, you have to give good service to the girls because then they like to stay. When times are bad and they don't make much money, they [might] say, "okay, but it is really nice here so we stay." The girls have to pay house rent only, just house rent. When they make 1,000 Euros in a day, we only [receive the] 120 Euro house rent [per day]. That's all . . . and sometimes we give our ears to the girls, when they have problems, or when they are sad or whatever. We are social workers a little bit, not professionals, but we are a little bit like this. Because when they have a problem with a friend, when they have trouble with a boyfriend or with a husband and they come and cry we say, "hey baby, it will get good." And that's it. Mostly we like our girls. Mostly. Some of our girls are shit, but that's normal. Some men are shit, and that's normal. They come from every country in the world, so there are many differences.

Bunsen frames himself as the client who serves the women, reflecting the German legal requirement that women be independent operators. It is only through building relationships with women that he can ensure a good working relationship between the sex workers who rent rooms and their regular clients.

The international clientele of the house makes for interesting human resource management strategies. But as Bunsen explains, he is more troubleshooter than employer:

> There are some countries, it is not good to have them on the same floor. We have problems. It is not possible to have Latino and German girls on the same floor. It is not possible. They work against each other. And it is not possible to put some blacks together because they hate each other. The Nigerian and Ghanaian girls, they don't like each other. Five or six years ago a Nigerian girl took a knife and "gave" it to a Ghanaian girl <stabbing gesture>. And the house was closed for two days because the police were here, and at first what they thought was that we [the managers] did that! No! You have to look for the roots [of problems] and learn it step by step.

For Bunsen, the experience of being in the house for years, learning "step by step" what works for his renters, is the key to being a successful manager of these "international relations." Here he highlights the differences among women that preclude any universal policy, emphasizing both their agency and their dependence—two principles of Germany's prostitution legalization.

When I asked Bunsen what makes a good renter, the fiction that he served independent operators slipped, as he described the characteristics of a "good woman":

> A good woman does what she promises at the door [to her room]. When she says, "I will do it for 50 Euros or 30 Euros in bed with you, she has to do it. And we have this problem sometimes when the man—there is a reason we have an office by the door—they knock and the men will say, "this girl, she told me a blow job and fucking for only 20 Euros and she only did a blow job." For me it is very difficult because I am not there, I am not in the room. The girls tell me other shit. He says, she says, and I can only [figure out] who was right when the girl does this two or three times. Then I say to the girl, "time for you to go to a different house, because you can go but I can't take the house to another place and I need the men who come here.

If Bunsen is not an employer, he does control access to the Eros Center work environment. For Bunsen, a good client is a man who returns to his establishment, and a good renter is a woman who is consistent and has stayed long enough that he can fairly adjudicate between these labor disputes when there are misunderstandings. Problems arise from regular workplace conflicts for Germans, and are not inherent to the business of sex work itself as Swedes or other abolitionist, radical feminists aver.

These same high rents often lead to ingenious room-sharing agreements among immigrant women, who sometimes sleep in a closet or behind a screen while a partner works a shift in the same room. Another common scenario is that three women will split the rents of an Eros Center room and a nearby flat. By staffing the Eros Center room at all times, they ensure that the expensive apartment is earning every possible dollar while women have a place to live and relax when off work, similar to flight attendants who share apartments near hub airports.

Of course, the visible prostitution in tolerance zones is only a small portion of Germany's commercial sex market. Frankfurt's status as Europe's largest convention center guarantees a steady stream of trade conventions that attract thousands of independent escorts who work the hotel bars.[23] Advertising is accomplished through escort agencies or fliers distributed in tourist kiosks (and in low-rent youth hostels frequented by graduate students).

The Frankfurt Roundtable

In 1999, police in full riot gear cordoned off one block of Frankfurt's main red-light district. Squads of officers with assault rifles and bullet-proof vests jogged up the stairs of the hotel-like Eros Centers, escorting lingerie-clad women into the chilly streets. Male clients were merely directed to leave the area. In the tumult and confusion, one woman attempted to escape by jumping out an upper story window, severely injuring herself. Within an hour and a half, hundreds of women were arrested and taken to the city jail, leaving the Bahnhofsviertel, or railway station quarter, eerily quiet. What prompted this unprecedented and unexpected city action in the city's largest and most prominent red-light district? Speculation ranged widely, from a ploy by the embattled CDU (conservative) mayor who was facing reelection, to long-needed actions to investigate human trafficking, to the fact that the Bahnhofsviertel was facing increasing gentrification pressures from international banks eager to acquire the stately nineteenth-century buildings.

The subsequent prostitution debates in Frankfurt centered not on issues of gender or violence, as in Sweden or the Netherlands, but on the legal status of workers. Debates were not about *whether* prostitution had a place in the city, just by *whom* it may be practiced, *where*, and *how*. After a series of actions called *raids* by critics and controls by its advocates, the Frankfurt City Council (the *Römer*[24]) called on all relevant parties to convene in a set of ongoing consultations as the Prostitution Roundtable (*Runder Tisch zur Prostitution*).[25] SDP (center-left) City Councillor Gregor Amann described the police actions in the railway station quarter as connected to the urban planning visions of the rival Christian Democratic Party:

> The hidden goal, in my opinion, was to get rid of prostitution in the Bahnhofsviertel, to realize their old dreams of having the Bahnhofsviertel as an entrée to the city, and a downtown area with banks and insurance and offices and so forth, lots of office spaces. I think that was the real reason behind it.

City officials responsible for carrying out the police actions vigorously denied any political motivation. They were compelled to act, they said, because of the Hesse state court ruling that employers were legally responsible for controlling the immigration status of their employees.

The controversy was still so fresh in 2003 that they provided a translator for my meeting with city officials of the *Ordnungsamt*, the Department of Public Safety (literally Public Order Office). Inside this office is the *Ausländerbehörde* (Foreigners Office), directed by Heiko Klein-stuber, responsible for administering federal migration law within this most-multicultural of German cities.[26] As his translator was at pains to stress:

> He wants you to **clearly** understand, very **clearly**, that the matters of the *Ordnungsamt* and the police department were never geared towards pros-titution at large, only illegal prostitutes. He wants you differentiate very carefully, because from the NGOs you will hear a little bit of a different story. Their measures were **never** geared towards prostitution at large, but those prostitutes who were **working**, working—the crucial fact is **working**—illegally, in those houses of ill repute, or cathouses, or whatever you want to call them.

Here it is not prostitution's morality that is at issue, but whether women have a citizenship status that allows them to work legally in Germany. Pros-titutes unable to provide evidence of legal working status were arrested not for any crime of prostitution, but to get at the more serious crimes behind them. As Kleinstuber, through his translator, described the arrests of women in the brothels:

> In order to get to the people behind that, the racketeers, they had to arrest those people and put them into jail. They didn't wish to harass the prostitutes who were here illegally, but in order, like I said, to catch the people behind it—the racketeers—they did have to take those people and put them into jail, the prostitutes, the **illegal** prostitutes.

As far as the city bureaucrats were concerned, then, the only problem with prostitution was about illegal workers, once the city office interpreted the State Court of Hesse's ruling as mandating that brothel owners—and city officials—had a responsibility to verify the legal status of their workers.

Brothel owners, who denied that the women were "their" workers, since such a contract was expressly forbidden by the 2001 German prostitution law, contested this controversial interpretation. Sex workers, their NGO allies, and brothel owners contested this definition even as the Frank-furt city officials began enforcing it through a series of *controls* that were derided by critics as *raids*.

This standoff between bordello managers and city officials lasted for several months, during which a series of raids were conducted within the Bahnhofsviertel. Over 1,000 sex workers were processed by police officials, hundreds were deported, fled, or were instructed to leave the city within three days.[27] The standoff ended in 2000 when the city council ordered a halt to the Immigration Office actions and convened a historic Roundtable on Prostitution to examine the views and interests of all involved parties and make policy recommendations.

The point of the roundtable was to find consensus not only between NGOs and the government, but also to find consensus among government agencies themselves, as well as among the major political parties. As the Conservative Democratic Party (CDU) representative Stephan Siegler, a former police officer, explained the Römer's action:

> Finally we made a choice that it was commonsense to have the parties in parliament to take a look at all these things and to start roundtable talks with NGOs and with all the people that are involved with the administration and the political parties. This roundtable founded some working groups and one of these was the group for city planning because we [decided] that if you want to improve the situation of the women working you have to improve the situation we have in the red light district.

Again, citizenship status for work was the focus of the committee work, which proceeded smoothly despite the fact that each attendee might bring several opinions to the table: their personal view, their organization's point of view, and those of its internal dissenters. As Siegler reported, the final result didn't represent any single point of view but reflected a consensus of all the positions brought to the table:

> We did not have any big frustrations. It is hard sometimes to meet for five-hour meetings with, as we now know, too many people sitting at this table. But finally the result was that everybody at the table says it's not *my* result, but we can accept it because everybody finds himself in this result . . . The situation was that even different branches of the city had different opinions and made their own politics <chuckles> . . . And with a topic that can be seen from so many positions, the first thing was to talk about the conflicts there and to find then a line of communication between all the people sitting at that table.

Siegler notes that government, embodied by the representatives of various city and legal divisions, themselves had no consensus about prostitution, much less between the police and NGOs opposed to their raid tactics. The end result, while no one group could claim it fully represented their position, was acceptable because it was a compromise in which everyone could see their influence and point of view—a consensus that was reached, perhaps, by excluding the one NGO representative who could not agree with the Roundtable. The multivocal consensus prized by the roundtable, like other similar German actions, did not reflect a gendered definition of prostitutes as victims, as in the Nordic countries. And though it resembled the kind of work-based consensus in the Netherlands, the German consensus lacked the self-conscious sense of being moral pioneers or beacons, as did the Netherlands, reflecting a German pragmatism grounded not in moral leadership, but local compromises.

This framing of prostitution in Frankfurt as a problem of undocumented workers was shared by NGOs working on their behalf. As Christiane Howe of AGISRA (Organization against International Sexual and Racial Exploitation) described her feminist counseling center's solution for the policing actions in the Bahnhofsviertel, "The only way to get out of that is to empower the women and to legalize it and to give rights. So that's why we also support the prostitution organizations here in Germany to change the law," the law that prohibits migrant sex work.

This version of events was not directly contested by the SPD city councillor who represented his part on the roundtable. The SPD's Gregor Amann protested the raids in the red-light district from personal experience: He had lived for years in the Bahnhofsviertel himself and had seen several previous CDU administrations try to remove its prostitution:

> GM: Why did it all of a sudden become an issue?
> GA: My personal opinion is because of the elections <laughs> I mean, the CDU has for many years, maybe not always but for one or two decades at least, wanted to rid the Bahnhofsviertel of prostitution. In the 70s they really tried to, when the city was run by the CDU . . . they just wanted to get rid of prostitution and this time they used a new court decision. *One* court decided back in the late 90s that the brothel owners have to check passports. So far, the brothel owners always said "we're just renting rooms, we're like a hotel. It's not our problem if the women are legal or illegal, we're just renting room. It's the woman's problem." And then one court in the late 90s decided that it is their responsibility.

For Amann, one court action was not sufficient to explain the sudden police raids, especially given the long-standing tradition of understanding the Eros Centers as hotels. One of the main reasons Amann found the Ordnungsamt rationale so unconvincing was the lack of raids on other sites known to have illegal workers:

> GM: So when they were doing the stuff, you know, talking about public order and illegal migrants, they weren't looking at illegal migrants anywhere else?
> GA: No it was all focused in that part of, the prostitution part of the Bahnhofsviertel. And a little bit in a [prostitution tolerance zone] close by. A little bit there as well. But mainly the Bahnhofsviertel.
> GM: It became clear that when it came down to illegal migration, public order, it wasn't all illegal migrants, it was prostitutes only.

GA: Exactly. I mean there is an office, a [separate] city department that goes after illegals for all this, in construction and so forth. But not for many years has that [activity] increased. I mean, all of [the city offices], they started going after the prostitutes.

The director of another city department also cast doubt on Ordnungsamt claims that only brothels were well-known employers of undocumented migrant workers.

Helga Nagel was the director of Frankfurt's Office for Multicultural Affairs (*Amt fuer multikulturelle Angelegenheiten*), representing it on the Prostitution Roundtable. Nonprofits are important partners in enabling the city to help families in the city, especially those of migrants, and especially the undocumented. The following conversation reveals the mutual interdependence between city agencies and NGOs in delivering essential services and sharing knowledge to all city residents, including the undocumented, in ways that still define citizenship through labor:

HN: The families who are illegal don't dare to get in contact with administrators—one of the rules is to be invisible, if illegal.

GM: How does your office deal with that, then? Do you have certain obligations because you are part of the city?

HN: Officially, no. This is a problem that the NGO deals with. We know and we are helping kids go to school. Schools are accepting. It is a human right to go to school, and you should not be punished because your parents have no status in the country they are. So the school directors, they don't have to ask the legal status of the kids.

GM: You're the city office for "you need to talk to the NGOs, we cannot help you?"

HN: Yeah, normally it's the NGOs who are near the community. You know the structures. You know that there are 10–20,000 people who are illegal, who have no documentation here in Frankfurt. And then there are the "naturals" [legal to stay, but not to work]. Look at the Polish people coming from Eastern Europe, they don't need a visa to come to Germany so they can come for 3 months [as a tourist, legally]. And it is not so far to go to Poland—8 hours by minibus, 100 Euros to go to Warsaw—so there are many making that journey now, even from the little villages. There are good, trained, middle-class housewives who don't get—or don't even want—a contract. They just want cash. One thousand Euros a month, cash. Which is good, without any tax.

GM: But what are they working at?

HN: They are working in families with elderly people.

The home health care industry, a huge need as German baby boomers age, is allowed to issue visas for immigrant workers. Home health care is, of course, both an occupation and a business. But for Director Nagel, it is through labor that local citizenship, at least, is crafted, and forms the basis for the duties of her office.

Prostitution, as only an occupation but with no legitimate industry recognized by the state, means that the migrant prostitutes who dominate the German sex sector are unable to receive the benefits of legalization.

> *GM*: Has there been any talk of making a similar green card scheme for prostitutes?
>
> *HN*: Not yet.
>
> *GM*: To say there must be some demand because they're all foreign?
>
> *HN*: Yes, this was one of the topics when we discussed it [in the Roundtable], to have a green card.
>
> *GM*: I didn't see any recommendation in there.
>
> *HN*: No. I think it's not a recommendation, but we talked about it.
>
> *GM*: OK.
>
> *HN*: In the meeting, no . . .
>
> *GM*: . . . consensus?
>
> *HN*: No consensus <nodding>. Same with the home health care women. A woman from Columbia, for instance, coming to Europe to [work in prostitution] because her family has to survive. She does not want to apply for this sort of job, obviously. This is the same problem, so she's leaving saying "I'm doing a job." But she is not talking about it. And this is one of the problems. I think we can find 1, 2 or more women to deal with it openly, but many of the women do it because they are looking for a job to get the money to go back to their town. And therefore, this is the dilemma to solve, especially for the foreign prostitutes: legality.

Thus for Director Nagel and the services of the Women's Office, there is no difference among undocumented women workers whether in the Eros Centers or as home health care aides. She thus implicitly disputes the Ordnungsamt's account that the document controls in the Bahnhofsviertel were simply about undocumented workers.

Brothel manager Josef Bunsen was more succinct in his agreement with this official and Councilman Amann's point of view in his explanation for the brothel raids:

> *GM*: How did raids start?
>
> *JB*: <humorless laugh> It is politics, that's all. I think the banks would like to have this house.

Banks, in Frankfurt, are not your ordinary drive-through branches: These are the headquarters of some of the world's largest financial institutions and the European Central Bank itself, housed in Europe's tallest skyscrapers mere blocks away. For them, the scruffy Bahnhofsviertel is not only the untidy face to their business district, but valuable real estate near the railway station lifeline.

Helga Nagel of the Office of Multicultural Affairs cast further doubt on the simple explanation of a court case forcing the Ordnungsamt's hand, questioning their sincerity and highlighting the uncertainty of prostitution's status as a trade but not a business:

> The politicians and the laws are very cloudy, and they have to work it out, and there are no guidelines to work it out. And it makes a lot of insecurity for the officials who don't have the courage to decide something. And they want the guidelines, perhaps, I don't know if they are really . . .

Even for a core participant of the roundtable like Ms. Nagel who helped draft consensus guidelines, implementing them still lies with the city officials who may lack "courage."

Since the brothel owners were unwilling to do their duty, the city was forced to do it, reckons Heiko Kleinstuber, head of the *Ausländerbehörde*. They issued fines for employing illegal workers and it led to the closing of the bordellos:

> *HK*: There were hardly any more prostitutes left.
> *GM*: So what happened to the clients?
> *HK*: The police came to the houses.
> *GM*: So the clients went away?
> *HK*: Yeah, yeah <general laughter> the clients—[we] took the prostitutes to the police department, and, well, if someone was walking through your bedroom, you stay away.

If the brothels had to close, then, it was because they had been employing illegal workers, leaving the city no choice but to remove them and disrupt the johns' "bedrooms."

Brothel managers, on the other hand, denied that they were in any sort of employment relations with the women who rented from them. As Josef Bunsen, manager of one of the Eros Centers in Frankfurt explained,

> We are the same as a hotel business. We have 30 *en suite* rooms, and the girls, the prostitutes, can make reservations and then they work here. If they like it and make money, they stay. Or when they don't like it, or they don't make money, they go . . . We are in the hotel business, but it is with security. The rooms have alarms and we can, when they have a problem with a client, they can [trip] the alarm and we go upstairs and we say to the client, "You have to go now, you have to leave." And when he is intelligent, he goes <laughs>.

That's it, eh? We don't like trouble, we don't like to beat them or whatever. But when they say, "No, I stay here," then we have to kick them out. And if they start to fight, then we fight with them. But it doesn't happen very often.

In describing his business, Bunsen stresses the absolute autonomy that women have over their working conditions. If a woman trips the alarm and asks for a client to be removed, staff do so without question, in part because, as Mr. Bunsen explains, "I cannot say 'you are right' or 'you are right,' sometimes it is a problem between the people." In such he said/she said situations, she wins.

This is not to say, Mr. Bunsen implies later, that the women do not have needs. But he frames these needs as a service he provides to retain their patronage, not as an intrinsic dependency caused by their work:

> In the bad newspapers, we take the girls and force them to work here, or we take their money or have [control over] the girls. We have nothing to do with the girls. In our house we have slow business at the moment, everywhere [else as well], but our house is so busy [as it is] because we have good service for the girls. They come in the morning—they like to eat when they are hungry—we make them breakfast. In this time [when business is slow] and they don't make much money, but they say "okay, but it is very nice here, so we stay." When they make 1,000 Euros in a day, we only get 120 Euros house rent. That's all. And this includes this kind of [service], a little bit to drink, and that's it. Well, sometimes we lend our ears to the girls when they have problems, or when they are sad or whatever. We are social workers <laughs> a little bit. Not professional, but we are a bit like this. Because when they have a problem with a friend, and we have to, when they have trouble with a boyfriend or with a husband and they cry we say, "hey baby, it will get good." And that's it. And mostly we like our girls. Mostly.

As Mr. Bunsen explains, his brothel is merely one hotel among many rented to individual women, who have the freedom to leave if another manager provides better support services. Therefore brothels, like hotels, should not be required to do such checks. The city, brothel managers stated, had merely crafted a catch-22 for them: Admit you are a pimp by recognizing sex workers as employees or refuse to comply with a government order.

For Mr. Bunsen, the same qualities that make for good sex worker–customers in the Eros Center also make good policemen:

> I like the police when they do their work. I do not like it when they not only do their work, but they do something interesting by themselves, you know? My opinion is there are three types of police. I know this because 20 years ago I was a policeman. One kind of police, they do it because it is a job.

They make their money and it is a normal job for them. They are ok [for me]. Then there are police who like to do some good for the world, and with them it is a little bit difficult because they are "special" and [usually] very young. They know nothing but they think they know it all. When they see us [brothel managers], they think we are bad men, you know? That is what they think, and they have to learn that it is not only black and white, there are some colors between. And then there is the third type of police, it is the type that are nothing without a uniform. You know, when they have a uniform they are cool and when they have no uniform, they are <pffttt> [nothing]. And that is the police I hate. Because they make trouble everywhere. We are here, we have to work together with the police.

In the opinion of Mr. Bunsen, for police officers as with prostitutes, the good ones do their jobs as normal work, not for the power trip of wearing a uniform. And normal work implies seeing shades of gray through everyday working relationships, the interpersonal knowledge that allows "working together" to solve problems. This is necessary for a business like an Eros Center:

> Here we work with trouble, and so you have to work together with police. And they say, "hey, this man, he only does his work. He doesn't like to beat up people, he's just doing his work." And then they say to the clients, "ok, now go and fuck yourself." <laughs>. That's it, we work together.

It is only through these sustained interactions of working together that the police can judge whether Bunsen is being fair. Good police, who see Bunsen and his colleagues every day, know that trouble is infrequent and deal with him in a manner he considers *professional*—just as the good women who rent in his Eros Center treat their clients in a professional manner.

As far as city officials were concerned, however, the law did have some advantages. As one of the officials[28] in the Ordnungsamt explained:

> OA2: Prior to the change in law—they are called hotel owners here, here they are not called pimps—if one of his . . . "girls" put out, maybe condoms or something like that, it was a criminal act because he participated in [facilitating] the act of prostitution.
> GM: By promoting it?
> OA2: Yes, he was promoting prostitution.
> GM: And that is the criminal act eliminated by the new law.
> OA2: Yes they liberalized that now.

Now that prostitution is a permitted trade, its workplace essentials no longer indicate criminalized immorality. This legal issue, at least, was settled by the national *liberalization*.

In the end, however, the Frankfurt Roundtable was unable to solve any of the broader legal issues prompted by the fundamental paradox in the national legislation between trade and business. As the city officials noted, legalized prostitution did not imply a legal contract between buyer and seller:

> In a legal contract, if you are the purchaser you have the right to determine how the service is being rendered. However in prostitution, that's not the way it is. You cannot go to court if you say you are not satisfied with the service I render you <general laughter>.

Much of the legal uncertainty stemmed from this distinction under German law between a business and a trade. While prostitution is permitted as a trade, it is not yet allowed to be a business with employment contracts. An official[2] of the Ordnungsamt explained further:

> Since the right to contract does not apply to prostitution per se as interpreted here by the law, it cannot be interpreted as a business, it has to be interpreted as some kind of work, but it is not a business per se. Under the laws of contract and the laws of business, it is not a business, eh? It is some kind of work, but it is a gray zone because it is totally contradictory to everything that contracts mean.

If prostitution is work, then Germans may legally engage in it, but foreigners may not because they may only "work" in Germany if they run a "business." This gray zone is all the starker against the black-and-white roadmap provided by German welfare legislation that bestows so many of the social rights of citizenship *through* businesses *to* employees.

Compounding the city's difficulties were contradictory decisions with neighboring countries at the European level. As the Ordnungsamt officials complained,

> *FRA OA:* Under the European law for common law members, you have to be legal to be engaged in prostitution, even if you are not a native of that country. In other words, there are two different laws, one for European nations that are governed—supposedly—by European law, which is contradictory to German law. Under European law, it says that if you decide, let's say you are Dutch and you want to engage in prostitution now. Then you can engage in prostitution if you are, let's say French, you belong to the Common Market too, you have the right to engage in prostitution **also,** yes? German comprehension of the law is different here.
>
> *GM:* In Germany, only Germans—
>
> *FRA OA:* —In Germany, the law says that only Germans can engage in prostitution. Other Common Market members can't be here for prostitution.

This ruling that only Germans can engage in prostitution reflects a legal interpretation that conflicts with a 2001 European Court of Justice ruling that self-employed prostitutes may work legally in any Common Market country that tolerates prostitution.[29] The Ordnungsamt policy has not yet been successfully challenged, however, owing to the long and protracted process. To this day, the situation facing German citizens and denizens involved in prostitution was uncertainty and a long wait for court cases to decide among competing definitions of work, trade, business, and contract that underpin the European project. This gray zone of "massive uncertainty" was what prompted the EU Network of Researchers on Fundamental Rights to issue their warning that such interpretations of prostitution threatened to become a wedge that would divide the Common Market.[30]

The Ordnungsamt officials disputed critical interpretations of their actions as lacking courage or decisiveness. For them, executive action was impossible without judicial definition:

> OA1: We are still in a kind of gray zone. Is [prostitution] a trade (*Gewerbe*) or is it not? We are still on unsettled ground.
>
> OA2: We are now waiting for legal decisions. First we waited for the roundtable results, then we waited for the prostitution law, and now we are waiting for a legal decision not at the local level but at the level of the highest court, it has to go up to the Federal Court of Justice or even the European Court of Justice, if the terms *prostitution* and *trade* are compatible with each other.
>
> OA1: The term must be clarified.
>
> OA2: Then we will be able, based on the existing laws to make decisions.

This waiting, in the Ordnungsamt interpretation, proceeded from the unique work status of prostitution in the 2001 Act and required further clarification from the courts or further federal legislation. But if this gray area was annoying to city officials, it seemed excruciating to sex workers, brothel managers, and NGO activists.

The European Court of Justice had already settled the work status of prostitution in the Netherlands. Frankfurt's sex workers' rights activists and NGOs saw this ruling as applying directly to Germany as well. But for the Immigration Office, the unique occupational status of prostitution in Germany required further clarification. When asked whether he knew of the status of such lawsuits in Germany, Herr Kleinstuber replied:

> As far as I know there are no lawsuits filed yet. In the European level there are lawsuits filed, mainly in the Netherlands, and there have already been decisions about that, but there haven't been any decisions about Germany, so we must still wait for those decisions. We haven't gone up to that high level

yet. It's not about changing the immigration law (*ausländergesetz*) which some people say, we still have all the laws that we need, it is all about defining the term, it's all about how the term *trade* [Gewerbe] is defined. Once this decision will have been made, we will be able to make positive decisions at once on the basis of existing laws.

Again, the paradox embedded in the prostitution law made prostitutes dependent on court decisions about whether sex was both a Gewerbe and a Betrieb.

The main outcome of the roundtable for the NGOs and city service offices was the assurance that prostitution was a historic and valued part of the Bahnhofsviertel, guaranteeing a measure of security for their work and the women they served. For the Ordnungsamt, the period of closure after the controls/raids gave the office leverage to enforce zoning ordinances for safety and appearance. My query about what kind of safety regulations had gone unenforced reveals the rectitude with which Herr Kleinstuber was held by his employees and the possibility that the necessary Eros Center improvements were only cosmetic:

> OA2: One of the positive things that came from the increased pressure onto the keepers of the houses of ill repute is that they fixed up the houses, they improved the conditions of the houses which were in a truly medieval situation previously. Together with the Ordnungsamt and City Planning they went along and looked at the houses and decided what was and wasn't okay with them. In other words, they were trying to improve the whole sector for safety, fire safety.
>
> GM: Did they have to have sprinklers as well?
>
> HK: No, no <brief quip in German, followed by general laughter>.
>
> Translator <gasping for air> Ha, I asked him about fire alarms and he said <hee> he said <hee hee> he said, well, he hopes they do because he is so frequently at that <ha ha> at the <ha ha> bordello.

Herr Kleinstuber's dry humor so tickled the translator, who could not imagine that he would ever be in the brothel for anything except a zoning inspection.

As his aides continued, the period of closure was actually a win for the brothel owners as well:

> OA1: The [hotel owners] took the opportunity and renovated the houses, this was a big deal, and through the improved facilities, legal prostitution established itself once again, and very few illegal prostitutes are left in Frankfurt simply through the architectural improvements, not the zoning laws, the general pressure so that [the prostitutes] would have better housing quality then they once had, and had better sinks to take care of themselves—

OA2: —Because the controlling measures that had been taken before, the number of bordellos had been reduced so it was now a favorable situation for the bordello owners to make investments. In addition, there have been signals from the political side that prostitution in the station quarter is enjoying a certain level of official protection, which allowed these investments to happen.

For the Ordnungsamt, too, the guarantee that prostitution would always have a place in the Bahnhofsviertel was one of the main benefits of the roundtable.

Helga Nagel of the Office of Multicultural Affairs reiterated this point that the consensus guaranteeing brothels a secure future in the Bahnhofsviertal was positive, although she stressed that it also meant recognizing its inevitable downsides, especially the concentration of IV drug users in the neighborhood:

GM: It sounds like in the end, the Roundtable made some statement of security toward the brothel owners [that they would not be removed from the Bahnhofsviertel].

HN: Yeah, but they are realistic. They know that if they say there is no future for prostitution in this area, they will have it in another area. They are realistic enough to know to control it by reality and not by moral feelings.

GM: Control?

HN: Yes, we prefer to control it in a special area than let it go <gestures everywhere>.

GM: So it comes down to, in the end, a measure of control.

HN: Yes. Once it's in a special area, and they want in the same time, the control and the quality of living in this special area gets worse and worse. But they have a special and a certain standard to keep the people who live there, to have diversity. My colleague, who is that administration and head of the department lives in this area, and one of the problems he is describing is drug-[addicted] prostitutes.

GM: Yes?

HN: I.V. drugs

GM: Yes, this is the problem that everyone complains to me about—brothel owners, prostitutes, store workers complain about it.

HN: Yes, yes, it is a problem that needs to be solved.

This exchange highlights the fact that tolerance zones, so abhorrent to Swedes and Finns, are not about tolerating exploitation but reducing and controlling it. The irony, of course, is that the drug-addicted prostitutes were the ones who could not benefit from the national legislation because the exchange of sex for drugs, food, or a place to sleep does not fit into the worker model of prostitution management.

Christine Heinrichs is the director of the "Women's Café" in the Bahnhofsviertel, or railway station quarter, where the main red-light district and streetwalking area is located. The professionalized sex workers who practice their trade in the Eros Centers are not her clients, as the Women's Café serves homeless women. Many of them are involved in sexual commerce, but not as a Gewerbe:

> The women—our clients—are between legality . . . [prostitution] is legal in the bordellos but we estimate that there are about 3,000 drug-using women who have touched prostitution in some way at some point. They are not prostitutes, but there are many kinds of prostitution. We see 500 or so a year. Many of our clients are homeless, 50–60% have Hepatitis C, around 20–30% are HIV positive. They live around here <sweeps her arm in a wide arc encompassing the railway station quarter>.

Ms. Heinrichs makes a distinction between prostitutes and prostitution, a distinction rooted in the fact that to work in a brothel or Eros Center, a prostitute must already be relatively independent, just as regular workers are. The clients at the Women's Café were not able to function independently in society, whether from abuse, addiction, or social marginalization. So while increased rights for sex workers is a good development, in her view, her work was with others who had touched the broader world of prostitution unimagined by the abstract reforms and their narrow focus on legalized bordellos and professionalized sex. These bordellos shared the Café's street, but not their reality. Legally speaking, prostitution by those who cannot be seen as independent workers—drug-dependent, mentally ill, or developmentally disabled—still existed in a legal limbo, illegal workers in a sex trade in which they had little claim to be professionals.

The existence of these underground sex markets creates further criminality, argued Christiane Howe of an NGO that worked for the rights of migrant women workers, AGISRA. For AGISRA's clients, whether prostitutes or home health care aides, it was the lack of a legal status for temporary work that creates the exploitation they face because they cannot report crimes against them. The European Common Market's exclusions against outsiders created the conditions for human trafficking:

> CH: We think that the law here in Germany or the law here in Europe supports trafficking because you have no rights to come here, so you come this illegal way. And this illegal way opens up other violence, there's blackmail, so because they have no legal way to do this, they have to use other ways.
>
> GM: So you think it's because there's no legal way to come here for a year work permit, it creates a market.

CH: Yeah, and this supports the violence and blackmail.

GM: Because it's all underground.

CH: Because you don't have any rights because the women couldn't go to the police or anywhere else to say, "Okay, I have paid this, he wants more money and says I have to do this, but I don't want to." They couldn't, so that's flowing from [that]. It's fluid because you have this labor migration in prostitution between places and it's [difficult to separate this from] trafficking because it depends on the person. So for most prostitutes, it's really dramatic because they have paid a lot of money to come here to work here and their family depends on the money and they're just exploited. And they often come with another passport, or not a legal passport because they need a loan, which is growing and growing. And the situation is more difficult for the women if they now don't like to work here. They really need legal papers. So there's two ways, up to now. To marry, this is not very easy, [nor] to get a passport from one of the European countries. So we have Columbian women who have Spanish passports because they really lived there for a while and worked there for a while and so they are of course now, many of which are more or less better or worse now, like Spanish passports.

GM: And a lot of these marriages, are they also just paper marriages?

CH: Yeah.

GM: Most or just some?

CH: Some, yeah, so they have to pay for it.

GM: Of course.

CH: Passports for the women. So the way we see it, the only way to get out of that is to empower the women and to legalize it and to give rights. So that's why we also support the prostitution organizations here in Germany to change the law. <bitter laugh> Really it's so little [what we do].

For Ms. Howe, the work of AGISRA seems almost futile in the face of the glacial pace of legal change and its distance from their everyday work, which focuses on empowering women to have the degree of autonomy necessary for them to conduct their trade.

For SPD Councillor Gregor Amann, Ordnungsamt claims that the raids solved the migrant prostitute problem rang hollow as well:

The *Ordnungsamt* said there's less of a problem of illegal aliens there now. I don't really believe that. I think, like I said, it's only, it's on paper. Like I said, there are more women now that are married to German men or something, having legal papers, but it's just been in order to find somebody who marries them. I personally met women who told me "I have papers but I don't even know who my husband is <laughs> I met him once at the city office." And so the numbers went down but in reality it didn't change that much. And if you look at the women there in the houses I don't find a lower percentage of foreigners there, I don't think that's realistic. We have a hard time finding

German workers for garbage collection and for certain jobs that are just . . . same as in the US and in other industrialized countries. They're just certain jobs where natives do not work anymore. Germans, Americans, so forth. And it's taken over by foreigners and prostitution just happens to be one of those fields and I just don't see any possibility of how you could increase the percentage of German women.

The roundtable-brokered consensus on the future of sexual commerce in the Bahnhofsviertel may have cleaned up the facades of the houses and the documentation status of the workers, but for Councillor Amann, nothing much had changed.

Brothel manager Bunsen also shares this skepticism that not much had changed, at least in terms of his day-to-day work:

> Well, nothing. It changed nothing. I don't know, for me this is only work, and it changes nothing. We [owners] are shit to [the other Prostitution Roundtable participants], I tell you. That's my opinion. We are shit for them, and they do what they want. And when they speak at the roundtable I see nothing coming from that, nothing. It's only for the newspapers and the politicians. They know what they're doing.

For him, the local changes had as little effect as the national legislation passed in the midst of the roundtable's work, in part because his views had little effect on the Roundtable's final consensus. He succinctly described the effects of prostitution legalization for him:

> Nothing. They only thing is that now—in the newspapers you can read this—now the girls have started to pay tax. That's the reason why they [changed the law]. But I think the girls [would] like to pay tax only if it is not just paying tax but if they have the rights, the rights of a normal job. But they stopped. First [politicians] say, "We make a new law for a normal job." And then they change from behind. And [the prostitutes] say "This new law means that it's NOT a normal job." You know, when you are intelligent then you can change all you want, write all you want, and when I read this, for me I say "Oh it is very good what you'd *like* to do." You know? But it is not what they like to do with the new law. It is, for me, okay that I work and live in this life. For me it is nothing. It is a service, a sexual service. It is a normal thing. When you are married or you have a girlfriend, and you like the blowjob, and your girlfriend, "Hey, I don't like to give you blowjob," it is normal, eh? What is the problem to be, "Ok, so I go to a girl and she is professional and she make it very good." For me it is a normal service. And when you are alone, and you are single, what is the problem to say, "Hey, time for a treat! I pay 30 Euros and I go to a girl. It is cheaper than to have a girlfriend."

Mr. Bunsen's desire to have brothels be part of normal work extends from the work done by the women in the rooms to his management of the house, and the life they both share. Making women pay taxes without having rights is fundamentally unfair. Having lived through several prostitution regulation strategies in Frankfurt, Bunsen doesn't trust that the national legalization will remain because politicians come and they go. "They are all the same. Some they have a good mind, but they know nothing about this job. And some politicians, they have a bad mind and want to stop prostitution in Germany." Like Councilman Amann, Mr. Bunsen has seen many attempts to manage prostitution in Frankfurt come and go.

National Consensus and Local Compromise

Germany's prostitution legalization, so hailed in the international press and derided by the Nordic countries, is different in principle than Dutch legalization. In the Netherlands, prostitution is treated as a business like any other, yet sex workers and NGOs struggle with prostitution's stifling social stigma of prostitution that cannot be legislated away. By Dutch standards, the German legislation appears to have faltered in granting rights to workers by protecting them from dependence upon an employer. Yet this compromise, consistent with the German nation-state project's other policies on abortion or citizenship, demonstrates the degree to which Germans accept the state as the adjudicator and guarantor of a balance between individual and societal rights. If this imposed a seeming compromise in employment law, it did so because prostitution is not (and may not be) an occupation like any other in the eyes of the German state.

Social Democratic Councillor Amann described the shared history of prostitution in Frankfurt and Amsterdam to draw an unfavorable contrast between the German and Dutch ways of legalizing prostitution:

> Frankfurt is interesting when it comes to the city politics side because the red light districts in Holland are the same for 150 years. And it's been, changes haven't happened there. Business goes on as usual. Whereas here there's been lots of different strategies tried and I don't know if people are happy with that.

The lack of clarity at the federal level means that a lot of strategies have been tried at the municipal level, a variety of sex bureaucracies that reflect local contexts in a diverse nation. While not recognizing the paradox that ensures the gray zone, he described his gut feeling that "the Netherlands is the model for decriminalizing and legalizing prostitution" without recognizing that German opacity is itself a model for a Federal framework that permits multiple local consensuses to be forged under a national umbrella of compromise.

Christiane Howe of AGISRA was one of the few who saw broader benefits to the roundtable, one achieved with one of the fundamental values of the German welfare roadmap:

> *CH*: We just had election in Frankfurt and we were really afraid that they would use this thing and compete, the Green Party and Liberals, use these controls and the prostitution and red light district for the election, and then "now what?"
>
> *GM*: Did that happen?
>
> *CH*: No! The problem is dead.
>
> *GM*: Strong language.
>
> *CH*: Yes, we got them with consensus!

Consensus, described as essential by Germans involved in prostitution reforms, was also a feature of Dutch prostitution talk, rendering it unsatisfactory as an explanation for the countries' differences. Such consensus is also embedded in the inclusion roadmaps of the German and Dutch corporatist welfare states, extending citizenship to prostitutes by incorporating them as workers. Where Germany differed from the Netherlands, however, was in seeing their national legislation as an essentially German compromise, and not as some international best practice to be exported to other countries.

Germans describe judicial decisions as causing the prostitution reforms of 2001, not factors outside of Germany. It is impossible to know whether or to what degree judges were conscious of those cases from outside Germany; their offices declined to be interviewed. Yet previous citations against brothels were not heard by judges or were unsuccessful: It was only in the wake of widespread European debates following the 1999 Dutch and Swedish prostitution reforms that two German judges, in two different administrative contexts, found the previous German prohibition of immorality untenable.

Abolitionists are incorrect when they contend that Germany, like the Netherlands, classified prostitution an occupation like any other, which, lumping in German legalization with the Dutch, misses important differences. Like the Dutch reforms, Germany extended the benefits of citizenship to sex workers by virtue of the employment status: a characteristic of corporatist welfare states. Another similarity was the program of consensus in which sex workers were actively included in local and national decision making as part of the consensus-reaching that is also a hallmark of the corporatist model of state-society relations. As the Frankfurt Roundtable shows, this included a wide range of organizations. While the reform has made it easier for individual prostitutes to ply their trade or enforce payments, they are not businesses and thus cannot employ or be employed. Prostitution is permitted as a form of self-employment, and sex workers have the benefits accorded to self-employed entrepreneurs— on paper, at least.

In practice, the reforms have had little effect as few sex workers have taken advantage of the reforms, reflecting a failure of the bureaucracy of sex as similar to the Dutch case as the Swedish. As the federal government's 2007 assessment of the law stated—in English, for an international audience—"The Federal Government believes that the Prostitution Act has only in a limited degree achieved the goals intended," citing "hardly any measurable, positive impact" on sex workers' labor conditions, that it had "not recognizably improved the prostitutes' means for leaving prostitution," nor were there any "viable indications that the Prostitution Act has reduced crime."[31] The policy thus seems to be a failure—unloved by domestic sex workers, a flawed, weak form of legalization in comparison to the Netherlands, and the legalization of women's exploitation, to the Swedes.

What frustrates Germans whose job it is to help prostitutes is not the reform, but the fundamental inability of law to achieve justice. As the director of the Vice Unit of the Berlin State Police described prostitution, "We are well aware we cannot abolish it altogether," she was not wishing for the old policies, or requesting more resources, but making a general statement about the limited ability of policing.[32] And for Christine Heinrichs of the Frankfurt Women's Café, the limits of law are its inapplicability to women on its very edges. By implication, the presence of more law about prostitution at the European level is similarly irrelevant to the German way of doing things, which can only be achieved through internal compromise that hinges on tacit understandings of the state. Thus while the German case may have be codetermined by events happening outside Germany, its prostitution reforms followed the inclusion roadmaps of past nation-state projects that had been institutionalized in its corporatist welfare state.

Similarly, German prostitution policy does not reflect approval of prostitution, but a recognition that the woman (prostitutes are almost always women in German debates) is best positioned to decide whether or not to sell sex, but under conditions that reflect societal interests in minimizing the exploitation of sex workers. In this framing, the state is the guarantor of women's individual choices, in part by enforcing their individualism by banning contracts with employers and sex businesses. The 2001 prostitution law protects prostitutes by offering them pension and independent health benefits as independent workers, maintaining the protections against exploitative employment that are key to social citizenship in Germany. No matter that German sex workers' rights groups reject this latter protection as patronizing.[33]

The reform also reflects the less radical feminist movement in Germany. Although the German feminist movement has long been associated with trade union activism, the conservatism of the country's Christian Democratic state has emphasized choice—in motherhood and work.[34] The feminism that is dominant within the state is a liberal one that contrasts with the radical tradition dominant in Sweden and Finland.[35] "Autonomous" feminist groups who spurn working under state strictures have a wider range of feminist opinions, encompassing feminisms from the former East Germany, the new women's movement of the Green Party, and others.[36] For example, prominent radical feminist Alice Schwartzer has been a tireless campaigner against Germany's legalization and a prominent supporter of criminalizing sex buyers, most recently with her book *Prostitution: A German Scandal!*[37] She is prominently cited as an opponent to the legislation, but she is one of the few to oppose it on feminist grounds. Schwartzer was also the leader of the campaign to decriminalize and legalize abortion in Germany. If the German compromise to prostitution seems similar to Dutch model's recognition of sex workers, it is also a gendered policy that renders prostitutes dependent upon the state for their own protection, just as the Swedish reform does. Legalization and abolition may be understood by their partisans as opposites, but in practice they are not.

6

Finland on the Fence: Abolitionist Compromise at the Edge of Europe

Figure 6.0   Erotic Bar/Fresh Meat Ostensibly private massage parlors and strip clubs escaped explicit regulation in Finland, while prostitution was curtailed in public by banning streetwalking, boycotting newspapers carrying sex ads, and policing hotels.

Source: author photo

In 2006, the Finnish Parliament outlawed the purchase of sex when the sale would "exploit the object of sex trade." This was a "watered-down" "compromise" for longtime advocates of Sweden's criminalization sex buyers that was greeted warily by their opponents. Unlike Sweden, Germany, or the Netherlands where new national prostitution regulations were the result of a compact period from proposal to enactment, Finnish debates about prostitution recurred almost continually from 1999 onward. Reforms were creeping and partial rather than a single piece of legislation, as in Sweden, or a single legislative response to other events, as in Germany. The Finnish compromise sits uneasily with its European neighbors. Some Swedes claimed it essentially legalized prostitution, while other commentators characterized it as part of a "Nordic unity" in criminalizing the purchase of sexual services after Norway and Iceland both adopted Swedish-style legislation in 2009.[1] If the new act did not go far enough for those who wanted to criminalize the purchase of sexual services, they successfully set the terms of the Finnish debate, steadily curtailing prostitution in public for abolitionist reasons (see Table 6.1).

Nordic Unity?

Finland features a strong, social democratic welfare state similar to Sweden's, with strong provisions for women's employment. Finnish nationhood, however, frames the country not as a moral beacon to the world,

Table 6.1   Finnish Prostitution Reform Timeline

1999	Revised Aliens Act (537/1999) allows Finnish officials to refuse entry to those who "may justifiably be assumed to obtain income through dishonest means or to sell sex-related services."
2001	Helsinki adds prostitution to the list of public nuisance crimes, along with public urination and letting snow slide off your roof to block sidewalks.
2002	Finnish Parliament defines prostitution a public nuisance in new national Public Order Act, extending Helsinki's ordinance to the entire country.
	A boycott by the Finnish National Council for Women causes all but one of the nation's largest newspapers to refuse sex advertisements.
2004	Trafficking in humans introduced into the Criminal Code (650/2004).
	Aliens Act amended (301/2004); prostitution remains reason to deport.
2005	Ministry of Justice presents government proposal to criminalize sex buying.
2006	Finland revises its prostitution code; criminalizes the purchase of sex when human trafficking is involved.
	Swedish-style criminalization of clients fails in committee and parliament.
2012	Criminalization of purchasing sex proposed by Justice Ministry; fails to leave committee.

Note: National legislative actions in bold.

as the Netherlands and Sweden do, but as a small nation sandwiched between two more powerful neighbors who are in turns feared, admired, or ridiculed. Where prostitution debates in Sweden were framed around universal standards of human rights and were quickly incorporated into Swedish foreign politics, Finnish debates were always deeply implicated in its international relationships with neighbors and other powers, especially the European Union, Russia, the United Nations, and the United States. Fraught relations with neighbors similarly tempered Finnish gender politics about prostitution, between perceptions of "effete" Swedes, hyper-feminine Russian women, and concerns about international reputation.

This dependence on global politics reflects the fate of a small nation caught between more powerful neighbors for whom globalization anxieties have been chronic since independence in 1917. Finland was part of Sweden until 1809, then Russia until 1917, then the fulcrum of a Cold War balancing act between NATO and the USSR. This had led Finns to spurn NATO membership but enthusiastically join the EU, the only Nordic country to join the currency union and maintain high levels of popular support for the European project. The Finnish case reveals the degree to which globalization anxieties may be most acute in countries that felt they controlled their destiny before the European projects. For Finns, always caught between larger powers, the nation-state project has always been one of trying to be a hinge and not crushed. For prostitution, this meant dealing with a problem to appease neighbors and allies, rejecting ideological solutions for pragmatic compromises.

Until the EU expansion in 2004, Finland was the sole border between Russia and the EU, a 1,000-mile one that Finnish diplomats leveraged as expertise in Russian affairs for Europe. It was the collapse of the Soviet Union, in fact, that is cited as the origin of the contemporary problem of prostitution in Finland.[2]

Red Whores

For Finns, prostitution is synonymous with the collapse of the Soviet Union. "Red Whore" is an epithet that goes back to the first days of the Soviet Union for its Finnish sympathizers.[3] "Russian" women (Ukrainians, Estonians, and other post-Soviet citizens were often glossed as Russians) began selling sex in Finland starting in 1992. This period is captured by a ubiquitous anecdote that is still repeated as fact, told in the manner of a joke, and probably apocryphal: "Did you hear about the woman standing in the marketplace parking lot with the sign, 'Pusy 50 marks'?"[4] Finns still find the story funny, the implication being that only a foreigner, idiot, or Russian could misspell a slang word for vagina, or would be so crass about what was being sold (50 marks in 1992 was under US$8). There is no small amount of *schadenfreude* in this humor over the fall of the Soviet Union even 20 years on. After being dominated by their neighbor during the Cold War years, there is still a palpable satisfaction that Finns can call the shots when some Russians are concerned.

Before these pathetic Russians invaded, Finns considered their relative lack of prostitution unique. In 1993 a feminist researcher claimed that prostitution had been all but eliminated by social welfare.[5] An economic historian who published a 1995 book on turn-of-the-century prostitution received late-night phone calls begging for contemporary contacts, so invisible had it become in most of the country.[6] There were no pimps, and meetups in restaurants or hotel bars or via contact ads were discreet and therefore uncontroversial. Infamous were the "afternoon coffee" (*päivänkahvia* or PK) contact advertisements in newspapers (including the nation's largest) in which women advertised that their "coffee pots were always hot" for "generous" male company. Such ads had double barriers for foreigners: the Finnish language, and the abbreviation, leaving the sex market largely by Finns for Finns.

Johanna Sirkiä was a founder and spokesperson for Finland's sex workers' rights lobby SALLI (*Seksialan Liito*), a contrived abbreviation that produces the Finnish word for "permit" or "allow." As she described those years, "When it comes to talking about prostitution before the 1990s, that means before the fall of the Soviet Union . . . it wasn't easy then, but it was less complex because then you could just talk about prostitution only as an issue of prostitution." She described how changing geopolitics introduced the complicating factor of human trafficking into discussions of prostitution:

> Foreign policy has changed, and we have lots of foreign women working as prostitutes, so the issue is much more complex. And there are lots of things that are not said aloud. Our relationship with Russia and Russians is very complex too and there are lots of things that are not said aloud . . . the basic attitude of the Finnish people is they don't like Russians that much. Or some Finns even hate Russians. Or maybe many Finnish people do. And they don't want to see that they [Russians], actually, are much like *you* [Finns].

Sirkiä makes an easy link between foreign policy and domestic prostitution policy. She also expresses a chronic suspicion among those opposed to the criminalization of sexual services that they were motivated by anti-Russian xenophobia. Contemporary debates about prostitution in Finland, then, are always complicated by implicit connections to international relations, migrant sex workers, and their effects on domestic sexual politics.

Sirkiä denied that it was prostitution itself that motivated the near-constant Finnish prostitution debates during the 2000s, attributing shifting gender roles to shifting geopolitics. In a conversation with her friend Ari Saukkonen, a Green Party Helsinki city counselor and chair of the city Social Welfare Board, they noted that other forms of illegal commerce were celebrated:

> AS: Of course you cannot say that it's okay that there are prostitutes on the street but it is quite a new thing for Finnish gentlemen to get sex easily.
> JS: Yes.
> AS: Of course, it's very clear.
> JS: Smuggling spirits is nothing new, buying—
> AS: —yes—
> JS: —from black markets, that's nothing new—
> AS: —nothing at all, we have done it all the time, it's nothing—
> JS: It's the national hobby—
> AS: —hobby, yes—
> JS: —smuggling spirits.
> AS: The new thing is that Finnish heterosexual men can have sex—
> JS: —as much as they want.
> AS: Yes.
> JS: If they just pay.
> AS: Yes.
> JS: Heterosexual women are angry because they're—
> AS: —they don't control sex—
> JS: —anymore.
> GM: I see.
> AS: Yes, and because these heterosexual women don't want to have sex, and now there are some women who give sex to these heterosexual men, and that's the point, I think. There's this new market, a new thing. But we have not sex here in Finland. Heterosexual men, they didn't have sex.
> JS: Until 1991.
> AS: Yes, yes, yes, yes, yes, that's true.
> GM: Okay.
> AS: You don't believe me?
> GM: No, I do.
> JS: Okay, this is oversimplified, but—
> AS: —no it's not—
> JS: —and you have to take into account that he has taken one brandy—
> AS: —No, no, no, no, no!—
> GM: <laughing>
> JS: But that's it, with one brandy you speak the truth. Because that you are.
> AS: But it's **true**, I'm **sure** that it's true.

Saukkonen approved of the 2002 ban on streetwalking, connecting it to gender politics rather than anti-Russian xenophobia or any attempt to recriminalize prostitution. For both Saukkonen and Sirkiä, the disruptive new market is not the one in which sex is for *sale*, but the *availability* of sex, disrupting the gendered balance of power. The post-Soviet smuggling and black markets did not upset Finnish domestic gender relations and were therefore uncontroversial.

Finns who sought to criminalize the purchase of sex cite the presence of prostitutes on the streets as their call to action. Although prostitution featured in newspaper stories and television reports steadily from 1992 onward, there were no national political proposals to deal with it until 2001. This gap is surprising. Given the upset caused by Russian streetwalkers on two streets in one city, it took nine years to do something about it legislatively.

The years between featured a score of competing narratives: about the shame of Finnish women in sexual commerce, the loutish behavior of Finnish men toward women on the streets, and the Russianness of prostitution. Finland entered a deep economic recession when their primary trade partner, the Soviet Union, collapsed. This time period coincided with the introduction of "sex bars" and "topless restaurants" in Helsinki: from zero in 1991 and 2 in 1992, the city had 9 by 1994.[7] Feminist commentators blamed "globalization" and "neoliberalism" for eroding Finland's gender equality, arguing that no Finnish woman would have considered such work before the economic downturn (see Figure 6.1).[8]

Figure 6.1   Erotic Bar/Fresh Meat Lola Erotic Bar catered to an international audience by advertising in English, alongside a streetside advertisement for fresh meat.
Source: author photo

Several confrontations between feminists and these sex clubs served to keep these businesses in the media spotlight. This pressure did not cause their closure directly, though it may have brought them to the attention of the tax and alcohol authorities who fined them for illegal business practices relating to payroll taxes and alcohol licensing rules.

Further evidence that it was Russian prostitution, and not prostitution generally, that motivated Finnish prostitution reforms was the open presence of massage parlors in major Finnish cities from the 1990s (see Figure 6.2).[9] These parlors, marked "Thai," "Asian," or "Oriental" more-or-less openly sold massages that included sex, but did not attract the attention of feminist groups, tax authorities, or neighborhood campaigners until 2011.

From 1993 onward, however, the nation's newspapers fed readers a steady diet of stories about Russian prostitutes in a compact area of two streets in Helsinki's Kallio neighborhood.[10] Some journalists clucked over the "sad

Figure 6.2   Saigon Massage Saigon Massage informed passersby that a new massage [sic] is open in Helsinki's Kallio neighborhood.

Source: author photo

Russians" trying to find customers, others the "circus" of "Hollywood-style" hookers that turned the Kallio "into a national monument of prostitution," in the words of the director of the National Council of Women. The tone of some of these articles was that sex bars and street prostitution represented a sort of cosmopolitanism, a "miracle" that "finally prostitution has arrived in Helsinki!" in the words of the director of the city's prostitution support center. A neighborhood activist group sprung up: "The People's Movement to Get Prostitutes Off the Street."[11] It allied itself with a charismatic retired police inspector to highlight the noise, traffic, and litter produced by the men cruising for prostitutes by foot or in cars.

The most salient feature of these reports was the description of Finnish men approaching Finnish women on the streets to ask them for sex: "How much do you cost?" This discussion was ubiquitous in my interviews, usually as something that had happened to an acquaintance. A report on this phenomenon by researchers who interviewed Kallio residents received national attention but its results were surprisingly inconclusive. While indeed 37 percent of Kallio women reported concern about being approached to sell sex by strange men, 31 percent of all women in the capital reported similar concerns—not a significant difference.[12] I never met any Finn who had direct experience with such a proposition, although everyone knew a friend of a friend who had, and all agreed that even the prospect of being accosted in this way was disturbing. This highlighted the anxiety about gender relations that produced its own reality.

While the Finnish discussion of prostitution during the 2000s focused on the potential street harassment faced by Finnish women at the hands of Finnish men, women who were actually receiving harassment received no attention. Immigrant women in Finland reported widespread harassment by men who took them for prostitutes, but only a few NGOs offered support and no newspapers covered the phenomenon until after 2006 when the last legal change was enacted. Natalia Aljosina was the director of Monika Naiset (Multicultural Women's Association), an NGO dedicated to helping migrant women in Helsinki. When I asked if being harassed was a problem for migrant women, she answered, "It's very common. If you for example go to a restaurant or ferry, if you have an accent when you speak Finnish it gives anyone permission to ask, 'how much do you cost?' That's *very* common." In other words, a circumstance that outraged Finnish women as evidence that gender equality had eroded was an everyday part of migrant women's experiences. Aljosina detailed her most recent experience:

> NA: I had a very hard day working here and I went to a bar, and like anyone else I ordered a coffee and a cognac, like anyone else, to relax. And the guy next to me started talking to me, and after a few sentence he asked me,

"How come you look tired? You have to be happy because you're working now!" He took it for granted that I was there working as a prostitute!

GM: This was a bar around here?

NA: It was [name] restaurant there in the city center.

GM: I just have to ask about this man, what was the matter with him that he thought you were working? Why was this man thinking you were working as a prostitute?

NA: I had normal clothes, just trousers on, just looking normal, not even like I was going to a party. But it is about the accent, really. If you are alone in the evening, in a bar, with an accent from somewhere else, you must be a prostitute.

GM: Has it always been this way?

NA: I don't have very many experiences with these kinds of situations because I obviously try to avoid them, but my friend says it has always been the same, she has lived here [since 1992], and it's been the same, you don't want to go to a restaurant or a bar because no matter how happy you are when you go in, you will be really mad when you come out!

Even the executive director of the organization whose mission is to help foreign women overcome isolation and make connections with social service agencies is the object of Finnish whore stigma,[13] signified by a foreign accent.

When my translator asked Aljosina why the women didn't fight back against this public abuse, she explained:

They are ordinary people living ordinary lives and it is a big surprise when they get an <sarcastically> offer, "How much do you cost?" It's not an issue that's talked about very much, but when a [Russian-speaking] family moves here it's not the first question in their lives, they have other problems . . . When they first get here their whole economy is shattered, they don't really have any money, much less to go out, so they don't come into contact with these attitudes so much. They have other problems, they will encounter this one later.

That my Finnish translator could not understand why any woman would endure such public abuse was a measure of his assumption that women in Finland were empowered to fight back, but also of general ignorance regarding the challenges facing women *migrants* to a country that, until recently, had hardly any.

If some Finns can heap abuse on individual "Russian" women in the streets, official attention focused on the geopolitical sensitivities of prostitution. News stories regularly detailed Finnish sex tourism for child prostitution across Russian border crossings ("Children in Viipuri [Russian Vyborg] Attest to Sex Trips by Finns," "Campaign against sexual abuse of children begins along eastern border"), buses of Russian women selling sex on the roadsides in Lapland ("Russian Mafia Ships Prostitutes to Helsinki"), the impact of street prostitution ("Helsinki Residents Clearly Disturbed by Sexual Harassment from Prostitution"), and concerns with Finland's image abroad ("Finns Deny Swedish Claim of Widespread Prostitution on Passenger Ferries," "U.S. Report on Human Trafficking Shows Finland in a Poor Light").[14] These stories summarize the set of concerns Finns had in public prostitution: the disruptions to the Kallio neighborhood in Helsinki and the ways prostitution or human trafficking might embarrass Finland internationally, including through the behavior of Finnish men abroad. The issue of gender relations upended by the sudden, public availability of commercial sex described by Aljosina, Sirkiä and Saukkonen was not.

Similarly, interviewees described Finnish legislative timelines as proceeding from domestic causes, without reference to the context either of these international pressures or the European Union attention to the issues. The legislative response to these varied concerns reflected globalization anxieties and a nation-state project of aligning Finland with international norms and protecting domestic gender relations.

The 1999 Aliens Act: Foreigners Barred from Selling Sexual Services

The first national act to control the movement of prostitutes was enacted without debate or consultation, and still poses somewhat of a mystery. When the new Aliens Act (*Ulkomaalaislaki*) was passed by parliament in 1999, it included a clause giving officials the right to deport[15] women suspected of prostitution, or bar their entry to the country. What was unique about this clause is that while selling sex is not a crime for Finns or European citizens who are members of the common travel Schengen Area,[16] it provided grounds to refuse entry for non-Schengen foreigners. As summarized by Jaana Kauppinen, director of Helsinki's prostitution help center (Pro-tukipiste):

> According to the Aliens Act, an individual from outside the EU can be deported from Finland if suspicion arises that he or she may be selling sexual services. As a rule, the deportation is often combined with a year's ban on entry, which can apply to just Finland or to the entire Schengen Area.

This power was not a negligible one. If a woman was denied entry to Schengen, this prevented her from entering 15 other European countries. Because passports were essential personal identity documents in Russia and other Eastern European countries, a denial-of-entry stamp on a single woman's passport was a literal scarlet letter, advertising a foreign morals offense to landlords, bank officials, or neighborhood politics.

It is unclear how article 37.1, section 3, of the Aliens Act got added to the bill in 1999. A senior official at the Finnish Immigration Services (*Maahanmuuttovirasto*) characterized the time as one of changes prompted by demands from outside Finland. He was one of the few interviewees who contradicted the more common story that the ruling was in response to the situation on the streets, though he was also more in a position to know:

> Just then we became a member of the European Union, so there was a lot of international work, cooperation, there would be a need for some different department to do that [new] work, and there was a need to have some kind of office that would make decisions.

Supporters and opponents of client criminalization agree that it got added without public debate or consultation, and both sides also agree that it should be removed.

The fact that the Aliens Act was amended without public discussion violated social democratic norms of consultation. Jaana Kauppinen of the prostitute support center Pro-tukipiste related her surprise:

> It was just there. For me it was surprising. Nobody asked "What do you think, or what would the course of actions be if this kind of measure was taken." Of course we have recommended many, many times since that this paragraph can actually hurt, promote crimes against prostitutes. For example, in trafficking cases it's a very effective way to keep [women] from coming up to testify. Also, selling sexual services and earning money in a dishonest way, they are under the same clause.

In other words, the 1999 Aliens Act lumped those selling sex—a legal activity in Finland for most EU citizens—alongside patently illegal activities like blackmail or cheating on taxes. This lack of consultation was a surprise because it violates the principle of mutual consultation in social democracies.

Regardless of how the line ended up in the act, its new powers were justified by claims that the Russian mafia had become involved in Finnish prostitution. Besides the xenophobic overtones of blaming Finnish prostitution on foreign Russians, such claims also called into question any woman's ability to consent to sell sex in Finland. Now that non-EU women—Russians especially—could be banned from entering most of Europe for selling sex, they needed help to cross into Finland. Mafia procuration services, at first of negligible value to Russian women, were now necessary to gain access to the Finnish market because of increased border control. By 2002, the Mafia had set up a rational, bureaucratic business with little apparent extortion or violence: Women come over on multiple "contracts" at their "choice" according to government and journalistic sources.[17] Johanna Sirkiä, head of SALLI, claimed, however, that "when the Aliens Act changed, then was an increase in violence and robberies against prostitutes." The act made foreign women more dependent upon others to hide their unauthorized status, emboldened criminals who preyed upon them, and for this reason was opposed by almost all feminist groups in Finland. Attempts to remove the clause on selling sexual services have been unsuccessful, though it was severed (now Section 148.6) from dishonest earnings (148.5) in a 2007 rewrite of the law.

Finland's first new national prostitution regulation thus made a firm distinction between domestic (permitted) prostitution and that performed by foreigners (forbidden). It strengthened the powers of police and border agents by giving them ability to turn away suspected prostitutes, without any definition about what constituted a suspicion. As a customs inspector told me, she would alert her supervisor to a range of discretionary observations:

> Oh it can be anything, you see a new [different] woman every week with the same man she calls "Boyfriend," or a full, **full** bag shows nothing in the X-ray because it is full of lingerie and 100 condoms in there, or you can see all sorts of interesting things [like] sex toys, then I say, "you have to wait a moment!"

The line in the Aliens Act made a distinction between the citizenship of EU women and outsiders, subjecting the latter to more intensive scrutiny of otherwise legal items and activities. Subsequent actions continued to make this distinction between authorized and unauthorized prostitution by steadily curtailing prostitution from the public sphere, actions that, like the abbreviated PK newspaper ads, privileged native Finns and punished outsiders.

Public Peeing and Prostitution

While the Aliens Act prevented foreign prostitutes from entering or remaining in Finland, the new Public Order Act (*Järjestyslaki*) in 2003 made it illegal to buy or sell sexual services in public places anywhere in the country. As described in an English-language informational brochure by the Police Bureau (*Poliisivirasto*) of the Ministry of the Interior, the Public Order Act "strives to promote order and security in public places," ranging from streets and sidewalks, to sports fields, office buildings and restaurants. Subheadings describing proper public behavior included "no intoxicants," "dogs and cats on a leash," "warnings of snow falling off a building," and "eliminating the nuisance of urinating and sex trade." This equation of prostitution and urination is explained as follows:

> Disturbing public order or endangering health by urinating and defecating in public places is forbidden. The Public Order Act bans buying sexual services or providing sexual services for a charge in public places. In this connection sexual services mean sexual intercourse and a comparable sexual act as referred to in the Penal Code of Finland.

The equivalence of the nuisance of public urination and prostitution was repeated often. Left Alliance MP Annika Lapintie summarized the ban on sexual services in public, "making it part of a law on public order means viewing prostitution as a nuisance similar to urinating in a doorway." The same link was made in the headline in the national paper, "Public prostitution, drinking and urination to become offenses."[18] Fines specified in the act were 20, 35, and 50 Euros, although only the violations of building safety codes or sexual services had the highest fines.

The 2003 act took three years from proposal to passage, in part because, unlike the Aliens Act, it had extensive subcommittee hearings that received testimony from over 100 individuals and groups. Finnish cities each had long had their own versions of a public order act. Now, due in large part to prostitution, national standards of definitions and fines were established because after the Helsinki City Council had introduced the nuisance misdemeanor of prostitution in public in 1999, streetwalking merely moved to the adjacent city, Vantaa. When Vantaa's city council then banned streetwalking, surrounding municipalities braced for displaced streetwalkers. Discussions then began in parliament to prevent prostitution from moving from city to city.[19]

The Public Order Act essentially copied Helsinki's public order ordinance (*Järjestyssääntö*) of 1999. As Interior Minister Ville Itälä explained, "In a sense, the ordinance of Helsinki will now be extended to the whole country."[20] That ordinance began as a way to strengthen the city code against "disorderly drinking" and its effects, but quickly became an opportunity for city councillors to curb street prostitution as well.

The few objections to the act focused on its implications for Finland's international agreements. The most-frequently raised issues were those of Professor[21] of Criminal Law Ari Hirvonen, who questioned whether "a complete prohibition of Conduct like prostitution or drunkenness is a form of government opposed by some of Finland's binding international human rights treaties."[22] In other words, objections focused not on whether prostitution in public was legal according to domestic Finnish law, but whether the act was legal according to international treaty, reflecting Finnish constant nation-state project of balancing internal actions with external powers.

The police opposed the ban on prostitution in public, citing a lack of personnel, but when it passed they duly began citing women selling sex in the Kallio. As a police superintendent noted sheepishly, "the residents of Kallio have praised us so much that it's embarrassing." If the residents were pleased, prostitutes were unimpressed: "One practitioner of the trade says that the scene in Kallio is the same." [23]

When the capital's municipal ordinance became national law in 2003, public prostitution became the target of agencies ranging from the restaurant licensing agency, the alcohol licensing monopoly, and police departments all over the country. The police began issuing fines to men looking to buy sex. As Lieutenant Reijo Muuri summarized, "To date, all cases are fines from the street. We have conducted surveillance in certain areas from time to time, 3–4 days a week, which means we have brought street prostitution under control as well." He continued, "The Public Order Act has more bite, bringing better regulation to prostitution because now we can scare buyers away from the street."[24] As with Sweden, it was not the amount of the fines, but the public shame of buying sex and the fear of arrest that gave the act its "bite."

The agency responsible for alcohol licensing, STTV (now Valvira), began investigations into restaurants that allowed prostitution on their premises in 2003. In other words, Finland's 2003 act made possible what the Berlin state court ruled unconstitutional in Germany only three years earlier. In February of 2004 STTV won on appeal from the Supreme Administrative Court that the National Order Act did give it the power to revoke alcohol licenses if prostitution had been permitted on the premises, which were clearly defined as public places in the law. This ruling in hand, STTV offices began a comprehensive review of licenses, shuttering several restaurants by September of 2004. As the Helsinki main daily newspaper explained, "If a restaurant's personnel does not prevent prostitutes from offering sexual services to customers in its premises, the STTV can issue the restaurant with warnings and restrict, suspend, or revoke its alcohol licenses." The act has proven effective, garnering national attention when it justified the revocation of licenses of two of Helsinki's most notorious sex bars in October 2011, ending an era of open sex bars that had begun in the early-1990s post-Soviet recession.[25]

The Public Order Act, then, gave existing state personnel the mandate to remove prostitution from the public sphere. While the Finnish legislation, unlike Sweden's, did not criminalize sex buyers or define advertising as a public from which prostitution must be excluded, this was accomplished in Finland not by legislation, but by activism.

You Can Buy a Cat or a Puppy, You Can Buy a Woman"

Just as the Public Order Act was being proposed in 2002, a national boycott removed sex ads from newspapers without legislation. The way in which these ads caused a national outrage is instructive as to what kind of problem prostitution is for Finns. As in Sweden, prostitution was interpreted as an offense against gender equality. Unlike Sweden, where offense was articulated on behalf of all women's comfort on the streets, in Finland it was the pedagogical impact on children that made prostitution incompatible with social democracy, especially when the public invaded the private sphere in the form of a newspaper.

In response to member complaints about sex ads in local papers, the National Council of Women of Finland (*Naisjärjestöjen Keskusliitto*) responded. With nineteenth-century roots in the first wave of "white slavery" antiprostitution activism,[26] it is an umbrella group of over 20 other women's organizations and a member of the European Women's Lobby discussed in Chapter 2. Its director, Sirpa Hertell, helped organize a boycott of the national paper *Helsingin Sanomat*. As Hertell described the message her members communicated to *Helsingin Sanomat*, the nation's (and Scandinavia's) largest newspaper:

> Please stop our subscriptions, and very many women did so. Because when I myself expressed my sentiment, I think it was the second or third day, I called and said that I am no longer interested in having it sent, and I want you to stop it because of these prostitution advertisements. And the [newspaper employee] said, "Oh no! There are so many that want to do that, please don't! . . . And of course I said I am from the National Council of Women."

The story was picked up by the television news, and Ms. Hertell was invited to speak on the national morning talk show. Within six days the senior editor-in-chief of *Helsingin Sanomat* published an editorial announcing that neither the paper nor its affiliates would accept advertising for sex services. The National Council of Women didn't stop there, but continued the campaign against other regional newspapers as well in response to growing anger that the ads had not been eliminated sooner:

> People are very angry about that. They call us and ask, "please will you do something? We don't want to have those newspapers at home and our kids are reading them." And that was the main reason why we were so angry and so worried about these prostitution advertisements because everyone wanted to have a newspaper. You would want to read it at home and you would want to give it to your kids. And in the same page you can buy a cat

or a puppy, you can buy a woman. And it is not nice to tell your kids that it is possible to buy a woman. That was the main reason.

When the content of newspapers disrupted the socialization of gender equality in children, teaching them that women are objects, then it constitutes an invasion of the public sphere that must be fought. Internet sites are not as offensive, Hertell explained:

> Internet? It was not necessarily so easy for children to go on the Internet and find the pages [for prostitution]. There you *can* buy women and buy prostitutes, but the newspaper is something you have at home and you want to have at home and you want to read at home and you want to [use to] teach your kids.

In other words, unlike in Sweden where abolitionism was intended as part of an international movement to eliminate prostitution everywhere, for Director Hertell, it was not the absolute existence of prostitution on the Internet, but concrete prostitution ads in the newspaper delivered into the home that caused offense.

The NCW boycotts brought further demands to curtail ads from other newspapers that invade the home. "At the moment we get quite a lot of phone calls and emails from people about those advertisements in those free daily or free weekly newspapers," Hertell explained. These offended because unlike subscription papers that could be stopped or started, they were pushed through mailslots indiscriminately, bringing sex ads into the home. Hertell described: "The text is so awful, it is [almost] funny. Before [this summer] I didn't read those, of course, I'm not interested in buying a woman. But at the moment when I see them with my own eyes, they are so awful" (see Figure 6.3).

The ads are quite small and, compared to the graphically explicit ads in other countries, discreet. Mixed among phone sex lines, the text from the issue she provided included ads for "Helena—only home visits," "Beautiful women. Home and hotel. 24 hours," "I lick and suck like a sex cleaner," "Young girls offering sex companionship to you," and "Uninhibited Estonian daughters offer afternoon coffee dates."[27]

Other newspapers followed suit in dropping the sex ads. Hertell laughed at the desperation with which some papers begged to be removed as NCW targets: "Savon Sanomat called me the next morning and said, 'this morning we have made the decision that we are going to have no more prostitute advertisements. If you are still on television, can you tell them?'" In all, five of the eight largest newspapers in the country changed their advertising policies immediately.

Figure 6.3   Finnish "Entertainment Lines" Sex Ads, 2002   Sex ads in newspapers
sparked a 2002 boycott of Finnish newspapers.

Source: Alueuutiset 2002 No. 62, Aug. 7, p. 21

The campaign was largely divided along gender lines. Hertell guessed
that for every 200 messages from women, she received 30 from men, of
which 10 "would say for the record: it is nice you are doing this." The other
20, however:

> SH: I got about 20 emails or text messages from men, and they were quite
> awful, all of them.
> GM: Really?

SH: Yes. I can give if you want to have copies. They told me that we are stupid, less [intelligent] than all feminists, who don't understand what Finnish men need. "Don't stop our hobbies!" But what was the most interesting for me because the worst these Finnish men could say is "you are a lesbo feminist." I am married, I have a husband and two children! I am not a lesbian! I have nothing against lesbians, but I am not. And yet, "you lesbo feminist!"

The battle of the sexes, then, is how Hertell understood men's extreme reactions to her leadership in the boycott, just as Saukkonen and Sirkiä understood the offense of prostitution on the streets. In Sweden, where gender equality is more institutionalized than in Finland, its principle as a good in itself justified the ban on sex purchasing. In Finland, equality empowered women to act and garnered results, even as it prompted this backlash. Where opposition to Sweden's sex purchase act put one on the side of sexual exploiters, in Finland opposition to banning the purchase of sex was possible.

After the Public Order Act became law, the rest of the sex ads were driven out of papers by legal interpretations that advertisements constituted public displays of prostitution. By that point, ads had long since moved to the Internet, especially the Finnish website "Secretary Academy" (see Image#). Now threatened by interpretations of accepting money for prostitution as pimping, it moved its operations out of Finland, where it prospered to become the dominant prostitution contact website for the Nordic and Baltic countries (see Figure 6.4).[28]

Although newspaper reports deplored the ease with which the advertising ban could be skirted in this way, sexually explicit ads in the newspapers disappeared for good. And the late-night television ads featuring Russian-looking

Figure 6.4   Finnish "Secretary Academy" Banner Ad The now-defunct "Secretary Academy" was the main Internet site for escort advertising for over a decade, not only for Finland but the Baltic region as well.

Source: http://www.sihteeriopisto.fi, Accessed April 30, 2004

women in a sauna, imploring the viewer to "add more steam" (*lisää löylyä*) by calling a phone number, also vanished.

"Finland Needs the Swedish Legislation"

Proponents of a Finnish ban on purchasing sexual services made at least three major attempts to put the measure before parliament in 2004, 2006, and 2012. To date they succeeded only in a 2006 compromise that banned the exploitation of sexual services, defined as banning the purchase of sex when involved with pimping or human trafficking.

Eva Biaudet was among the first politicians to call for a Swedish-style ban on purchasing sexual services. She rose from MP to lead the Swedish People's Party[29] into government, becoming twice Minister for Health and Social Affairs and also twice her party's nominee for president. For good and ill, the issue of combating human trafficking and criminalizing the purchase of sexual services has become identified with Biaudet personally, not feminists or her party: "The media said we lost the elections because of me <laughs>." Though her party did not share that opinion, she noted that human trafficking was one of three issues that garnered death threats against her and her family:

> EB: There was one person that wrote to me that at least in Sweden they know how to handle politicians like me [who are] state terrorists, like how they killed [Deputy Prime Minister] Anna Lindh, which was quite scary, and they wished that my children would die of cancer, or something. The other two issues that I got life threats on were the issues of foreigners and immigration . . . and the registration of homosexuals, you know, the civil unions. On these three, I got threats. And no other issues has raised as much although we have really political debates about nuclear energy, and never have I gotten any threats.

As social minister, Biaudet persisted in carrying the controversial issue, describing it as a difficult issue because it revealed the lie of Finnish gender equality:

> You get brought up with a very high recognition of equality for women, and it is the basis of this society, but of course when you grow up this is not the case. It's not really there. Even if many things are okay, it's not the same. There's not equality in many issues and it really comes [visible] when you have children while working. The idea, we believed there would not be a way of looking at women to make it possible to have prostitution to be so common, such a big phenomenon. I don't know if you

understand what I mean, but none of us felt this could be possible. We felt that the Finnish men were not like that. It's quite naïve that we believed it <rueful laugh>.

For Minister Biaudet, the presence of streetwalkers suddenly exposed the fact that the same men women worked alongside had viewed women as objects to be bought all along. And as she was quick to add, it was not out of prudery that sex commerce offends, but its objectification of women: "It's completely different if somebody would say, 'would you like to share the night with me?' it's completely different. It's not about sex, it's about the *thing* part, that you are just an object and just something that can be purchased." If the lie of gender equality was an insult to women balancing work and family, to work alongside men who wanted to buy sex was added injury.

Minister Biaudet also blamed anti-Russian prejudice for opposition to the criminalization of buying sexual services. But where opponents of the sex-purchase ban said it was to punish Finnish men for desiring Russian women, Minister Biaudet attributed xenophobia to punishing the Russian streetwalkers as a surface solution to a deeper problem:

> *EB*: But this was against the easy way, to say it was only these foreigners. We tried to raise [the issue]: why are our men like this? Why do they do this? They haven't done it before. How come they have accepted it so easily, that they would take advantage of other people's misery in such a way and use them as things?
>
> *GM*: hmm.
>
> *EB*: But this debate never, never . . . <trails off>. So it was easier to say, "it's because of this [Russian] trash. It's their fault. Once we get rid of them, the problem is out."

Biaudet implied that because the debate was so focused on the style of Russian women, it was difficult to reorient the debate toward men's behavior, which the sex-buying criminalization was designed to address.

And yet even among feminist activists for the ban on sex-buying, the appearance of Russian women—prostitutes or not—was an offense that could not go without comment. One interviewee described the poverty in Russia that drove women from their country into sexual exploitation and gendered violence in Finland. As she continued, "But have you seen their shoes? Such high heels and makeup all over and tight clothes, they look like trash, like real Hollywood hookers." These two lines of commentary did not quite blame the Russian women for their own victimization. But it highlighted the puzzle for Finnish women of why Finnish men would find such "Hollywood hookers" attractive. Underlying this discourse about the Finnish battle of the sexes was the implicit claim that Finnish women's practical style embodied egalitarianism. Russian women, in contrast, had big hair, exaggerated makeup, tight clothes, and high heels. The desirability of this style was a question I put to Sirpa Hertell of the Finnish Council for Women:

> GM: But I don't understand, why would Finnish men want Russian women?
> SH: <laugh> Well, it's a good question. It starts with, well, our society is quite equal. And the Finnish men can pay the Russian women for something where it is not so equal . . . And a Russian woman who looks so much like a woman is something *very* womanly.

In this brief exchange, exaggeratedly feminine style dramatizes the inequalities between Finns and Russians, their national economies, and gendered power relations.

Minister Biaudet noted the public backlash to the proposal to criminalize the purchase of sex exposed gendered politics that feminists had not previously perceived:

> I think men in Finland have some kind of gap between the rational and the real life, the way they talk together. You know, some kind of hidden male thing. It might be that it has been allowed between men to make fun of these issues, to tell stories about experiences. But it has not been something that they have [been open about], you know . . . or there is a different code among men, or feel there is, and they feel very much threatened by this, that this debate says that "you are bad, you are immoral, you are the abuser." Because I can't understand it otherwise, why it is so personal. When I ask any one of my male friends what do they think about [prostitution], when they think of their family they think it is horrendous. They would never like to see any one of their close ones, never like to see one of their daughters.

As social minister, she worked to correct this gendered imbalance by first commissioning a series of reports on prostitution and trafficking from the then–National Research and Development Center for Welfare and Health (STAKES). STAKES was one of two national research institutes for public health, alongside one for medical research. Its reports were issued not only in Finnish, for domestic consumption, but also in English for wider audiences and EU lobbying.[30] These early reports directly grappled with competing feminist views on prostitution, including a wide range of authors.

Biaudet also described how Finnish advocates of the Swedish model had to contend with competing models of feminism, something Swedish advocates did not. But where an American might describe a liberal versus a radical feminist position, Biaudet distinguished between feminism concerned with solidarity and a radical feminism concerned with freedom, what in the United States would be called liberal feminism:

> *EB*: We say you cannot give consent to violence. [But] his is how the radical feminists think: they think a woman is not free unless she can decide for herself. Of course my argument is that this free will is very much depending on the circumstances that you haven't chosen, you haven't. This is, of course, a moral/intellectual debate. These people that oppose criminalization, they are not in favor of prostitution. They think you should work against it but you shouldn't do it in this way.

For Biaudet, free will is an intellectual crutch in situations of extreme exploitation, a view echoed internationally by such radical feminists as Janice Raymond, Sheila Jeffreys, and Catherine MacKinnon. Though Biaudet disagrees with the liberal feminist view in Finland that privileges individual rights over women's solidarity, she does recognize that they are not in favor of exploitation, but favor different methods to combat it. But where Biaudet rightly sees this distinction between chosen work and gendered exploitation as a core distinction between feminist ideologies, she doesn't recognize that the default feminism is in harmony with Finnish social democracy, while the liberal one fits the worker rights of Dutch and German states, as explored further in Chapter 7.

The ability of such "radical" (liberal) feminist positions to be heard was greater in Finland than Sweden because women parliamentarians defended them. One such opponent to client criminalization was Rosa Meriläinen, MP for the Greens. She described her ability to oppose her own party as due to her outspoken feminist views on other topics, and to her party's pluralistic views on other topics:

> *RM*: Most of my own parliamentary group, the Greens, they favor criminalization. I quite strongly oppose.
> *GM*: You quite strongly oppose?
> *RM*: Yeah.
> *GM*: Which puts you in quite the minority.
> *RM*: Yes. From the feminist approach there's two ways of looking at this issue. The other ways may be the ways of a moral attitude that the world should be so that no woman should be forced to sell herself. Well, I'm quite a pragmatic person. I don't [care] about morals, moral statements. One way also of looking at this issue is what it does to the safety for normal women, like if we are walking on the streets of Helsinki. Are there

going to be men who try to buy sex from us? It can be so that if buying sex is criminalized it's that this buying and offering thing is more rare. So. We can say that for most women it is better, but for me, my point of view has been the point of view of prostitutes and how to improve their safety. I think that's a feminist attitude also.

MP Meriläinen, like Minister Biaudet, also recognizes plural feminisms, one that hardly exists in Sweden. But like Johanna Sirkiä and Jaana Kauppinen earlier in this chapter, she qualifies her liberal feminism with "think" or "like," underscoring its underdog status among the default feminism in Finland.

I asked Meriläinen what it was like to be a contrarian feminist, and she contrasted hers with the social democratic form:

> GM: What is it like trying to represent a feminism that isn't the approved or majority feminism here?
>
> RM: I think for me it's easier because I'm being quite strongly and openly taking feminist positions in many other things. So people still think I'm a feminist here even though I have a wrong opinion in this issue . . . Maybe in the Green group it's easier because we are used to this kind of debate and whose feminism, like I have a right to say, for example, Social Democrats who are more like, "feminism is something that you demand that women have to work like men." And we have been more like, "well, feminism is women can choose what they want to do and if you choose to be at home, well, that's feminism too." I think being in the Green group is easier. We are used to having ideas which are not considered feminist. But still we think we are feminists.

The distinction Meriläinen makes between feminism centered on equal work opportunities and one that maximizes women's choices reveals how support for criminalization garnered broad support by political party, but also provoked dissention with them.

Banning the Exploitation of Sexual Services: The Finnish Compromise

The Finnish compromise, as I am calling it, used the Swedish model to create domestic punishments for human trafficking in accordance with international norms, building on previous laws that had curtailed prostitution from the public sphere. Unlike the other three countries, where one or two bills accomplished the national legislation, in Finland it was the accretion of alterations to the Aliens Act, the introduction of the national Public Order Act, and the 2004 and 2006 revisions of the criminal code that constituted Finland's response to prostitution and human trafficking.

It was against this broad template of opinions, party decisions, feminist divisions, and dissenting opinions that proponents brought to parliament a proposal to ban the purchase of sexual services. In 2004, advocates of the Swedish example failed to have a ban added to a revision of the criminal code that added human trafficking as a separate crime. That statute also created the crime of aggravated trafficking, punishable by further fines and prison time, statutes that brought Finland into compliance with EU norms and addressed some of the US State Department concerns that listed the country in Tier 2 of its annual TIP reports, the controversy discussed in Chapter 1.

Advocates of client criminalization had another chance in 2006, when the compromise was struck as the end game of the first Swedish model proposal in 2002. Then it was remanded to a Ministry of Justice working group, which in 2003 issued a report based on consultation with a wide range of state and nongovernmental organizations, collating its deliberations in a report entitled "Human Trafficking, Pimping, and Prostitution" (*Ihmiskauppa, paritus ja prostituutio*).[31] The report summarized the legal preferences of the broad array of groups who submitted statements:

18 in **favor** of the proposed criminalization of buying sexual services (a lá Sweden)

6 in favor of criminalizing the purchase *and* sale of sexual services (as in the United States)

21 **opposed** to the general criminalization of buying sexual services, of which

11 favored a limited ban in cases of exploitation or human trafficking (the compromise)

3 with reservations about the criminalization of buying sexual services, and

6 that needed further clarification before they could make a decision.

Even this summary is deceptively simple, as many footnotes mark organizations riven by internal dissent and objections.

As might be expected from a proposal originating in government, proponents of the Swedish-style general ban included the Ministries of Foreign Affairs, Education, Social Welfare and Health, the Ombudsman for Equality, and the Council for Gender Equality. Most of the feminist associations that filed statements also supported criminalization of buying, including the Women's Studies Institute of Helsinki University (*Kristiina-institutuutti*), the radical-feminist *Unioni*, the National Council of Women, and the Women Lawyers Association. Administrative bodies that supported the abolitionist law included the Finnish Local and Regional Association, the Turku City Social Services, and the Helsinki City Health Department.

If high government offices mainly supported the government proposal, the organizations who would have to enforce it or deal with the aftermath on the streets largely opposed it. These included judicial entities like the Associated Courts of Appeal, District Courts, Prosecutors' Offices, and associations of public defenders. The Helsinki Police Department and the national Central Bureau of Investigation also filed briefs in opposition. Organizations for sexual rights all came out against, including the Finnish Association for Sexology, Johnna Sirkiä's SALLI, Jaana Kauppinen's The Prostitutes Support Center, and the Sexpo Foundation (akin to Sweden's RFSU or the United State's Planned Parenthood). Significantly, the boards of directors for both state churches (Orthodox and Lutheran) also filed briefs in opposition, in part because church organizations are the major training organizations for social work in Finland, as in many European countries. Those who favored criminalizing sexual commerce for buyers and sellers included the social conservative Free Church Council of Finland, the community activist People's Movement for Prostitution off the Streets, three police organizations including the trade union Finnish Police Association, and the Finnish Association for Mental Health.

Similar divisions occurred in the Finnish Parliament's Legal Affairs Committee when it deliberated upon these working group reports. In a nail-biting series of moves that attracted breathless news coverage, a movement to defer the proposal failed 10–7, one to abandon the bill altogether failed 13–4, and one to amend the government-proposed criminalization of purchasing sex succeeded 15–5, banning the "purchasing of sex in cases in which the provider of the services is a victim of pimping or trafficking in humans." When this "limited ban" was presented to parliament, it passed easily 123 to 19, creating the Finnish compromise. Headlines cheered Finland's promotion to Tier 1 in the State Department TIP Reports after passage of the compromise bill, which survived a 2012 attempt to enact a total ban on purchasing sex.[32]

Finland on the Fence

Though Finnish proponents of Swedish-style criminalization of sex buyers were unable to achieve their legislative goal, abolitionists set the discursive agenda. Although Finland's abolitionism does not look like Sweden's, its actions were justified by the need to remove prostitution from the public sphere to preserve gender equality. While there is palpable Swedish disappointment with Finland's "failure," international observers might be forgiven for not noticing Finland's half-hearted abolitionism at home given its international leadership on abolitionism in the new prostitution politics. President Tarja Halonen highlighted abolitionism during Finland's term as the rotating Presidency of the European Commission, and Finnish negotiators at the United Nations worked against prostitution's legalization, discussed further in Chapter 7. Minister Biaudet went from being National Rapporteur on Trafficking in Finland to the first appointee to the newly created post of International Anti-Trafficking Coordinator for the Organization for Security and Cooperation in Europe (OSCE), a post she held until she returned to government in Finland. Her successor was her Swedish colleague Kajsa Wahlberg, demonstrating the success of abolitionists in occupying high-profile posts in intergovernmental organizations (IGOs), despite the lack of support from police or prosecutors back in Finland for the criminalization of sex buyers.

This strong sense that abolitionist policies were possible and desirable in Finland, I argue, was grounded in the gender equality rooted in Finland's social democratic welfare state that posited visible prostitution as a threat to all women. The inclusion roadmap for social democratic social citizenship meant that all women were vulnerable to street harassment from men asking "how much do you cost?" and the visible sign of eroding gender equality had to be curbed. Seeing prostitution as the Finnish state required a gendered skepticism that was yet informed by its long history with Russia and concerns over migration.

The protracted nature of Finland's deliberations and its stubborn insistence on going its own way reflects a nation-state project that has long relied on pragmatism over ideology in assuaging the concerns of neighbors and allies. Finland is the most enthusiastic of Nordic EU members but refuses to join NATO out of commitment to international neutrality and the concerns of neighbor Russia. It proudly boasts its role in the Helsinki Accords for international human rights but eschews international interventions or criticisms, hewing closely to the realpolitik by which it survived the Cold War.

This realism is seen in the wider range of feminist discourses in Finland than in Sweden, which includes the dominant radical feminist equation of prostitution with violence against all women and the liberal feminist notion that women may be making the best choices available to them. In the years 2002–6 when client criminalization was being debated, Finland had a woman president, two women prime ministers, a mayor in the capital city, and the highest percentage of women in parliament among EU countries. These strong and capable women, however, were present on the opposing side as well, marking their success at having their side heard in public debates more than in Sweden. The compromise, palatable to few of the feminists on either side, removed the prostitution advertisements and streetwalkers that bothered most Finnish women, even as it left unmolested the "Oriental" massage parlors.

This realism is present in the Finns' characterization of their country as a small one dependent on foreign powers, yet when it comes to describing their responses to prostitution, all but the most bureaucratic insiders described the Finnish legislative timeline as a response to domestic events. This is despite the fact that streetwalking prostitutes had been present in Helsinki for eight years before the city council acted, a delay I have suggested may be *schadenfreude* over the sudden reversal of fortunes between poor Finland and rich Russians. The Helsinki City Council only acted *after* Swedish and Dutch Parliaments had garnered international headlines and the German courts attracted attention for throwing out Germany's morality statute. Only then, amid headlines about plans for EU harmonization of social welfare and criminal law did Finns act to curtail prostitution from public space, starting with the streets of Helsinki and the pages of its newspapers, and subsequently to the nation as a whole. Proposals to enact Swedish-style legislation were floated several times but parliamentary compromises meant that, legislatively speaking, Finland prohibits prostitution in public to protect the right to public space by women and girls. This means that, as in Sweden, prostitution only ever means women sellers and male buyers, a gendered approach that reflects social democratic values. This gendered approach means that the problem of prostitution was always framed over harm to women and girls, but almost never about how to raise boys to be more egalitarian men, a battle-of-the-sexes approach that differentiated Finland from Sweden.

Instead of an ideological solution to prostitution, the Finnish compromise represents a realistic fence-straddling, neither "fully feminist" like the Swedish solution nor fully able to address the migration of Russian women into the country. The Nordic model of abolitionism is thus a range of policies that differ in their tone and implementation, leading two prominent researchers to declare the Nordic model a "myth."[33] For Finns, making a virtue of the necessary to endure difficult circumstances is captured by the national character "*sisu*." This concept, sometimes translated as "stubborn endurance," is to Finns what freedom is to Americans. A crude joke captures the dark side of *sisu* and its harsh assessment of Finland's place in the world:

A Russian and a Swede are walking through the fields when they come upon a sheep with its head caught in the fence. The Russian cries "aha!" unzips his trousers, and immediately begins to screw the sheep. With a satisfied groan he pushes off the sheep and steps back, telling the Swede, "now it's your turn." The Swede goes up to the sheep and puts his head into the fence.

Funny on its face, when told by a Finn the joke forms part of a genre about the neighbors between which Finland is trapped—just like the sheep.

One of my informants described gay rights in Finland with a parallel for-mula: "Sweden is a country where policemen and the army walk in the Pride parade. Finland is a country where policemen would never walk in the Pride parade. Russia is a country where policemen beat the Pride parade people." Encoded in these stories is a whole gendered national poli-tics, reflecting not only European stereotypes about rapacious Russians and effete Swedes, but the *sisu* implicit in my interviewees' accounts for why they struggle against legal compromises that are unlikely to change. Finn-ish globalization anxiety is different than in the other countries, because Finns are not surprised that their nation cannot control its destiny, just as the Finnish prostitution compromise reflects a small nation straddling Europe's fence between West and East, between Swedish idealism and the reality of being a small neighbor of the largest sending country of migrant prostitutes. Only countries with nation-state projects organized around autonomy had the luxury to imagine that they were ever in control.

7

Seeing *as* a State: Transnational Problems through National Lenses

Figure 7.0   Police/The Secrets of Love A German billboard displays a magazine issue on "The Secrets of Love" under directions to police headquarters.

Source: author photo

In Chapters 3 through 6, I showed how 4 of the 15 European Union countries became so concerned about prostitution and human trafficking that they passed new legislation removing sexual commerce from municipal and ad hoc regulation and imposed new national reforms. Each case study showed how prostitution was framed as a social problem along two similar conceptual regimes—workers versus gendered victims—but with national variation. Understanding these cases has implications for how we understand the ways social problems come to be defined as such, the efficacy of state policies to manage them, and the enduring power of national culture in an era of transnationalism and globalization. Claude Fischer describes national culture as a shared mentality, "the shared, loosely connected, taken-for-granted rules, symbols and beliefs that characterize a people . . . ways of thinking, feeling and behaving that individuals typically share with others in their nation." While sociologists distinguish between culture and structures of the state, the interrelationships between shared meanings, state structures, and the definition of social problems are often opaque.[1] Here I describe how social problem framing as a important project of the nation-state, shoring up domestic values in part by defining what is unacceptable, unfair, or unjust.

European welfare state policies lie at the crux of understanding this interrelationship between nationally shared meanings, state structures, and cultural politics. Cultural definitions of welfare, and the institutions and policies they underpin, affect the ways that citizens see and address threats to their way of life. In this chapter I introduce the metaphor of "seeing as a welfare state" to capture the interrelationship between the way that the state "lives" in its citizens, whose aggregate preferences reproduce its institutions and enact its policies in everyday life. This metaphor is based on an extension of the concept of social citizenship, one welfare state scholars use to describe the financial entitlements that states guarantee their citizens, from health care, education, pensions, or unemployment protections. I argue that these policies have institutionalized and thus reproduced cultural conceptions of the good life, and thus are cultural as well as material, helping citizens see "as" the state, an institution produced each day as much by citizen "common sense" and everyday expectations as the actions of politicians and bureaucrats.[2] I conclude by discussing the implications of the seeing metaphor for comparative policy analysis, state theory, and feminist analyses of prostitution.

As I introduced in Chapter 1, one of the most influential characterizations of the variety of welfare states is that of Norwegian political scientist Gøsta Esping-Andersen.[3] He found three clusters of policies and outcomes so different that he characterized them as three "worlds" of welfare: social democratic, corporatist-conservative, and liberal-residual. Social democratic welfare states provide universal benefits for all citizens, placing emphases on equality and broad social solidarity, as in Finland and Sweden. Corporatist-conservative regimes provide benefits through the workplace or the family, preserving social distinctions through existing social institutions, as does Germany and the Netherlands. Liberal-residual welfare states like the United States or United Kingdom provide benefits based on lifetime contributions or, when families or the market fail, means-tested benefits as a temporary safety net.

These worlds of state policy differ in the degree of universal benefits they offer, but are united by their special concern for vulnerable citizens: veterans, mothers, children or the poor.[4] These categories are especially intertwined with gendered expectations and sexuality—whether through heterosexism, maternalism, or family breadwinner models.[5] The officials who administer and implement them, however, mediate the provision of these concrete material benefits with the "intellectual processes" of the "policy imagination" that instituted them. The social rights of citizenship instituted by law are not objectively "out there," but only become real when they are institutionalized as particular interpretations of the law backed by bureaucratic action. In other words, welfare states provide support systems for vulnerable citizens but also frame the *meaning* of vulnerability for the officials who administer and implement them. Social citizenship thus can describe both the institutional supports that provide a material foundation upon which citizens do the cultural work of planning, assigning meanings, and acting—and the cultural meanings that feed back into policy discussions. Citizenship is thus a cultural repertoire, a set of strategies and meanings that people can draw upon to create solutions to problems—seemingly novel solutions that still make common sense to fellow citizens because their welfare state context is underpinned by shared cultural meanings of indexical concepts.[6]

This richer understanding of social citizenship highlights the cultural dimensions of the welfare state by focusing on the ways citizens see social problems and the ways citizens are socialized to self-regulate themselves in accordance with social norms. Welfare states create institutions by which citizens reproduce self-regulating individuals through day care, school, courts, and transfers to families. Self-regulating individuals are thus seemingly harmonized with the expectations and benefits of citizenship in their society.[7] And if they disagree, they do so within the terms of a debate that have already been set by the shared expectations of the majority. This model for social reproduction was developed to describe the interrelationships of individuals in society, but could just as well describe the interactions among European nations and the supranational European institutions and its budding civil society.

For sociologists, the concept of social control refers to the way societies train individuals in self-regulation such that coercive measures are unnecessary. Welfare states frame the expectations that citizens have for state action, legal rights, and the "normal troubles" that have routine diagnoses and institutionalized responses. For example, truancy laws direct police to seize wayward school-aged children or fine their parents, but school attendance is more efficiently realized when parents take these responsibilities upon themselves and inculcate them in their children. Sociological research on social control suggests that the public reaction to a social problem need not be related to any material or empirical change, but to the public's perception of the necessity for change. Phenomena become social problems when they are perceived as widespread failures of self-regulation—yet another example of the Thomas theorem that what people take to be real is real in its consequences. Or, as W. I. Thomas long ago asserted, morality itself is "the generally accepted definition of the situation, whether expressed in public opinion and the unwritten law, in a formal legal code, or in religious commandments."[8]

No social problem is so complex that it stands for all evils because no society is organized around *all* potential meanings. Societies work because there are a limited number of shared meanings, just as change comes about because there are always multiple, not single meanings for a thing. Culture is itself the set of meanings possible in a society—some more likely than others—that underpin communication and collective action. The specific remedies that a citizenry imposes upon itself tell us about the kinds of social problems its citizens see.

The welfare state, as an institution that sanctions behavior and bestows benefits, is in an ideal position to produce moral and political consensus. Thus, social citizenship considered materially and culturally builds upon the insights of other international-comparative projects to understand political culture, such as "language repertoires" or national "policy styles" or "knowledge regimes." In contemporary democracies, language repertoires must be considered alongside the policy regimes from which they spring and subsequently reproduce, the duality that social citizenship captures.[9] Social citizenship is both culture—the feeling of belonging and the cognitive categories that police the borders of "us" and "them"—and the structures institutionalized in state institutions and social policy to protect those categories and the benefits attached to them.

Though I cannot say with certainty why any of my countries acted the way they did, what I have shown is that the terms of the debates about prostitution in each of the four countries was consistent with a general cultural repertoire. This repertoire, embedded in welfare state policies and citizen expectations, showed cross-nationality similarities even as it was not deterministic, allowing for nuanced outcomes between countries with similar welfare states.

Seeing *as* a State

The metaphor of seeing *as* a state more accurately captures the relationship between citizenry, culture, and the state. This riffs upon James Scott's famous description of seeing like a state, with a twist. Seeing *like* a state implies that the state is separate from the citizen who sees; seeing *as* a state captures their mutual interdependence. The former implies that when the police are called, the citizen who did so was only temporarily adopting the perspective of governing; the latter insists that the state lives within us as the "shared ways of thinking, feeling, and behaving" that characterize national culture.[10] Previous characterizations of state rule described it as "penetrating," "making legible," or "embracing" the societies they govern.[11] These metaphors are inadequate because they frame the ruling class as almost omniscient elites who constitute the state, absolving the governed from any responsibility for state authority. A theory of modern democratic states must account for the reproduction of these elites, the source of their influence, and the ways social structures influence the way they apprehend social problems. In this chapter, I propose acculturating the state by means of the visual metaphor of the "state gaze"—highlighting the dialectic by which citizens make demands of their bureaucracies and bureaucracies socialize citizens. Understanding that citizens can view the state as something outside their lives even as they take actions *as* the state helps bridge the gap between cultural and structural understandings of the state. This gaze of the state illuminates national differences in the commonsense ways social problems are framed.

Beyond the policies that undergird state institutions, however, "there must also be auxiliary institutions of mass representation at the local level to ensure that the welfare agencies perform effectively and responsibly." These include the "policy entrepreneurs" of state-funded NGOs and research institutes that pursue state goals and grant them legitimacy by translating them in broadly accepted scientific and cultural terms. But culture itself, considered as a structure, is itself an "institution of mass representation" by which citizen expectations make demands upon those very agencies.[12]

In strong welfare states, policy entrepreneurs are more likely to come from within the state or from state-funded institutions than from the private sector (whereas they come almost exclusively from the private sector in liberal-residual welfare states). Strong welfare states implicate more bureaucracies in the work of the welfare side of the state, and by definition the social workers, auditors, day care workers, and border officials that staff them. These buttress a social citizenship that represents taken-for-granted notions about policing, social care, and personal autonomy.

For social problems like prostitution, the social citizenship embedded in welfare state citizens provides them with shared ways of seeing vulnerable women that that constrain the possibilities for responding and highlight certain creative moves as most useful. Although there are many ways prostitution can be a social problem, not all communities care about all problems at all times. For example, prostitution is variously perceived as a(n): avenue of women's illegitimate social mobility, trajectory for disease, threat to marriage, useful diversion for husbands, blight on property values, inappropriate sight for children, threat to sons' purity, untaxed economy, pacifier for single men, source of unwanted immigration, among many others. These problems tend to be organized by the "mass representation" of welfare states, defining prostitution as a problem of gendered violence in social democracies, of worker protection in corporatist states, and as an issue of property in liberal-residual states.

Social Democratic Citizenship

Of countries that have adopted the Swedish model, all are social democracies: Sweden, Iceland, Norway. Their rejection of free versus forced prostitution parallels decisions embedded in the early days of their welfare state development that made gender equality "integral to Scandinavian citizenship."[13] When confronted with a labor shortage after World War II, Scandinavian countries activated women's labor. In a move of radical social solidarity, work outside the home was made the measure of personal development for women and men. No one should be forced to do degrading work, however, preserving the dignity of working daughters, wives, and mothers. These policies were both egalitarian—opening up the world of work to women—and nativistic—choosing domestic labor over foreign. Scandinavian political scientists often frame their policy heritage in national-cultural terms rather than the results of political choices, describing their cultures as "women-friendly" and citing long traditions of women's authority. This radical solidarity incorporated women into the state in gendered terms, producing a norm of full female employment made possible by the extraordinary supports of the social democratic welfare state, including universal childcare and generous parental leave, in ways that removed sex considerations from the workplace, especially in the public sector.[14]

The hallmark of the social democratic welfare countries like Sweden is their rejection of any distinction between free and forced prostitution. This has become a contentious issue in the international movement to combat human trafficking where the Nordics are part of a powerful minority of countries who equate human trafficking with contemporary slavery along with the United States, the Vatican, and Saudi Arabia. Unique to social democracies, however, is the resonance such a perspective has among their citizenry and the robust social support that virtually eliminates poverty as a cause of prostitution. That there might be other reasons for prostitution is almost unthinkable to Swedes (except among those whose work brings them into contact with prostitutes).

In social democratic welfare states, men and women can be equal workers when society—via the state—ensures that women have support for full employment. They can be equal workers only when sex and fertility is removed as a barrier to women's full participation in the public sphere. Sex work is thus an oxymoron. From the perspective of social democracies, the corporatist welfare ideology that permits a distinction between free and forced prostitution is abhorrent because social acceptance and protection of prostitutes makes the state into the biggest pimp of all.

And yet, the social democratic model is not so monolithic that there is no variety. The case of Finland demonstrates that while it shares the commitment to gender equality of other Nordic states, it did not need to follow the Swedish model to demonstrate it. And yet, that model definitively framed the debate, with at least four parliamentary proposals for client criminalization and none for any other policy. Finland's criminalization of the purchase of sex from victims of human trafficking is obviously modeled on the Swedish legislation, and other Finnish measures mirror those in other social democracies, including the prohibition of selling sex in streets or newspapers, both to protect all women in public from men's bad behavior.

Corporatist Social Citizenship

Of EU-15 countries that have legalized prostitution in some form, all are corporatist welfare states: the Netherlands, Germany, and Austria. That the corporatist framework allows variety t is demonstrated by the divergence of Germany from the "full" legalization of the Netherlands. Yet the states that had parliamentary debates on legalization included primarily corporatist states: Luxembourg, Spain, Italy, Greece. As with Finland, I cannot cite *the* reason why the German legalization foundered on the key distinction between a business (*Betrieb*) and trade (*Gewerbe*) As Chapter 5 suggested, this may have been as a compromise with most conservative parties or out of concern for the influx of foreign sex workers. Both of these are framed in the language of corporatist social citizenship: crafting consensus for workers.

For corporatist policy makers, however, to refuse state recognition to sex *workers* is a recipe for exploitation and inequalities that require welfare state intervention. The defining characteristic of the corporatist welfare state is "its ceaseless effort to accomplish a settlement between possibly opposed social interests" of workers and employers.[15] This is traditionally interpreted in terms of workplace consultations, where the state plays a role of friendly referee in consensus building between workers and employers. It also extends to the realm of social policy, however. The strong Christian heritage of corporatist welfare states, be they Calvinist in the Netherlands or Catholic in Italy, means that there are different moral stances on controversial issues such as prostitution. But all parties are resigned to the fact that they will not be able to impose their view on the others and that compromise is not just inevitable, but the most desirable political solution. This is reflected, for instance, in the fact that the Dutch reached consensus on state programs to combat human trafficking in the early 1980s, over 15 years before any other European country took up the cause.

For corporatist welfare states, the distinction between free and forced prostitution parallels other labor market distinctions. Most important, corporatism makes "a distinction between social rights attached to citizenship (as in the case of health) and social rights attached to performance on the labor market (as in the case of pensions)."[16] Participation in the labor market is the basis on which social benefits are allocated, and these are negotiated through unions ("corporations") that represent workers' interests. To prevent large-scale strikes and unrest, the state acts as a good-faith arbiter of labor and business concerns. The state has the responsibility to ensure that workers labor under safe conditions and have jobless benefits to allow them to move out of undesirable jobs, ensuring their dignity and choice. The value of worker choice is enshrined in the state treatment of women workers as well, providing opportunities for women to work part-time, full-time, or not at all when raising small children. For women, workers and prostitutes, the state supports individual choice to maintain a domestic labor market that is both fair and flexible.

Liberal-Residual Social Citizenship

Thus far I have described that broad support for prostitution reforms at the parliamentary level must be framed in ways compatible with social welfare meanings of autonomy, vulnerability, and legitimate aid. Since prostitution reforms were not enacted in the third category of welfare states, liberal-residual, in this section I propose an interpretation based on a review of secondary literature. Liberal-residual social citizenship, with its focus on private property ownership and common-law interpretations of bodies as property, sees prostitution as a misuse of personal property. The implementation of criminalization and decriminalization in liberal-residual states are virtually identical, punishing public forms of prostitution and largely ignoring indoor forms or freelance escorts. This reinforces general social hierarchies: prostitutes who are able to maintain their own private property benefit from the residual-liberal states' laissez-faire social controls and rewards for entrepreneurism, while those who cannot maintain private property or public propriety are punished, even when this means fining prostitutes who must sell more sex to pay off their fines.

To say that the United States has no social citizenship, as many scholars do, is to make normative the standpoint of strong welfare states. I implicitly bow to the dominant view within welfare state scholarship by using the "strong" designation, as if the United States and the UK are "weak." It is more accurate to say that the social citizenship of residual-liberal states like the United States is oriented around different values than those of other welfare states (or that American social scientists are partisans of a particular welfare state not supported by their countrymen). This makes the United States, for example, a stronger residual-liberal welfare state than the UK when comparing their liberal reliance on the market and kin networks to provide social security. In residual or laissez-faire welfare state societies, civil society is defined primarily as a buffer for citizens from both markets *and* states. Thus the dominant paradigm for understanding welfare states à la Esping-Andersen entails a culturally specific understanding of the relationship between state cultural influence, state structures, and civil society.[17]

Prostitution scholarship about prostitution in the United States, United Kingdom, and Canada links the common law concept of property rights to these societies' response to prostitution without situating it within the cultural or state contexts of welfare. Feminist theorists of prostitution in Anglo-liberal countries note how the common law concept of property rights defines a citizen's autonomy in terms of control over one's body. Though empirical studies within the sociology of property rights ignore prostitution, empirical studies by feminist researchers demonstrate how the bodies of prostitutes are treated as misused property by criminal law. Under America's criminalization regime, for example, prostitutes have neither the legal protections as citizens nor the rights of workers, leaving them open to violence but without recourse in the courts. A study by Lisa Sanchez explicates this residual-liberal common sense that prostitutes are not taking care of the property that is their body. A prostitute thus cannot be a victim of rape under this logic because something cannot be taken from her that she gives away indiscriminately. State protections of the body as property are predicated upon the reasonable care of that property before the state will defend, much less actively enforce a citizen's rights.[18]

These studies suggest that property is core to residual-liberal citizenship, what Ananya Roy characterizes as a "paradigm of propertied citizenship."[19] As property, bodies confer both rights and responsibilities—the right to an abortion but also the responsibility to be circumspect about sexual propriety. In corporatist and social democratic welfare states, bodies are fragile vessels that must be shielded from the full might of the market. In corporatism, the state should coax them into unions—families and trade associations. Under social democracy, bodies are sheltered through the radical solidarity of universal, total reliance on the state in case the family fails. In residual-liberal welfare states, bodies are the means of participation in the labor market, which the state safeguards. Thus citizens of residual-liberal welfare states are loath to grant benefits to those who abuse their bodies because they reveal themselves unworthy to participate in public life, as through such bodily abuses as drug use, premarital sex, cigarette smoking, obesity, or risky sex.

Social Citizenship Frames Social Problems

Social citizenship, considered materially *and* culturally, presents a fruitful way to describe the interaction of states, culture, and citizens by thinking about a shared state gaze. I have shown how social citizenship frames social problems, particularly prostitution, in countries with different welfare regimes. The homology between prostitution regulation discourse and the policy solutions was not only about the institutional tools at hand to address the problem, but reflects the cultural meanings that gave rise to such compromise formations, legitimizes them, and reproduces citizens who support them.[20]

Seeing citizenship as an inculcated gaze that focuses or blurs structural dilemmas of Western governance has much in common with the focus on cultural repertoires in cultural sociology, the sometimes-contradictory elements that individuals draw upon to interpret social life and/or solve problems.[21] In settled times, these shared tools provide more or less conventional ways of thinking, feeling, and acting. In unsettled times, these tools are used to interpret the new reality and make it conform to established institutional order—they are the switchmen of history. In this case, the unsettling prospect of EU enlargement and constitutional harmonization set the stage for prostitution's role as a potent symbol of a vulnerability increasingly felt by all citizens. This globalization anxiety called into question the state's ability to protect national ways of doing things from perceived incursions.

This perspective sheds an institutional light on European controversies over prostitution, casting otherwise gendered and moral politics as a politics of welfare state competition within Europe. Recurrent (false) claims that German welfare offices require women to consider work in the sex industry, for example, attract more attention outside Germany than within. Spurious allegations that international sporting events facilitate prostitution or human trafficking are regularly leveled by social democratic countries against corporatist ones, as recent World Cups, Olympics, and European Football Championships attest.[22] Rather than seeing these as feminist disagreements over the best way to address vulnerable women, I argue these should be seen as struggles over welfare policy in the midst of government retrenchment and an integrating Europe. Or if we see them as disagreements among feminist positions, we must recognize the state contexts that give these ideologies their meaning and reproduce them institutionally.

The dispositions that are social citizenship are the internationalization of the structural realities of the state. The state is one of the key institutions of the "imagined we" by which a nation constitutes and governs itself.[23] Its bureaucracies are repositories of institutional memory—such as laws and social policies, but also of informal meanings such as liberty, vulnerability, or solidarity—by which citizens continually rededicate themselves and in which they find daily meaning. Welfare states in particular play a critical role in shaping the habitus of its citizens, their dispositions toward seeing social problems in similar ways. Thus when we speak about national character, differences between cultures, or the "culture shock" we experience when dealing with them, we are in part describing the differences in meaning that are produced and reproduced by state institutions and the expectations citizens have of them. Social citizenship—as a shared national disposition and ongoing nation-state project—represents a compromise solution to the structural dilemmas for which there is no right answer, only temporary measures to address intractable debates. When citizens draw upon cultural tools to address structural dilemmas, they reproduce the state in their everyday lives by drawing upon values that the state's reproductive machinery makes most salient. Part of this process means that the state is incarnate in individuals, part of their innermost assumptions and unexamined habits in shaping the way citizens see as the state—state bureaucrats, civil society activists, citizens, and long-term denizens alike.

8

The Truly Trafficked Woman, and Other Globalization Anxieties

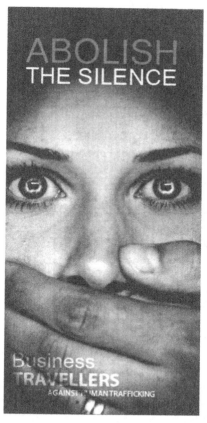

Figure 8.0   The Traffick in Talk Stories of truly trafficked women justify the intensification of state powers.

Source: circa 2006 from http://www.businesstravelers.org

The idea that silence around human trafficking needs to be abolished, as the image above suggests, is odd. Trafficking and prostitution are stories that demand telling, even if, so-called globalization often takes the blame for causing problems that civic officials confess were already there to begin with—undocumented migrants selling sex, unregulated brothels, the lack of social rights (welfare) or responsibilities (taxes) for prostitutes, and the shift of national power to the supranational European Union. Globalization, then, has brought unresolved political problems to the public's attention. It is not clear whether this lack of resolution was due to a failure of migrant integration, conflicting definitions of morality for the intimate sphere, or the maintenance of EU- and state-funded programs to ameliorate social inequality. The EU itself is a striking incarnation of the anxieties caused by globalization: the erosion of the state, the homogenization of national cultures, lost control over domestic politics, and subjugation to distant, uncaring overseers. In international meetings about human trafficking, however, the politics of these local contexts can be swept aside in favor of a story with clearly defined victims and villains. Trafficking talk allows for international agreement in the face of diverse globalization anxieties, and underpins moves to strengthen the moral capacities of the state by hardening its borders and giving its agents new powers to surveil, assess, and inscribe.

The Truths of Popular Culture

"People think prostitution is like [the Julia Roberts movie] *Pretty Woman*, but really it's like *Lilja-4-Ever.*" "Have you seen this Moodysson film *Lilja 4-ever*? Prostitution is like that, it's not some *Pretty Woman* story." "I really resisted seeing it for a long time, but it wasn't as bad as I thought it would be but it was still pretty black and white, as bad as *Pretty Woman*." This comparison was told to me many times, both in formal interviews and informal conversations during my four years of fieldwork. *Lilja 4-ever*, by Swedish director Lucas Moodysson, was a hit in Europe, featuring a fatalistic story of young Lilja, a Russian girl whose entire life has set her up for prostitution. It is told via a mix of styles that veer between magical realism and the gritty realism of handheld camerawork of the kind pioneered by Lars von Trier's "Dogma 95" movement and made ubiquitous by *The Blair Witch Project*, MTV, and YouTube.

The movie recounts Lilja's life in the rusting hulk of Murmansk, once home to the Russian Navy's proud Arctic fleet but now a decayed, disintegrating port devoid of sailors, including the one who fathered her. Her mother leaves with a boyfriend at the beginning of the film, leaving the 16-year-old Lilja in the care of an abusive aunt. There is no school, and her time is spent either with her mentally handicapped friend Volodja or with a girlfriend who has begun turning tricks at the local disco. When she is suspected by the housing project roughs of being a prostitute, this friend accuses Lilja, whose red-faced embarrassment seems to confirm the lie. After being gang raped by the neighborhood boys, Lilja begins prostituting herself in the disco until she finds temporary refuge in the arms of Andrej, who she believes to be her boyfriend. Alas, Andrej's promise to get her out of Murmansk is fulfilled; Lilja is spirited to Sweden where she is locked in a room, beaten, and forced into prostitution, graphically portrayed with camera angles from Lilja's point of view. Eventually she escapes to a local gas station but, frightened of a policewoman who has pulled up in a patrol car, she flees to the highway overpass where the film began.

This film was referenced by many of my interviewees, from all four countries, often seen as truthful compared to the obvious fiction of *Pretty Woman* but also criticized for being rendered in black and white that obscures the gray areas of real life. In the film *Pretty Woman*, failing businessman Richard Gere picks up Julia Roberts on a backstreet stroll only to be disgusted by her frank sexual advances. He purchases her time for the weekend, transforming her into his fair lady by buying her boutique clothes. On her own, however, she is shunned by the store clerks and faces stigma for her low-class ways. Gere's faith in her allows her to blossom, her love redeems his failures, and his love allows her to transcend her seedy past. "So what happened after he climbed the tower and rescued her?" "She rescues him right back."

But if *Pretty Woman* is a film that succeeded by appealing to a broad global audience's taste for redemptive love stories, Lucasson's film had some state-sponsored help. Nominated by the Swedish Film Board as its nominee for the 2002 Academy Awards, it was also featured in schools as the center of a campaign to reduce violence against women; the curriculum was authored by *Kvinnoforum*, a state-sponsored women's NGO on whose board sat Commissioner Anita Gradin.

What both movies share is an aversion for ambiguities, shades of gray that are similarly denied by advocates for national legislative solutions to prostitution. The earnest commentary my interviewees heaped on these films could be interpreted as standing in for their anxieties about globalization: domestic truths versus foreign lies, local values versus transnational commerce, and a defense of local ways of protecting the weak.

Prostitution without Prostitutes: Workers and Victims

I have suggested that the wave of national reform projects that swept the EU between 1998 and 2002 were a response to European integration. As the acme of vulnerable citizens, female prostitutes came to symbolize the ability of states to shield their citizens, especially the weak. That men were conspicuously absent from these debates as victims, but omnipresent as the cause of prostitution, helps reveal the tacit images of citizenship that motivated prostitution reform. The four countries in this study enacted prostitution reforms not only to bolster domestic prostitutes' citizenship rights, but also to strengthen state protections for all women and children—the paradigmatic clients of state protection.

Two broad policies were enacted in these four countries, creating new legal statuses for prostitutes. The Netherlands and Germany legalized prostitution from a labor standpoint, consistent with the corporatist social citizenship their countries embraced after World War II. This created three legal statuses for prostitution in these two countries: sex workers, illegal sex workers, and the victims of sex crimes ranging from forced prostitution to human trafficking. Finland and Sweden attempted to abolish prostitution, redefining it as the product of rape, sexual slavery, human trafficking, and the crime of "the purchase of sexual services." This created the legal victimhood of prostitutes in these countries, foreclosing the very possibility of voluntary prostitution and making the term *sex work* an oxymoron.

These reforms strengthened national responses to human trafficking, an issue that exploded in international politics during this time. Trafficking became the bogeyman of globalization, becoming the focus of international accords on moral pressure. As the timeline in Chapter 2 shows, a wide range of international organizations reached accords on the definitions of and appropriate responses to human trafficking. The United States, as befitting its status as the lone superpower, established its own criteria for ranking countries' antitrafficking efforts, naming and shaming them in its annual State Department Trafficking in Persons Reports.

Despite the increased amount of international agreements on human trafficking, local agencies in all four countries reported inadequate responses on the ground. By 2006, only the Netherlands allowed suspected victims of human trafficking the immediate possibility of a temporary visa or the possibility of permanent residence if it was unsafe for them to return to their native country. If this procedure was so difficult as to be impossible in the Netherlands, it was not even a legal possibility in the other countries. During the period in which Sweden and Finland were placing human trafficking on the EU agendas, neither country had any program in place to aid victims of human trafficking, some of whom were deported even before police departments could take statements from them against their traffickers. If all four countries were equal enthusiasts of *trafficking talk*, all of them failed to walk the walk, if domestic NGO critics are to be believed.

The spread of trafficking was not unique to these countries, nor was it the only similar outcome of national prostitution reforms. As I have already suggested, they rationalized prostitution by enforcing uniform categories across the country, eliminating local custom and meanings. These new meanings were derived from the situations in these countries' largest cities. And these new policies explicitly eliminated the category of migrant prostitution, defining it either as illegal sex work resulting in deportation, or human trafficking resulting in repatriation.

The increase in trafficking talk represents a success of sorts. It is an evil on which everyone can agree. All EU countries have enacted comprehensive antitrafficking reforms in their customs services, external border controls, and national police services. For all of the resistance to "dictates from Brussels" that the EU has induced in national populations, reforms to help victims have been eagerly embraced by EU Member State politicians and citizens alike. Human trafficking and national prostitution reforms create stronger states, not weaker ones.

The Traffic in Trafficking

As 100 years ago the phrase *traffic in women* galvanized international social movements and intergovernmental agreements, so today the words *human trafficking* show the same ability to unite coalitions from the political right and left. Meanwhile, community-based organizations are divided over the appropriate local response to impersonal forces they attribute to globalization. These elites from civil society link the public sector's inability to fend off sexual commodification (topless bars and streetwalking) to the welfare state's declining services and employment protections. Others identify *globalization* as the increasing penetration of capitalism into our intimate lives. Some draw links to general increase in international migration since the fall of the Soviet Empire in 1991 and resulting wars in Africa and the Balkans. Civic and political leaders agree that the nation-state is ill-poised to make any dent in this trafficking. Yet despite this agreement that international cooperation is necessary, agreement remains elusive.[1]

Unlike those of 100 years ago, most prostitutes in Europe today are not nationals of the country in which they sell sex. And yet, as little evidence about human trafficking exists today as it did about the white slaving of a century ago. Numbers of those trafficked into the 15 EU Member States as of May 2004 ranged from 50,000 to 700,000. Scanty evidence exists—neither now nor when the new prostitution politics emerged in 1998—showing that trafficking is conducted in a way different from ordinary chain migration or that it is monopolized by organized crime.[2]

Though the story of trafficking and prostitution are really two sides of the same coin, the historical understanding of migration is rarely applied to migrant prostitution. Many local explanations for the changes that occurred after 1991 emerged: *schadenfreude* over poor Russians in Finland, fears that old-fashioned, unequal sexuality would blossom in Sweden, Germany's necessary challenges in reuniting the two Germanys, and reestablishing Dutch values in its red-light districts. None of these found traction in international agreements, but all are now understood as part of each country's antitrafficking policies and strategies for national prostitution governance.

Until 15 years ago, with few exceptions, Western industrialized nations governed commercial sex in a somewhat paradoxical way. On the one hand, selling sex was decriminalized to avoid punishing vulnerable women, a value enshrined in the 1949 United Nations (UN) "Convention for the Suppression of the Traffic in Persons and the Exploitation of the Prostitution of Others." This liberalizing move dismantled the primary form of regulating commercial sex through the police surveillance and/or registration of prostitutes. On the other hand, this same treaty prohibited prostitution legalization. Laws against pimping were maintained to ensure the prostitute received the whole sum of her earnings by preventing any form of organized prostitution (such as brothels, pimps, or crime syndicates).

At the level of international agreements and transnational advocacy networks, abolitionist politics have shown remarkable success.[3] The organizations that work primarily at the transnational level are overwhelmingly abolitionist regarding prostitution. These include several United Nations agencies, the Nordic Council, the European Women's Lobby, or the Massachusetts-based Coalition against Trafficking in Women. They have enshrined their feminist approach in the 2001 UN Protocol against Trafficking in Humans, Especially Women and Children by forging coalitions between the United States, the Vatican, Muslim countries, and many of the Nordic states.[4] Governments that have made explicit interventions are also explicitly abolitionist, such as the United States, Finland, and the Vatican. The Foreign Ministry of Sweden has been the most active, however, in making ministerial proclamations denouncing "pro-prostitution" actions in other countries, as well as coordinating and galvanizing abolitionist sentiments within the Nordic Council, EU, and UN. As detailed in this book's introduction, all of these actors coalesced around Athens's decision to enforce existing brothel legislation in advance of the 2004 Olympic Games, prompting criticism even from Greece's European Commissioner, Anna Diamontopolous.

At the community level, however, civil groups that actually work with prostitutes are, with few exceptions, advocates of legalizing prostitution. *Pastoral NGOs* offer services such as sex worker health services, counseling, legal assistance, and even political lobbying for prostitute's rights. They too stress a feminist approach, though one that differs from the feminism that operates mainly at the transnational level, a difference that might be described as *liberal* versus *radical* feminism. They are often joined by other civic institutions, such as local women's offices, health clinics, or the women's caucuses of political parties. Indeed, one of my findings is that organizations that work directly with prostitutes on a regular basis are invariably suspicious of abolition and supportive of legalization—including police and church groups. This even includes, discreetly and quietly, organizations within nations with abolitionist policies as well.

These competing politics of prostitution—for *victims' rights* or *sex workers' rights*—operate at these very different levels. When parliaments debate these issues, however, they are stymied by the groundswell of opposition from highly respected NGOs and civic groups whose work is threatened by these broad definitions of women's rights. Interviewees with the employees of women's shelters and migrant support services confided that they often provided advice that was technically illegal, telling migrant prostitutes that their only option to get out of a legal bind was to change cities, tell their story congruent with trafficking narratives, or marry an EU citizen. For example, one German NGO leader confessed:

> This money we get, of course we would use it for trafficking work if we had legal victims of trafficking, but so far no case like that has come our way. We help our migrant women get out of scrapes . . . but we are client driven, so we are not sending them home <pffft!> like that, helping them get what help they can from the police if necessary, but mainly we are helping them learn German.

Another NGO director concurred:

> Because we receive those [state funds from the EU] we have agreed to work closely with the police to monitor migrant women. But I will never turn any of my women in to the police. Never!

Ideologies that make sense at the national or transnational level often falter in the messy realities. The establishment of national policies does not mean that states have the ability to monitor the way their preferred policies are enacted on the ground.

State ability to deal with prostitution in such comprehensive ways only became necessary and possible under certain conditions. Abolitionist and pro-legalization coalitions powerful enough to influence national policy emerged only in social democracies able to leverage substantial welfare state resources against the disorder posed by un(der)regulated markets for sex. Both models represent a logical extension of the modernist project of governance from successes in science, railways, and mapping into sexuality.[5] State authority is extended over bodies in the domestic sphere on the basis of international human rights law, or at least, justified on that basis. What is important is what these states are not: They are not the classical liberal economies of the United States or third-world countries under the influence of World Bank or International Monetary Fund demands. In those places, domestic nationals are still the majority of prostitutes and welfare structures are undeveloped. Both European models intervene—with associated state spending—for the health and well-being of prostitutes, their clients, and society at large, marking a shift from the strictly moral controls on prostitution that focus strictly on the demands of *good* citizens. Yet ironically, they do so at a time that few prostitutes can take advantage of these benefits because few are domestic nationals.

As extensions of their welfare states, prostitution controls are the bailiwick of armies of Swedish and Dutch bureaucrats, public health personnel, and social workers. In theory at least, abolitionism and normalization have sidelined the role of the police. This marks the first instances where the custody of this social problem has been salvaged from the criminal realm and made a matter of citizen welfare. And, as I discussed in the introduction, the elites in charge of these policies are overwhelmingly women, from police chief up to president. It also marks the first instance in which prostitutes are taken to be citizens at all.

Another similarity among various national debates is the paucity of public discussion about the fact that it is *migrants* who are overwhelmingly involved in European prostitution. When feminists in community-based NGOs discuss prostitution in terms of a right to work or a woman's right to control her own sexuality, this invariably plays into broader discussions about the impact of globalization on local state benefits or the status of women's rights at home but disconnects it from debates about international development aid. For example, in Finland, there was a bifurcation of media accounts of prostitution: popular accounts of Russians and Estonians, and political debates that discussed prostitution as an affair of domestic oppressors and domestic victims.

The state context of national prostitution policies is important to recognize because opposing regimes of prostitution control are often critiqued from a gendered or feminist perspective, such as the insensitivity of a "German tolerance for sexual slavery" or a Finnish "outlandish denial of women migrant's rights," as two interviewees described them. These claims are framed in gender-neutral language that implies benign neglect or a malicious patriarchy in the other state. In reality, it is a different feminist ideology that is being criticized, a different way of conceiving of individual autonomy and protecting it, whose architects and upholders are women as well.

Finally, both models use the language of international human rights to justify their domestic legal changes, appealing to international authority to guide local decisions. Common to both approaches is the explicit or implicit link to the concerns of domestic women, such as the penetration of the economy in our everyday lives, migrant competition for female job sectors, and community standards of sexual behavior. Supporters of abolition and normalization appeal to universal standards, whether they be a right to work or a right to one's body, or a right to freedom from slavery or sexual violence. The different conceptions of these rights is a tension that cannot be resolved in the international agreements themselves, however, but leaves them as potent political tools against opponents in this struggle for the acme in high moral ground.

For example, in 1998 Finland's Ministry of Social Affairs and Health launched a five-year Program for the Prevention of Prostitution and Violence against Women. Though framed as a program for research and developing a broad range of public–private cooperation, research philosophy reflects key tenets of abolitionist philosophy. Prostitution is defined as inherent violence against women: "Doing research on powerful and sensitive issues such as men's violence against women, including sexual violence, prostitution, and the violence in male culture, meets various obstacles in societies and academia. These obstacles represent the resistance of patriarchal societies against *de facto* equality and women's human rights."[6] A Finnish minister of parliament goes further in describing the program's intent, indicting countries that legalize prostitution for eroding women's human rights:

> The countries that have legalized or otherwise regulated prostitution are precisely the countries into which most women are imported through organized channels . . . Even if there is a desire to eliminate abuses, the "legalizers" have not, in my view, grasped the fundamental reality that a system of prostitution is in itself an abuse. I want to conclude by pointing out that the countries which have not embarked on the wrong road of legalising prostitution, but instead see it as a violent breach of women's human rights, are in a key position in work to ensure that prostitution and human trafficking are taken up in political debate and decision making.[7]

This "us versus them" language is a particularly potent rhetoric for coalition building, putting Finland and all the countries that haven't yet made a decision on prostitution naturalization on the same side against Germany and Holland within the EU.

Prostitution legalizers vigorously refute the charges that their system leads to abuse or migration. Indeed, the Dutch system of prostitution reform was specifically crafted to get a handle on the illegal migrants in the red-light district there. They also use the language of human rights, highlighting not the right to control one's body as an American campaigner might, but the human right to a safe and hygienic workplace.[8] Consider the language used by the coordinator for Germany's national clearinghouse to coordinate countertrafficking efforts that was established and funded by the Federal Ministry for Families:

> The 38 consulting agencies and NGOs in Germany which I represent for the KOK [which stands for], the "Federal Association Against Trafficking in Women and Violence Against Women in the Migration Process" . . . we approach trafficking in persons and trafficking in women from this basic standpoint: as a violation of human rights.

The KOK's apparent agreement with abolitionists is undone by the conclusions drawn from the human rights basis of the offense:

> The legalization of prostitution and more generally the creation of legal avenues of migration, so people traffickers can no longer criminalize their victims and threaten them with deportation.

In other words, the 38 agencies that represent the vast majority of Germany's antitrafficking efforts advocate the creation of temporary work visas for sex workers. These include organizations that receive funds from the Evangelical Lutheran Church of Germany, the European Commission, and the Catholic social work foundation Caritas. These diverse organizations and funders are united by the very German sense that workers need protection—congruent with the corporatist social citizenship Germans enjoy.

Consistent with the opposing laws they champion, these groups construct very different images of prostitutes. Civil groups see migrant women struggling under tremendous handicaps to send money back home, while self-described radical feminists and transnational NGOs see actions facilitating the exploitation of women in an increasingly unstable and laissez-faire international order. Neither view helps explain the failure of *both* sets of law to cause any measurable change in the degree of prostitution that occurs in these four countries, or any evidence of harm reduction.

The fact that most prostitutes in Holland or Germany are foreigners prevents them from ever taking advantage of the new protective legislations. Neither Sweden nor Finland ever had many prostitutes to begin with. Even officials involved in executing the new laws note that it has had little effect, focusing instead on the importance of the law's symbolic statement of values. These contrasting viewpoints and parallel conversations show a struggle for moral control of the European Union itself, in which all Member States feel their ability to maintain their way of life is under threat from globalization or by Brussels. Yet the threats to their local values emanate neither from the Euro capital nor the globalization nodes of New York, London, or Washington. Threats to local values in the battle over prostitution come from the centers of competing value systems, be they feminist, economic, or political. Thus Berlin and Amsterdam are a bigger threat to Swedes or Finns, and vice versa. What brings them together is the European project—but unlike the amorphous and anarchic forces of globalization, the EU is globalization via democracy, pooled sovereignty with consent. And because Europe guarantees "freedom" among friends and neighbors, it is thus harder to oppose—and more insidious. Discourses of universal human rights are increasingly deployed with this irony: The reasons given for state intervention and surveillance are increasingly—*progressively*—modern and scientific, but the legal results bring benefits to few and potential harm to many.

Despite the wildly divergent paths that are being mapped out, debates over the publicness of legalized prostitution are still discussed as if the new policy proceeds naturally from domestic political culture itself—whether the new policy is de facto criminalization or state recognition of prostitution as a legitimate occupation. More broadly, legalizing or abolishing sexual commerce is almost always treated as a single thing assumed to have discernable effects by both pro- and antiprostitution activists. In practice, the recent changes that have been taking place show that legalization never led to a laissez-faire attitude to commercial sex, and legalization has often been more restrictive than the informal policing in jurisdictions where prostitution is illegal.

Globalization Anxieties, Cultural Responses, State Institutionalizations

In Chapter 1, I described European prostitution reforms as sharing the characteristic of attempting to rationalize and standardize sexual commerce. If only the state has the administrative resources to even attempt to reorder the sexual lives of its citizens and denizens, only the nation has the cultural resources by which such actions make sense. As *nation-state projects*, each of these European prostitution reforms were framed by their supporters along their country's *inclusion roadmap* with its ready definitions of social citizenship that include worker, fairness, and gender relations. Yet all these reforms failed on the ground, at least at the level at which their ground-level administrators were able to enact them. What utility do sexual reforms have if that don't always—or even rarely—work?

In Chapter 1, I recounted how the theorist Michel Foucault defined sexuality as the domain by which individuals create subjective selves that are aligned with the ways that governments imagine their citizenry. Sexuality,

I claimed is one of the ways that citizens and their governments re-enchant a world of impersonal standards that Max Weber described, one further constrained by *globalization anxieties* about distant forces of market flows and undemocratic transnational institutions.

Telling sexual stories is one of the ways we re-enchant our rationalized world of impersonal standards and distant authorities. The new prostitution politics were always embroiled in, and lurking underneath, the politics of human trafficking. As Ken Plummer as written, "sexual stories are maps for action—they look into the future, tell us how we are motivated, guide us gently into who we will be."[9]

Trafficking talk, with its potent morals of abject victims and heartless villains, is also a form of standardization and rationalization, smoothing out the ambiguities and gray areas of life and replacing it with the melodrama that feels like truth. The *truly trafficked woman* demands our sympathy and awakens a sense of purpose, rededicating us to our values. If these values are national and not universal, so much the better: the standards are not impersonal, but *ours*, and in their conflict with others we find a potent map for action as individuals and a sense of collective purpose.

It has become axiomatic to tell stories about the nation as being destabilized by globalization. Such stories include such unverified truths as: local autonomy eroded as neoliberal capitalism makes decision-making centers increasingly separated from the far-flung individuals who are affected; cultural ideas are being torn from the places that generated them and plunked down in new contexts, and commercialized pap or Hollywood-diffused American ideas are filling the gaps; technology increasing the pace at which people and ideas circulate, pulling apart local communities and creating an uneven new world order of the transient privileged and those left behind; or transnational organizations spelling the death knell of the liberal nation-state that is being eroded by a borderless world.[10]

These *globalization anxieties*, as I call them, have generated a cottage industry of competing concepts and theories to explain how fast, new, different, and strange the new global order is. But these truths of the way things are being accepted faster than evidence can be found to support them. Sociologists are suspicious of these kinds of claims because our discipline was founded upon very similar claims—back in the nineteenth century. The threat to what is seen as *authentic* local cultures is part of a long history of social thought—when we hear new versions of the old story of modernity, we ask ourselves to what degree the changes we are experiencing are just part of our unfolding history since the Enlightenment and the Industrial Revolution. But while historical sociologists make cases about the technical and administrative reach of globalization—trade, political interdependency—little has been written about many of the current globalization anxieties that have to do with the impact on local culture.

That these anxieties have material effects on the world—in flows of money, voting patterns, or strengthened border police—shows that even myths can have real effects in the world. That prostitution regulation often fails does not mean that it was without purpose—when a nation feels better, this effect may indeed have addressed the original cause of anxiety. To paraphrase a sociological theorem coined by W. I. Thomas, what people take to be real is real in its consequences.

One of these globalization anxieties, I proffer, is the resurgence of fears about the trafficking in women. In this book I have examined the role of trafficking in women as a discourse of globalization anxieties, one that highlights challenges to citizenship and the liberal nation-state. I have chosen not a typical case, but an unusual one, one designed to show the tensions in these understandings of trafficking and its presumed effect on the ways we organize our lives. To do this, surveys of trafficking or citizenship shifts in many countries is not sufficient. Sexuality as a concept is a dense site of power and underpins many other ascribed identities, including ethnicity and citizenship.[11]

In the debates about trafficking and migrant prostitution, globalization takes the blame for causing problems that civic officials admit were already there to begin with. *Globalization* was recognized when these latent political problems became public issues due to the active lobbying of stakeholder groups. They pushed for the rationalization of prostitution—eliminating the cultural ambivalence toward it in favor of a single meaning and set of policy responses. Trafficking stories boost funding for local community organizations *and* bring together transnational feminist networks; they also fund border control surveillance *and* prostitute help centers.

What is consecrated by society as public versus what must remain private tells us not merely about the sexual peccadilloes of a particular country. They tell us about their ideals for intimate relationships and proper conduct in the public sphere, and the way politics can be conducted to resolve disagreements and create consensus. This is why it is so difficult to import or export these policy solutions—they are buttressed by a complex architecture of state policies and shared cultural ways of seeing. Though many countries have studied the Dutch and Swedish models, the first countries that followed them crafted compromises that show national differences within similarities of social citizenship: Germany's solution resembles the Dutch's because both share a corporatist welfare state and its social citizenship; both Finland and Sweden are social democracies.

The question I am most frequently asked about my research is which system works best for regulating prostitution. My analysis of prostitution regulation as the product of social citizenship—underpinned by bureaucratic institutions and deep cultural beliefs—reveals my skepticism that these policies are transposable. Abolition makes sense in a social democracy where the elimination of poverty and gender equality and core precepts of social citizenship. State recognition of a prostitutes' union makes sense in a corporatist country where all benefits come from occupational groups and society is governed through the consensus of state, worker, and employer. In a rationalized world, these policies might even work in states that were composed only of national citizens.

In a world of migrants, however, abolitionism and legalization represent compromises with the specific social policy foundations in these societies. Undocumented migrants are vulnerable in a host of ways, but especially because they are excluded from both social programs *and* labor markets. Red-light districts, occupying gray areas of the law and facilitating black markets, once provided a source of subsistence until migrants could integrate themselves into society in other ways. Now that these have been rationalized under abolitionism and legalization, national standards for prostitution must be seen as an extension of state control over the boundaries of community membership.

Ultimately, the politics of sexual morality are a metaphor for our hopes and fears about autonomy itself. Despite the emergence of international human rights institutions, individual autonomy is not something that can be protected by international treaties or documents specifying rights. Autonomy is guaranteed by the institutions that give it support and the cultural beliefs that animate it. When citizens feel that globalization is eroding their autonomy, they push the state to strengthen national moral boundaries. Strengthening the state in this way has the ironic effect of causing the kinds of cultural homogenization that globalization is feared to cause. Far from undermining the nation-state, globalization involves its reinforcement in the moral and territorial realm. Stories of horribly brutalized victims who receive state succor, or of workers happily overseen by smoothly functioning bureaucracies, are both responses to globalization anxieties. But, because the stories of prostitution that we treat as real are real in their consequences, the victims we get, we deserve.

9

Methodological Afterword: Identity Work and the Interviewer

"Prostitution (and its study) treads into unconsciously threatening waters, remaining marginal and comparatively untheorized precisely *because* something about it is so central and meaningful."

—Lynn Chancer[1]

Figure 9.0   Reflections   Neon signs for a Berlin club in the Stuttgarterplatz tolerance zone.

Source: author photo

Interviewing about Prostitution Regulation

Researchers have long described how cultural ambivalence about sexuality makes its research fraught, especially regarding prostitution. This methodological postmortem describes my strategies, both premeditated and improvised, for dealing with this ambivalence during my investigations. In particular, probing personal questions and gendered miscommunications dogged me during my research:

> "Do you know about the conference in October later this year, it's also in Brussels?
> "Yes," I replied.
> "Are you going?"
> "No."
> "Oh? It's only for sex workers, you know."
> "I know."
> "Is there a reason you're not going?"
> . . .
> "Were you frightened to come here?" My respondents leaned into the table eagerly.
> Feigning ignorance, I replied "Noooo, it was perfectly safe, I just walked over the bridge from my hostel, it's a perfectly safe neighborhood."
> "No no," they interrupted. "Were you scared to interview the scary feminists?"
> "Are feminists scary?"
> "We are!" they laughed.
> "Who says this?"
> "All the men," they replied, disappointed in my reaction.

If being a scary feminist was a joke, I missed the opportunity to demonstrate my insider humor. If it wasn't a joke, my respondents expected that I would know people who thought feminists were scary. Either possibility implied that I couldn't myself be a feminist.

Cultural ambivalence toward sexuality produces special challenges for the researcher. Scholars have long noted the stigma from professional colleagues that renders sexuality research "dirty work," according to Janice Irvine. Such research work is necessary, yet stigmatized. Feminist researchers in particular have noted the gendered double standard of this stigma by which women who research sexuality are presumed to be sexually available. I have not had the experience described by female researchers of being sexually propositioned or shamed by colleagues, but I have shared the experiences of having my research trivialized by colleagues, prompting awkward sexual confessions from them, or eliciting queries about my personal life rather than my work. This included several unsolicited admonitions from the president of one of my academic institutions about my "wacky" and "out-there" courses and to "be careful about what I publish." These signals heighten the stakes of sexuality research and slow professional advancement. I confess that I'm relieved this book appears after I was awarded tenure.[2]

Prostitution is a particularly fraught topic, despite its similarity to other sensitive topics that sociologists regularly investigate, such as personal income-generating strategies, child-rearing, or domestics. As Lynn Chancer claimed:

> To analyze prostitution unavoidably raises *both* the ongoing specter of gendered oppression in patriarchal societies and our often-schizophrenic—part-acknowledged, part-tabooed—passions about sex: in combination, the two may evoke highly ambivalent and disconcerting sets of reactions.[3]

This ambivalence manifests, in part, in the intense interest around prostitution research even as the researchers are trivialized.

The stakes are especially high given prostitution's role in ongoing "feminist sex wars" over the meaning of sexuality, between radical feminists who strive to abolish it along with pornography and sadomasochism, and liberal or sex-positive feminists who argue there are no fixed meanings of sexuality. These wars position individuals as either apologists or allies for each side, making neutrality all but impossible.[4] The cultural politics of the EU's sex war over prostitution reforms had unacknowledged nationalist overtones, posing countries with the "wrong" policies as enemies, and positioning countries with even vaguely similar policies as allies. In the second vignette above, the framing of feminists as scary, which precluded me as a feminist, also removed me from the front lines of that war by virtue of my nationality and gender. In the first, vignette, my interviewer seemed to be angling to know whether my interest in prostitution was because I was a sex worker.

We know little about the presumptions placed upon male researchers of prostitution. Ronald Weitzer, one of the most prolific international experts on prostitution, does not address his experiences as a male researcher in his books. His analysis of what he rejects as the "empowerment" and "oppression" paradigms of prostitution identifies them as the product of idological commitments, but frames them in opposition to his "polymorphous" paradigm that is the product of strict empiricism. Such a false opposition sidelines a long tradition of feminist and LGBTQ scholarship that is both empiricist and informed by cultural politics.

In what ways was being a man relevant to my research? Several interviewees were surprised upon meeting me, admitting they had expected a woman, despite the fairly conventional English-language gender markers of my name. Such reactions, and those I related at the start of this chapter, made sense in the context of the field of prostitution politics, a field in which almost all of the experts were women. Whether magistrates or ministers of parliament, social workers or police chiefs, the majority of the policy administrators and prostitution reformers were women. One of my male interviewees, a researcher, cautioned me about the social implications of my research and described the late night phone calls he endured from women who objected to his research and men asking for referrals to sex workers. Such experiences differed sharply from those Chancer experienced from colleagues after writing her essay: "Each commented enthusiastically about the essay's potential 'importance' but went on to ask in confidence, as though relevant, whether I myself had been a prostitute." Prostitution, in the way it is currently understood, necessarily implicates the personal lives of its experts in ways that expertise on the European Union or theories of the state does not.[5]

A man who is openly interested in prostitution is especially suspect:

> Before I could complete the nutshell description of my research suitable for elevators and cocktail parties, she sternly interrupted me. "No. What is your involvement in prostitution? Who is funding your research, what are its . . . what are you using it for? How many women have you bought?"

Among radical feminists such as these, pointed questions about my personal relationship to prostitution, sometimes presumed I had bought sex. This part of a general stigma described by anthropologist Don Kulick: "that adheres to men in radical feminist contexts, especially in countries that have criminalized the purchase of sex."[6] Among sex workers' rights activists, there were sometimes discreet invitations to disclose whether or not I was a sex worker, indicated by oblique queries about how long I had been "in this world." I understood these awkward, telling moments as litmus tests of my politics that posed a potential barrier to getting the interview, or at least as hurdles to establishing rapport and trust.

Because I was interviewing about contentious topics, I used mirroring language to use interviewees' "definition of the situation" to describe their organization's work.[7] For example, my first questions would be about their group's mission or how they came to be involved in their programs. Such language showed respect for my interviewee's commitments, allowing them to describe their programs for sex workers, victims of human trafficking, or women involved in prostitution. Situations where I made a mistake were instructive, demonstrating the importance of terminology as signaling political positions in a sex war:

GM: When you're doing street outreach to sex workers . . .
INT: [interrupting] We don't use that word. They are victims, sex is not work.
. . .
GM: Do the prostitutes you serve use the services of other organizations in the city?
INT: Why do you use that word, so clinical? Our clients prefer sex workers.

While I used "prostitution" as a general, less-political label for the regulation of sexual commerce, my interviewees had no qualms at correcting my lapses in mirroring their language.

"That's all the questions I have. Do you have any questions for me?" This was my standard denouement to an interview, allowing interviewees to return to any questions they'd tried to ask earlier and allowed them to challenge my identity work or probe behind my mirroring language. It sometimes doubled the length of the interview, moving from my semistructured questions to an unstructured conversation.

These questions invariably covered my interviews with "the other side" across national and/or feminist boundaries. I inadvertently became tasked with explaining their definition of the situation. Dutch interviewees wanted to know if I understood why the Swedes did what they did, in part to know how to counter their arguments in international meetings. Swedes wanted to know if I could shed light on German policy and why they were so "anti-woman." My role as a bridge between these worlds illustrates not only how I was not a neutral presence but involved in the conflict, but also the possibility, however slight, that I helped to foster mutual understanding. But for me, these moments were stressful because I felt inadequate to fairly represent the other's sides arguments and passion. Invariably I found myself convinced by the interviewee in front of me, won over by her passionate convictions. After each interview I found it difficult to remember how I had been won over by their opponents only days before.

Identity Work and the Interviewer

Moving among the combatants was made possible by my own divided loyalties and my status as an outsider, but complicated by the ethical requirement that I treat all sides ethically and betray none of them. In comparative research, a researcher is by design an outsider to most of the research settings, but I quickly learned that local contexts defined more thoroughly than my American nationality or academic motivations. I was continually surprised at how little patience many interviewees had with my scholarly explanation for interviewing them. After one long interview I closed the session by asking my interviewee if she had any questions for me, prompting the following exchange:

INT: So why did you come here?
GM: I'm interested in the work of [your organization], because . . .
INT: [interrupting] No, why Finland?
GM: Well, Finland has the only EU border with Russia, and has outsized influence in . . .
INT: [interrupting] No really, but why Finland? And in January?
GM: <shrugging> It just fit along with the academic calendar to come here after the semester was over, and after when I received my funding.
INT: But why Finland?
GM: Well, I'm Finnish-American.
INT: Ah! Your relatives, where are they?

This led into a discussion of the region where my father's relatives live, my time in the provinces, and a discussion of possible people we knew in common. It was common in Finland for rapport to be established on the basis of my tenuous claim to a shared ethnicity, in part because of the widely held understanding that Finland did not merit scholarly attention.

My reactions to these kinds of queries were improvised and took the form of "identity work," a concept used by social movement scholars to describe the "range of activities individuals engage in to create, present, and sustain personal identities."[8] Through my deployment of other aspects of my identity to claim a researcher identity, I was doing something similar. At first, without being too deliberate about it, I responded to their questions about my identity by deploying other aspects of my identity to deflect their presumptions, introducing personal details to explain my interests. This included highlighting my student role under a dissertation advisor who studies love and relationships,[9] that as a Finnish-American I was interested in Northern European cultural politics, or that as a gay man I was interested in parallels between the government regulation of prostitution and homosexuality. Disclosures of being gay often seemed to reassure sex workers' rights activists, especially given the way the abolitionist frame is organized around rigid definitions of male and female or the longtime affiliation between sex positive feminists and queer politics. Affiliation with the University of California at Berkeley also assuaged Europeans, standing in as a generic cipher for radical politics of all stripes. Only later did I realize that my improvised identity work had implied that some aspect of my identity naturally articulated some moral or political position, especially insofar as it was congruent with my interviewees' own.

My interviewees often responded to my mirroring language by trying to verify my sympathy with their ideology, as when this interviewee used "you know?" during the interview to check for my understanding or agreement:

> *INT*: These pro-prostitution countries, or I call them like that, or maybe that's not quite accurate but you know what I mean?
>
> . . .
>
> *INT*: You know, our NGO system, plenty of money goes from this [foundation] to organization who support prostitution legalization . . .
>
> *INT*: I think the definition [of human trafficking] is quite enough and even though it's very complicated it takes this language from [the 1979 UN convention on women] so, you know.

Such language was echoed by one of this interviewee's opponents, who lumped her in with other feminists by stating: "You know how they are, they're so illogical and unreasonable. I wouldn't trust anyone who listens to them." Of course I knew how they are, because this interviewee knew I had spoken to most of them and was asking whether I was trustworthy—a question I was constantly asking myself.

These examples of impression management or "identity work" highlight the suspicion of objectivity among my interviewees and the paradoxical persuasiveness of my on-the-fly claims of self-interested subjectivity. These situations challenged my status as a neutral researcher and required me to reassert a self that was congruent with my interviewees' political worldviews. I did this by referencing my own identity in essentializing ways, that is to say, I would describe myself in ways that I believed would explain my research interests, assuming that *who I was* would explain *why I was interested*. This highlights the way in which identity work involves "giving not only information about one's self but, along with that information, a scheme for interpreting it."[10] The fact that I was deploying my identity in such an essentialist way—assuming that it explained things, and did so without deliberation—was, upon reflection, surprising, given my intellectual commitments to social constructionism, the scholarly position that sexual meanings must be studied inductively and not assumed. That such tactics worked, however, demonstrates the (rightful) suspicion of scholarly objectivity that made my on-the-fly demonstrations of a self-interested subjectivity so persuasive.

Studying Up

My identity work strategy emerged from some challenges between my naive framing of my research given that I was "studying up," and my interviewing elites whose social positions and time were more valuable than a foreign graduate student's or junior professor's. My training and the ethical requirements of my research prepared me not to exploit subjects, but left me ill-prepared to deal with these challenges to my identity as a researcher. My interviewees, experienced in managing the impressions of their professional selves and their organizations, often refused my simple presentation of self as a neutral foreign researcher, insisting I be inside their local political framework. My response was to remove myself as far as possible from that frame or to insert myself so deeply that I was unimpeachable through essentializing, indexical citations of self.

Despite calls since the 1970s to increase the amount of social scientific research on elites, sociologists less often study "up," and there is much less formal guidance about the dilemmas involved in studying those more powerful than the interviewer—the most powerful being the ability to refuse being interviewed in the first place.[11] Even for interviewees who did consent to be interviewed, it was sometimes difficult to reach them through layers of gatekeepers. I couldn't even reach the secretary for a director of refugee services, so I had to enlist the help of the front desk receptionist, as this excerpt from my field notes recounts:

> The receptionist led me downstairs and we were waiting at the elevator, I was telling her in our half-English half-German conversation why it was that I needed her to come down there with me. She clucked her tongue with a raucous, smoky laugh and thick accent: "ha ha ha, they think you have no brain! that you are like the others waiting there! Ho ho ho!" The four to five people I'd approached with her note in my hand and my business card outstretched didn't realize that I wasn't a *real* refugee. She continued, "Of course it should not be so. All are same, equal. In principle. Ha ha ha!" I smiled nervously and reorganized my notepad while she got the desk officer to buzz us into the inner sanctum.

The difficulties of navigating multiple reception desks and intercom systems with my clunky Finnish and rudimentary German were mild because at least I got the interview. Many key respondents did not answer my inquiries, possessing the administrative staff to deflect my emails and phone calls. Even within the interview situation, these staff could cut short the interview. My response was to try to interview their peers and use referrals to gain an interview and, when this failed, to use their publicly available quotations to provide their perspective in the text.

All of my interviewees signed consent forms on official University of California Berkeley or Oberlin College letterhead informing them of their rights and my responsibilities in research. These forms included three lines: consenting to research, consenting to being audio recorded, and consenting to be quoted by name. All signed the first two; only one inter-viewee declined to be quoted by name. This posed a challenge of its own; in this chapter I list only the organizations at which I interviewed and not the names of my interviewees to shield this respondent.

Interviewee concerns about being audio recorded centered on their English language skills. I contacted offices on the basis of newspaper coverage of controversies over prostitution reforms, sending bilingual interview requests in Finland and Germany but not Sweden or the Netherlands where English proficiency was far more common. Offices directed me to English-speaking respondents or sometimes provided a translator. I have cleaned up the transcripts to remove hesitations or fumbling for words when these were not related to the topic of the interview. These are professionals who I had in many cases contacted by virtue of their public statements in newspapers, and their concern that they would sound dumb was legitimate and unrelated to the topic of my research.

The legalistic human subjects consent forms required by Institutional Review Boards (IRBs) mystified my European interviewees and made them quite suspicious, and perhaps rightly so. IRBs arose to protect human subjects but have sprawled in their remits and requirements to also cover legal liabilities toward colleges and universities.[12] While sex workers may be a vulnerable population who deserve special consideration, IRBs ask me to treat national leaders and government employees with the same consideration. I provided bilingual consent forms to German and Finnish speaking respondents. Many misunderstandings centered around a suspicion that the form gave me legal rights over them or the organizations they represented. Despite these concerns, I was never contacted through the information on the consent form, nor to my knowledge was either of my institutional homes during the course of the research.

My mirroring language and identity work raised the possibility that I was misleading interviewees to assume I was a partisan on their side of prostitution policy disputes. Even after signing the consent form, with the tape recording running, several interviewees made pointed personal attacks on colleagues or opponents or disclosed legally questionable activities. After one NGO director told me that in the five years her organization had received antitrafficking funds they had yet to encounter someone who met the legal definition of a victim of human trafficking, I asked how the organization used the funds:

> TM: We use the [national and EU] trafficking money to offer services to the women, it's about doing what's best for the women, really.
> GM: Can you give me an example?

> *TM*: We offer language classes to help them with their business, and we have a tea time when they can meet amongst themselves and talk and get social support, one in [one language] and another in [another language]. I suppose if there was any trafficking we would hear it, but really this is using that money for a good purpose . . . rather than chasing ghosts.

The lack of any "truly trafficked women" meant that funds for rescue and support were put to more quotidian uses. Other organizations similarly described providing accounting classes for migrant prostitutes and even helping to broker marriages with locals to help a woman obtain legal status to remain in country. None of these activities were what legislators had intended when bolstering antitrafficking coffers, but NGO workers repurposed them. This included confessions that they were withholding information they were legally obliged to pass along to police or immigration authorities. As one NGO involved in a state-run coordination program to help trafficking victims confided, "I will never collaborate with the police, they will never snatch one of my women, no never!"

Telling me about these activities on tape, after signing consent forms, demonstrates the degree to which respondents' activities were part of taken-for-granted everyday ways of enacting their own definitions of prostitution, even when it contradicted national policy. It may be precisely because I was interviewing elites and had low status and authority that these disclosures occurred—after all, I am a foreign nobody with little connection to their professional networks. My identity work that often foregrounded my student status may have facilitated this.

Identity Work and Ambiguity in Research

"For it is with ambiguity as it is with naïveté: it ceases to exist when recognized."
—Rose Laub Coser[13]

It is difficult to resist the urge to confess when describing the ethics of research. In that in a sense, researcher tales function along the broad tropes of sexual stories: accounts of key moments of identity and boundary-work.[14] It was naive of me to confuse neutrally worded questions with a neutral political stance, especially in the middle of a sex war.

My pretense at neutrality was naive, as were my assumptions that I had no relevant personal experience either for governing prostitution or for the feminist sex war. The gay world and prostitution have never been that far apart. Being gay in the city means being propositioned for sex with money, dating guys who have sold sex, and having matter-of-fact conversations with strangers in bars about it. The very fact that gay men didn't consider such things prostitution per se is evidence of its depoliticization among men, highlighting its stigma as the ultimate act of public shaming of women.[15]

It was (and still is) important to me that I did not answer these questions, nor deny their importance. A simple answer to such loaded questions would not necessarily indicate my political stance—there are plenty of former sex workers or repentant johns who became antiprostitution activists, just as there are Catholic nuns who support sex workers' rights. Denying the importance of these questions would ignore the stakes of these battles in a feminist sex war. For feminists, prostitution has long been a cipher for identity politics, plumbed for the meaning of gender, markets, and modernity. Prostitution has so many complex meanings that the answer to a simple question cannot capture the complex opinions and assessments I have about it. I also did not want to explicitly or implicitly cast aspersions on those who are against buying sex, or have sold it, or on anyone, not because I wanted to have greater access to the field, but because my purpose as a researcher was to understand and not to condone or condemn. It was also important—ethically, professionally, and personally—not to deceive my respondents. I also reject a strong empiricist program that refuses to treat ideologies as unworthy of or antithetical to social scientific study. Rather, it is these ideologies I try to explain through the context of national political economies—the nation-state projects embedded in welfare state ideologies.

It would have been better to have explicitly insisted on my researcher status, even to the detriment of rapport in the interview situation. In that sense, I was inconsistent in my commitments even as they generated data of their own, as this chapter attests. The research encounter, like sexuality, is a zone of ambiguity, in which identity work is inherent to the rules of engagement for which the researcher improvises using whatever cultural tools at hand.

Notes

Chapter 1

1. Communication and Political Research Society and Greek Helsinki Monitor, "Sex Workers Rights in Greece," 2006, http://cm.greekhelsinki.gr.
2. Grandell, Tommy. 2003. "Northern Ministers Criticize Plans for Olympics Brothels." *Associated Press.*
3. Pangalos, Philip. 2003. "Prostitutes Protest Brothel Crackdown." *UK Reuters.*
4. BBC News. 2003. "Anger over Greek Olympic Brothels." Manninen, Mari. 2003. "Sweden Fights Prostitution at Home and Abroad." *Helsingin Sanomat International Edition.* UK Reuters. 2003. "Sex Row Is a Storm in a Teacup Says Athens Mayor." Embassy of Greece. 2003.*Athens Municipality Denies Increase in the Number of Brothels.* Washington, DC: Press Office.
5. Jana Hennig et al., "Trafficking in Human Beings and the 2006 World Cup in Germany," 2007, http://www.popline.org/node/200308. See also Julie Ham, *What's the Cost of a Rumour?: A Guide to Sorting Out the Myths and the Facts about Sporting Events and Trafficking* (Global Alliance Against Traffic in Women (GAATW), 2011); Kathleen Deering and Kate Shannon, "Fears of an Influx of Sex Workers to Major Sporting Events Are Unfounded," *BMJ: British Medical Journal* 345 (2012); Marlise Richter et al., "Female Sex Work and International Sport Events - No Major Changes in Demand or Supply of Paid Sex during the 2010 Soccer World Cup: A Cross-Sectional Study," *BMC Public Health* 12, no. 1 (September 11, 2012): 763.
6. Jo Doezema, *Sex Slaves and Discourse Masters: The Construction of Trafficking* (London: Zed Books, 2010); Gretchen Soderlund, *Sex Trafficking, Scandal, and the Transformation of Journalism, 1885–1917* (University of Chicago Press, 2013); Brian Donovan, *White Slave Crusades: Race, Gender and Anti-Vice Activism, 1887–1917* (Urbana: University of Illinois Press, 2006).
7. Mara L. Keire, "The Vice Trust: A Reinterpretation of the White Slavery Scare in the United States, 1907–1917," *Journal of Social History* 35, no. 1 (2001): 5–41.
8. Linda Gordon, *Women, the State, and Welfare* (Madison: University of Wisconsin Press, 1990); Mary E. Odem, *Delinquent Daughters: Protecting and Policing Adolescent Female Sexuality in the United States, 1885–1920* (Chapel Hill: University of North Carolina Press, 1995); Stephanie Limoncelli, *The Politics of Trafficking: The First International Movement to Combat the Sexual Exploitation of Women* (Stanford University Press, 2010).

9. Soderlund, *Sex Trafficking, Scandal, and the Transformation of Journalism, 1885–1917*; Jessica R. Pliley, *Policing Sexuality: The Mann Act and the Making of the FBI* (Cambridge, Massachusetts: Harvard University Press, 2014); Judith R. Walkowitz, "Male Vice and Female Virtue: Feminism and the Politics of Prostitution in Nineteenth-Century Britain," in *Powers of Desire: The Politics of Sexuality* (New York: Monthly Review Press, 1983); Barbara Meil Hobson, *Uneasy Virtue: The Politics of Prostitution and the American Reform Tradition* (New York: Basic Books, 1988).

10. Julia O'Connell Davidson, "New Slavery, Old Binaries: Human Trafficking and the Borders of 'Freedom,'" *Global Networks* 10, no. 2 (April 1, 2010): 244–61; Limoncelli, *The Politics of Trafficking*.

11. Barbara G. Brents, Crystal A. Jackson, and Kathryn Hausbeck, *The State of Sex: Tourism, Sex and Sin in the New American Heartland*, New Ed (Routledge, 2009).

12. Lin Lean Lim, *The Sex Sector: The Economic and Social Bases of Prostitution in Southeast Asia* (Geneva: International Labor Organization, 1998).

13. Janice G. Raymond, "Guide to the New UN Trafficking Protocol" (North Amherst, Massachussetts: Coalition Against Trafficking in Women, 2001).

14. HSIE, "U.S. Report on Human Trafficking Shows Finland in a Poor Light," *Helsingin Sanomat International Edition*, 2003, http://www.helsinki-hs.net.

15. Patterson, Tony. 2005. "Germany Backs Bigger Brothels to Fight World Cup Sex Explosion." *The Independent*. DW. 2005. "Scoring in the Soccer Love Shack." *Deutsche Welle*. CBS News. 2006. "Vatican Laments World Cup Prostitution." Cooper, Helene. 2006. "Ahead of World Cup, U.S. Warns Germany about Sex Trafficking." *New York Times*. DW. 2006. "Feared Surge in World Cup Prostitution Proves Unfounded." *Deutsche Welle*. Kucharz. 2006. "Nun Puts the 'Red Card' on Forced Prostitution at World Cup." *ABC News*. Landler, Mark. 2006. "World Cup Brings Little Pleasure to German Brothels." *New York Times*.

16. Felicity Schaeffer-Grabiel, "Sex Trafficking as the 'New Slave Trade'?," *Sexualities* 13, no. 2 (April 1, 2010): 153–60.

17. Paris: Jon Henley, "Defending Their Honorarium," November 6, 2002; Elaine Sciolino, "French Prostitutes Walk the Streets--in Protest," *International Herald Tribune*, 2002.; Belgium: Noelle Knox, "In Belgium, Brothels Are Big Business," *USA Today*, 2003; Clare Murphy, "Making Sex Pay," *BBC News*, 2003.; Italy: The Economist Global Agenda, "Sex for Sale, Legally," *The Economist*, 2003.

18. Shore, Cris. 2000. *Building Europe: The Cultural Politics of European Integration*. New York: Routledge, p. 25.

19. James C. Scott, *Seeing Like a State*, Yale Agrarian Studies (Yale U., 1998); John Torpey, *The Invention of the Passport* (Cambridge University Press, 2000); Stuart Woolf, "Statistics and the Modern State," *Comparative Studies in Society and History* 31, no. 03 (1989): 588–604.

20. Greggor Mattson, "Nation-State Science: Lappology and Sweden's Ethnoracial Purity," *Comparative Studies in Society and History* 56, no. 02 (2014): 320–50.

21. Timothy Mitchell, "The Limits of the State: Beyond Statist Approaches and Their Critics," *The American Political Science Review* 85, no. 1 (March 1, 1991): 77–96.

22. Benedict Anderson, *Imagined Communities* (London: Verso Editions, 1983); Ernest Gellner, *Nations and Nationalism* (Ithaca, New York: Cornell University Press, 1983); Michael Billig, *Banal Nationalism* (New York: Sage Publications, 1995).

23. Patrick Carroll, *Science, Culture, and Modern State Formation* (U. California, 2006); Frank Dobbin, *Forging Industrial Policy: The United States, Britain, and France in the Railway Age* (Cambridge England; New york, NY, USA: Cambridge University Press, 1997).

24. Ann Swidler, "Culture in Action: Symbols and Strategies," *American Sociological Review* 51 (1986): 273–86; Stephen Vaisey, "Motivation and Justification: A Dual-Process Model of Culture in Action," *American Journal of Sociology* 114, no. 6 (May 1, 2009): 1675–1715.

25. e.g. Steve Derné, "The (Limited) Effect of Cultural Globalization in India: Implications for Culture Theory," *Poetics* 33, no. 1 (February 2005): 33–47; Roland Robertson, *Globalization: Social Theory and Global Culture* (Taylor & Francis, 2003); Robert J. Lieber and Ruth E. Weisberg, "Globalization, Culture, and Identities in Crisis," *International Journal of Politics, Culture, and Society* 16, no. 2 (December 1, 2002): 273–96.

26. Max Weber, Hans Heinrich Gerth, and C. Wright Mills, "Science as a Vocation," in *From Max Weber: Essays in Sociology* (Oxford University Press, 1946), 139.

27. Michel Foucault, *The History of Sexuality, Volume I* (New York: Vintage Books, 1978).

28. Nancy Cott, *Public Vows: A History of Marriage and the Nation* (Cambridge, Mass.: Harvard University Press, 2002).

29. David T. Evans, *Sexual Citizenship: The Material Construction of Sexualities* (New York: Routledge, 1993); George L. Mosse, *Nationalism and Sexuality* (NYC: Howard Fertig, 1985); Elizabeth A. Povinelli, "Sex Acts and Sovereignty: Race and Sexuality in the Construction of the Australian Nation," in *The Gender Sexuality Reader: Culture, History, Political Economy* (New York: Routledge, 1997); Ann Laura Stoler, *Carnal Knowledge and Imperial Power* (U. California, 2002).

30. Foucault, *The History of Sexuality, Volume I*; Luce Irigaray, *This Sex Which Is Not One* (Cornell University Press, 1985); Claude Lévi-Strauss, *The Elementary Structures of Kinship* (New York: Beacon Press, 1971); Gayle S. Rubin, "Thinking Sex: Notes for a Radical Theory of the Politics of Sexuality," in *The Gender Sexuality Reader: Culture, History, Political Economy* (New York: Routledge, 1997).

31. Here I follow Michel Foucault, *Discipline & Punish: The Birth of the Prison* (New York: Pantheon, 1977); Michel Foucault, "Governmentality," in *Power: Essential Works of Foucault 1954-1984* (New York: The New Press, 2000), 201–22.

32. Gøsta Esping-Andersen, *The Three Worlds of Welfare Capitalism* (Princeton, New Jersey: Princeton University Press, 1990); Paul van Seters, "Legal Moralism, Liberal Legalism, and the Tangled Web of Law and Morality," in *Regulating Morality: A Comparison of the Role of the State in Mastering the Mores in the Netherlands and the United States* (Antwerp: Maklu, 2000), 23–34.

33. e.g. Philip S. Gorski, *The Disciplinary Revolution: Calvinism and the Rise of the State in Early Modern Europe* (Chicago: University of Chicago Press, 2003); Charles Tilly, *Coercion, Capital and European States, AD 990-1990* (Oxford: Blackwell, 1992); Michael Mann, *The Rise and Decline of the Nation State* (Oxford: Basil Blackwell, 1990).

34. T.H. Marshall, *Citizenship and Social Class, and Other Essays* (Cambridge University Press, 1950).

35. Rogers Brubaker, *Citizenship and Nationhood in France and Germany* (Harvard U. Press, 1992); Yasemin Nuhoæglu Soysal, *Limits of Citizenship: Migrants and Postnational Membership in Europe* (Chicago: University of Chicago, 1994).

36. Michele Lamont, *Money, Morals, and Manners: The Culture of the French and the American Upper-Middle Class* (University Of Chicago Press, 1994).

37. Myra Marx Ferree et al., *Shaping Abortion Discourse: Democracy and the Public Sphere in Germany and the United States* (Cambridge University Press, 2002); Myra Marx Ferree et al., "Abortion Talk in Germany and the United States: Why Rights Explanations Are Wrong," *Contexts* 1, no. 2 (2002): 27–34.

38. George M. Thomas and John W. Meyer, "The Expansion of the State," *Annual Review of Sociology* 10 (1984): 461–82; John W. Meyer, "The World Polity and the Authority of the Nation-State," in *Institutional Structure* (Sage, 1987).

39. See neo-Weberian discussions of state-interest subversion Joel S. Migdal, *State in Society: Studying How States and Societies Transform and Constitute One Another* (Cambridge University Press, 2001).; state moral values Morris Janowitz, *Social Control of the Welfare State* (New York: Elsevier, 1976), xi.; conflict between professional and bureaucratic values Alvin Gouldner, *Patterns of Industrial Bureaucracy* (New York: The Free Press, 1954), 22–25.; on the individual invocation of "the system" Michael Herzfeld, *Cultural Intimacy: Social Poetics in the Nation-State, 2nd Ed.* (New York: Routledge, 2005).; on gender and women's interests Lynne Haney, "Homeboys, Babies, Men in Suits: The State and the Reproduction of Male Dominance," *American Sociological Review* 61, no. 5 (1996): 759.; on street-level bureaucrats Michael Lipsky, *Street-Level Bureaucracy: Dilemmas of the Individual in Public Services* (New York: Russell Sage, 1980).

40. Valerie Jenness, *Making It Work: The Prostitute's Rights Movement in Perspective* (New York: Aldine de Gruyter, 1993).

41. Meyer, "The World Polity and the Authority of the Nation-State."

42. Swidler, "Culture in Action: Symbols and Strategies."

43. Nicholas Hoover Wilson, "From Reflection to Refraction: State Administration in British India, circa 1770–1855," *American Journal of Sociology* 116, no. 5 (March 1, 2011): 1437–77; Gorski, *The Disciplinary Revolution: Calvinism and the Rise of the State in Early Modern Europe*; Mara Loveman, "The Modern State and the Primitive Accumulation of Symbolic Power1," *American Journal of Sociology* 110, no. 6 (2005): 1651–83.

44. On unsettled times and toolkits Swidler, "Culture in Action: Symbols and Strategies."Ann Swidler, *Talk of Love: How Culture Matters* (Chicago: University of Chicago Press, 2001).

45. Although Greece legalized prostitution at the same time as the Netherlands, it did so with so little public debate and implementation, as the 2003 outcry in Athens demonstrated.

46. Timothy Mitchell, "Society, Economy, and the State Effect," in *State/Culture*, ed. George Steinmetz (Cornell U., 1999), 76–97; Mitchell, "The Limits of the State."

47. Esping-Andersen, *The Three Worlds of Welfare Capitalism*.

48. Helga Maria Hernes, "Welfare State and Woman Power: Essays in State Feminism" (Oslo: Norwegian University Press, 1987); Dorothy E. McBride and Amy G. Mazur, *The Politics of State Feminism: Innovation in Comparative Research* (Temple University Press, 2012); Ruth Neilsen, *Equality Legislation in a Comparative Perspective—Towards State Feminism* (Copenhagen: Women's Research Center in Social Science, 1983).

49. Here I follow American analyses of feminist ideologies e.g. Catherine A. MacKinnon, *Toward a Feminist Theory of the State* (Cambridge, Mass.: Harvard University Press, 1989); Chantal Mouffe, "Feminism, Citizenship, and Radical Democratic Politics," *Social Postmodernism: Beyond Identity Politics*, 1995, 315–31; Judith Lorber, *Paradoxes of Gender* (New Haven, CT: Yale University Press, 1994).

50. Gunilla Ekberg, "The Swedish Law That Prohibits the Purchase of Sexual Services," *Violence Against Women* 10, no. 10 (2004): 1187–1218; Helga Maria Hernes, "The Welfare State Citizenship of Scandinavian Women," in *Welfare State and Woman Power: Essays in State Feminism* (Oslo: Norwegian University Press, 1987), 198; MacKinnon, *Toward a Feminist Theory of the State*; Joyce Outshoorn, "Debating Prostitution in Parliament: A Feminist Analysis," *European Journal of Women's Studies* 8, no. 4 (2001): 472–90; Joyce Outshoorn, *The Politics of Prostitution: Women's Movements, Democratic States, and the Globalization of Sex Commerce* (Cambridge University Press, 2004); Carole Pateman, *The Sexual Contract* (Cambridge, Mass.: Polity Press, 1988).

51. Joseph R. Gusfield, *The Culture of Public Problems: Drinking, Driving, and the Symbolic Order* (Chicago: University of Chicago Press, 1981).

52. Manuel Castells, *The Rise of the Network Society*, The Information Age: Economy, Society and Culture Vol I. (New York: Blackwell Publishers, 1996).

53. KOK, "Bundesweiter Koordinierungskreis Gegen Frauenhandel Und Gewalt an Frauen Im Migrationskreis e.V.," January 6, 2004, http://www.kok-potsdam .de/; Uta Ludwig, "Experience Gathered from Cooperation with Government Authorities," in *European Strategies to Prevent and Combat Trafficking in Women* (Berlin: Senatsverwaltung für Arbeit, Berufliche Bildung und Frauen, 1998), 68–89; Claudia Burgsmüller, "Necessity for and Limitations of Cooperation with Criminal Investigation Authorities and Specialized Counseling Centers from the Perspective of the Joint Plaintiff Counsel," in *European Strategies to Prevent and Combat Trafficking in Women* (Berlin: Senatsverwaltung für Arbeit, Berufliche Bildung und Frauen, 1998), 182–203.

54. e.g. David Paternotte and Kelly Kollman, "Regulating Intimate Relationships in the European Polity: Same-Sex Unions and Policy Convergence," *Social*

Politics: International Studies in Gender, State & Society, March 26, 2013, http://sp.oxfordjournals.org/content/early/2013/05/30/sp.jxs024; David John Frank, Bayliss J. Camp, and Steven A. Boutcher, "Worldwide Trends in the Criminal Regulation of Sex, 1945 to 2005," *American Sociological Review* 75, no. 6 (December 1, 2010): 867–93.

Chapter 2

1. Austria was an exception, with legal brothels and licensed prostitutes in most provinces of the Federal Republic: Maggie O'Neil, "Prostitution, Feminism and Critical Praxis: Professional Prostitute?," *Austrian Journal of Sociology* Winter (1996). Wagenaar, Hendrik, Sietske Altink, and Amesberger, Helga. "Final Report of the International Comparative Study of Prostitution Policy: Austria and the Netherlands." The Hague: Platform 31, July 2013. http://www.platform31.nl, p. 47.
2. Neil Fligstein, *Euroclash: The EU, European Identity, and the Future of Europe* (Oxford University Press, 2008).
3. Adrian Favell, *Eurostars and Eurocities: Free Movement and Mobility in an Integrating Europe* (John Wiley & Sons, 2011); Thomas Risse-Kappen, *A Community of Europeans? Transnational Identities and Public Spheres* (Cornell University Press, 2010).
4. Mark Leonard, *Why Europe Will Run the 21st Century*, annotated edition (PublicAffairs, 2006); T. R. Reid, *The United States of Europe: The New Superpower and the End of American Supremacy* (Penguin (Non-Classics), 2005); Jeremy Rifkin, *The European Dream: How Europe's Vision of the Future Is Quietly Eclipsing the American Dream* (Tarcher, 2005).
5. Fligstein, *Euroclash: The EU, European Identity, and the Future of Europe*; Simon Hix, *What's Wrong with the Europe Union and How to Fix It* (Polity, 2008); Walter Laqueur, *The Last Days of Europe: Epitaph for an Old Continent* (St. Martin's Griffin, 2009); Walter Laqueur, *After the Fall: The End of the European Dream and the Decline of a Continent* (Thomas Dunne Books, 2012); David Marquand, *The End of the West: The Once and Future Europe* (Princeton University Press, 2011).
6. Alberto Alesina and Francesco Giavazzi, *The Future of Europe: Reform or Decline* (The MIT Press, 2008); Etienne Balibar, *We, the People of Europe? Reflections on Transnational Citizenship* (Princeton University Press, 2003); Irène Bellier, "A Europeanized Elite? An Anthropology of European Commission Officials," *Yearbook of European Studies* 14 (2000): 135–56; Mabel Berezin and Martin Schain, *Europe Without Borders: Remapping Territory, Citizenship, and Identity in a Transnational Age* (Baltimore, MD: Johns Hopkins University Press, 2004); Mabel Berezin, *Illiberal Politics in Neoliberal Times: Culture, Security and Populism in the New Europe*, 1st ed. (Cambridge University Press, 2009); Juan Díez Medrano, *Framing Europe: Attitudes to European Integration in Germany, Spain, and the United Kingdom* (Princeton University Press, 2003); Neil Fligstein and Frederic Merand, "Globalization or Europeanization? Evidence on the

European Economy since 1980," *Acta Sociologica* 45, no. 1 (January 1, 2002): 7–22; Fligstein, *Euroclash: The EU, European Identity, and the Future of Europe*; Frédéric Mérand, "Soldiers and Diplomats: The Institutionalization of the European Security and Defense Policy, 1989–2003" (University of California, Berkeley, Department of Sociology, 2004); Stephanie Mudge, "Precarious Progressivism: The Struggle over the Social in the Neoliberal Era" (University of California, Berkeley, Department of Sociology, 2007).

7. Pierre Bourdieu and Loïc J. D. Wacquant, *An Invitation to Reflexive Sociology* (University of Chicago Press, 1992); Pierre Bourdieu, *The Logic of Practice* (Stanford, Calif.: Stanford University Press, 1990); Neil Fligstein and Doug McAdam, *A Theory of Fields* (Oxford University Press, USA, 2012).

8. The Bourdieusian framework emphasizes conflict as an inevitable by-product of cultural formation and boundary work. The European debate is heavily influenced by Jürgen Habermas's theory of collective action (Habermas 1991 [1962]) and his notions of the public sphere, which emphasizes concord, an observation ade by Neil Fligstein. Examples of Habermasian discussions indicating widespread debates about the ability of the EU to create a public sphere included Jos de Beus, "The European Union as a Community: An Argument about the Public Sphere in International Society and Politics," in *Communitarianism and Law* (Rowman & Littlefield, 2005); John Downey and Thomas Koenig, "Is There a European Public Sphere?," *European Journal of Communication* 21, no. 2 (2006): 165–87; Klaus and Bernhard Giesen Eder, *European Citizenship : Between National Legacies and Postnational Projects* (New York: Oxford University Press, 2001); Erik Oddvar Eriksen, "An Emerging European Public Sphere," *European Journal of Social Theory* 8, no. 3 (2005): 341–63; John Erik Fossum and Philip R. Schlesinger, *The European Union and the Public Sphere: A Communicative Space in the Making?* (New York: Routledge, 2007); Ruud Koopmans and Jessica Erbe, "Towards a European Public Sphere? Vertical and Horizontal Dimensions of Europeanised Political Communication" (Berlin: Wissenschaftszentrum Berlin fur Sozialforschung, 2003); Thomas Risse, "An Emerging European Public Sphere? Theoretical Clarifications and Empirical Indicators," Annual Meeting of the European Union Studies Association (EUSA), 2003; Thomas Risse, *Social Constructivism and European Integration* (Berlin: Freie Universität Berlin, 2002); Marianne van de Steeg, "Rethinking the Conditions for a Public Sphere in the European Union," *European Journal of Social Theory* 5, no. 4 (2002): 499–519.Habermas applied his theories explicitly to the EU in his advocacy in favor of the doomed constitution for Europe: Jürgen Habermas, "Why Europe Needs a Constitution," *New Left Review* 11, no. September (2001): 5–27.

9. Eva Biaudet, "Opening Address by the Minister of Social Affairs and Health," in *Recommendations of the E.U. Expert Meeting on Violence Against Women*, Reports of the Ministry of Social Affairs and Health (Jyväskylä, Finland: Finnish Ministry of Social Affairs and Health, 1999).

10. Ibid., Tarja Halonen, "Address by the President of the Republic of Finland," in *Stop Child Trafficking: Modern Day Slavery* (Helsinki: United States Embassy to Finland, 2003).

11. Laura Keeler and Marjut Jyrkinen, *Who's Buying? The Clients of Prostitution* (Helsinki: Council for Equality: Ministry of Affairs and Health, 1999); Laura Keeler, *Recommendations of the E.U. Expert Meeting on Violence Against Women* (Jyväskylä, Finland: Finnish Ministry of Social Affairs and Health, 1999).

12. Biaudet, "Opening Address by the Minister of Social Affairs and Health"; see also Keeler, *Recommendations of the E.U. Expert Meeting on Violence Against Women.*

13. Security and Justice DG for Freedom, "The Daphne Experience 1997–2003: Europe Against Violence Towards Children and Women" (Luxembourg City: European Commission, 2007).

14. Ibid.

15. Licia Brussa and Pia Covre, "A Brief History of TAMPEP," in *Services in the Window: A Manual for Interventions in the World of Migrant Prostitution* (Trieste: Asterios Editore for the European Commission, 2001), 7; Licia Brussa, "Community Based Experience in Western Europe in Support of Trafficked Women," in *European Conference on Preventing and Combating Trafficking in Human Beings--A Global Challenge for the 21st Century* (Brussels: EU/IOM, 2002); Licia Brussa, "Migrant Sex Workers in Europe: The Experience of TAMPEP (Transnational AIDS/STI Prevention among Migrant Prostitutes in Europe)," *International Conference on AIDS* 15 (2004): 11–16.

16. Available contemporary research included: Sandra Wallman, "Global Threats, Local Options, Personal Risk: Dimensions of Migrant Sex Work in Europe," *Health, Risk & Society* 3, no. 1 (2001): 75–87; TAMPEP, "TAMPEP Position Paper on Migration and Sex Work" (TAMPEP Charter, 2002); Helka Mongard, "AIDS/STD Prevention Among Sex Workers in the Context of Transnational Prostitution," in *AIDS & Mobility: New Policy Directions in Finland* (Tampere: The Migrants Association for Social and Health Promotion, 1999), http://www.map.vip.fi/working_group_2.htm; John Davies, "The Role of Migration Policy in Creating and Sustaining Trafficking Harm," in *European Conference on Preventing and Combating Trafficking in Human Beings--A Global Challenge for the 21st Century* (Brussels: EU/IOM, 2002); Laura María Agustín, "Challenging Place: Leaving Home for Sex," *Development* 45, no. 1 (2001): 110–16. (Agustín 2001b; Davies 2002; Mongard 1999; TAMPEP 2002; Wallman 2001).

17. e.g. Jenny Wennberg, "EU Financial Support for Projects and Organisations Which Advocate the Legalisation and Regulation of Prostitution" (Strasbourg: Office of Marianne Eriksson, MEP (GUE/NGL), 2002).

18. Ibid.

19. Quoted in Karin Alfredsson, "No Prostitution and Trafficking" (Stockholm: Swedish Institute, 2005), http://www.sweden.se.

20. Ibid.

21. Janice G. Raymond, "Public Hearing on 'The Impact of the Sex Industry in the E.U.,' Committee on Women's Rights and Equal Opportunities" (Brussels: European Parliament, 2004).

22. Veronica Munk, "Migration and Sex Work," in *The Impact of the Sex Industry in the EU: Public Hearing at the European Parliament* (Brussels, 2004).

23. Laura Maria Agustin, *Sex at the Margins: Migration, Labour Markets and the Rescue Industry* (London: Zed Books, 2007); Brussa, "Community Based Experience in Western Europe in Support of Trafficked Women"; Wendy Chapkis, "Trafficking, Migration and the Law: Protecting Innocents, Punishing Immigrants," *Gender and Society* 17, no. 6 (2003): 923–37; Jo Goodey, "Migration, Crime and Victimhood: Responses to Sex Trafficking in the EU," *Punishment and Society* 5, no. 4 (2003): 415–31; Khalid Koser, "Asylum Policies, Trafficking and Vulnerability," *International Migration*, no. 1 (2000): 90–111; Gretchen Soderlund, "Running from the Rescuers: New U.S. Crusades Against Sex Trafficking and the Rhetoric of Abolition," *NWSA Journal* 17, no. 3 (2005): 64–87.

24. Wuokko Knocke, "Migrant and Ethnic Minority Women: The Effects of Gender-Neutral Legislation in the European Union," in Gender and Citizenship in Transition: (New York: Routledge, 2000), 139–55; Elina Penttinen, Corporeal Globalization: Narratives of Subjectivity and Otherness in the Sexscapes of Globalization (Tampere: Tampere Peace Research Institute, 2004); Raimo Väyrynen, "Illegal Immigration, Human Trafficking, and the Organized Crime," in Poverty, International Migration and Asylum (Helsinki: World Institute for Development Economics Research, 2002), http://www.wider.unu .edu/conference/conference-2002-3/conference%20papers/vayrynen.pdf.

25. Turkey (Içduygu 2002), Finland (Lehti and Aromaa 2002b), Indonesia (Surtees 2003), the Netherlands (Koser 2000), the Dominican Republic (Brennan 2003), Israel (Lemish 2000), Germany (Henning 1997), between the Philippines and Belgium (Van Impe 2000).

26. Parallels between white slavery and human trafficking Jo Doezema, *Sex Slaves and Discourse Masters: The Construction of Trafficking* (London: Zed Books, 2010); Soderlund, "Running from the Rescuers: New U.S. Crusades Against Sex Trafficking and the Rhetoric of Abolition."; white slavery as myth Frederick K. Grittner, *White Slavery: Myth, Ideology, and American Law* (New York: Garland Publishing, 1990).; 10 percent estimate from Ruth Rosen, *The Lost Sisterhood: Prostitution in America, 1900–1918.* (Baltimore: The Johns Hopkins University Press, 1982).

27. Agustín, "Challenging Place: Leaving Home for Sex"; Laura María Agustín, "A Migrant World of Services," *Social Politics* 10, no. 3 (2003): 377–96; Koser, "Asylum Policies, Trafficking and Vulnerability"; European Commission, "Proposal for a Council Directive on the Short-Term Residence Permit Issued to Victims of Action to Facilitate Illegal Immigration or Trafficking..." (Brussels: Information and Communication Unit of the Directorate-General Justice and Home Affairs, 2002), http://europa.eu.int/comm/justice_home/index_en.htm, .pdf GREEN CD; Martti Lehti and Kauko Aromaa, "Trafficking in Human Beings, Illegal Immigration and Finland" (Helsinki: European Institute for Crime Prevention and Control, 2002); Mongard, "AIDS/STD Prevention Among Sex Workers in the Context of Transnational Prostitution"; John Salt, "Trafficking and Human Smuggling: A European Perspective," *International Migration*, no. 1 (2000): 31–56; John and Jeremy Stein Salt, "Migration as a Business: The Case of Trafficking," *International Migration* 35, no. 4 (1997): 467–95.(Agustín 2001a; Agustín 2003; Koser 2000).

28. For accounts of these processes in the United States Nicola Beisel, *Imperiled Innocents: Anthony Comstock and Family Reproduction in Victorian America* (Princeton University Press, 1997); Kristin Luker, "Sex, Social Hygiene, and the State: The Double-Edged Sword of Social Reform," *Theory and Society* 27, no. 5 (1998): 601–34.

Chapter 3

1. Chrisje Brants, "The Fine Art of Regulated Tolerance: Prostitution in Amsterdam," *Journal of Law and Society* 25, no. 4 (1998): 621–35; Lotte C. van de Pol, "The History of Policing Prostitution in Amsterdam," in *Regulating Morality: A Comparison of the Role of the State in Mastering the Mores in the Netherlands and the United States*, ed. Hans Krabbendam and Hans-Martien ten Napel (Antwerp: Maklu, 2000), 97–112.

2. Manuel B. Aalbers, "Big Sister Is Watching You! Gender Interaction and the Unwritten Rules of the Amsterdam Red-Light District," *Journal of Sex Research* 42, no. 1 (2005): 54–62.

3. NBTC, "Cityguide: Quaint Quarters, Red Light District," *The Amsterdam Site*, February 22, 2008.

4. Sharon Zukin, "The Social Production of Urban Cultural Heritage: Identity and Ecosystem on an Amsterdam Shopping Street," *City, Culture and Society* 3, no. 4 (2012): 281–91.

5. RNW English Section, "FAQ- Prostitution in the Netherlands," Radio Netherlands Worldwide, September 18, 2009, http://www.rnw.nl; Ministry of General Affairs, "Prostitution," Government of the Netherlands, 2014, http://www.gov ernment.nl/issues/prostitution.

6. Katie Nguyen, "Netherlands Leads Way in Battle Against Sex Slavery," *Pittsburgh Post-Gazette*, Nvo 2014.

7. Corinne Dettmeijer-Vermeulen, "Introduction" (Monitoring mechanisms in the fight against human trafficking, The Hague: National Rapporteur on Trafficking in Human Beings and Sexual Violence against Children, 2010), http://www.dutchrapporteur.nl.

8. (ibid.)

9. C. E. Dettmeijer-Vermeulen, "Foreword," in Trafficking in Human Beings: Ten Years of Independent Monitoring (2010: Bureau of the Dutch National Rapporteur, 2010), 7–8, http://www.bnrm.nl.

10. Corinne Dettmeijer-Vermeulen, "Press Conference" (Improvement of National Anti-Traffic Policy through Transfer of Know-How, Experience and Good Practices, Sofia, Bulgaria: National Rapporteur on Trafficking in Human Beings and Sexual Violence against Children, 2012), http://www.dutchrappor teur.nl.

11. Corinne Dettmeijer-Vermeulen, "At the Occasion of Conference 'Putting Rantsev into Practice'" (Putting Rantsev into Practice, Amsterdam: National Rapporteur on Trafficking in Human Beings and Sexual Violence against Children, 2012), http://www.dutchrapporteur.nl.

12. Menno van Dongen, "Prostitutiewet: Bestuurders Te Naïef," De Volkskrant, March 1, 2011, http://http://www.volkskrant.nl.
13. On the religious basis of *gidsland* James C. Kennedy, "Recent Dutch Religious History and the Limits of Secularization," *The Dutch and Their Gods: Secularization and Transformation of Religion in the Netherlands since 1950*, 2005, 36.; on the tempering of its zeal since the 1990s Frank J. Lechner, *The Netherlands: Globalization and National Identity*, 1st ed. (Routledge, 2007).
14. Eva Biaudet, "Opening Address" (Alliance Against Trafficking in Persons Conference: "National Monitoring and Reporting Mechanisms to Address THB: The Role of National Rapporteurs, Vienna: Organization for Security and Co-operation in Europe, 2007), http://www.osce.org.
15. Eelco Tasma, "The Social Dialogue in the Netherlands" (Amsterdam: Dutch Trade Union Confederation (Federatie Nederlandse Vakbeweging), 2010), http://www.fnv.nl.
16. Joyce Outshoorn, "Pragmatism in the Polder: Changing Prostitution Policy in the Netherlands," *Journal of Contemporary European Studies* 12, no. 2 (2004): 165–76.
17. Ybo Buruma, "Dutch Tolerance: On Drugs, Prostitution, and Euthanasia," *Crime and Justice* 35, no. 1 (January 1, 2007): 78.
18. Kees van Kersbergen, *Social Capitalism: A Study of Christian Democracy and the Welfare State* (New York: Routledge, 1995); R. H. Cox, "Liberalising Trends in Welfare Reform: Inside the Dutch Miracle," *Policy & Politics* 28, no. 1 (2000): 19–31.
19. Outshoorn, "Pragmatism in the Polder: Changing Prostitution Policy in the Netherlands," 166.
20. e.g. Joyce Outshoorn, "Debating Prostitution in Parliament: A Feminist Analysis," *European Journal of Women's Studies* 8, no. 4 (2001): 175; Gert Hekma, "How Libertine Is the Netherlands?," in *Regulating Sex: The Politics of Intimacy and Identity* (New York: Routledge, 2005), 209–23; Hans Krabbendam and Hans-Martien ten Napel, *Regulating Morality: A Comparison of the Role of the State in Mastering the Mores in the Netherlands and the United States* (Antwerp: Maklu, 2000).
21. Suzanne Daley, "New Rights for Dutch Prostitutes, but No Gain," *New York Times*, 2001.
22. Bureau NRM, "Trafficking in Human Beings; First Report of the Dutch National Rapporteur" (The Hague: Bureau of the Dutch National Rapporteur on Trafficking in Human Beings, 2002), http://www.dutchrapporteur.nl.
23. A. L. Daalder, "Prostitution in the Netherlands Since the Lifting of the Brothel Ban" (The Hague: Wetenschappelijk Onderzoeken Documentatiecentrum, 2007), 73.
24. Her actual title is General Coordinator (*Algemeen coördinator*), a title without a direct American English equivalent.
25. Daalder, "Prostitution in the Netherlands Since the Lifting of the Brothel Ban."
26. e.g. Ibid.
27. For Australia Barbara Ann Sullivan, *The Politics of Sex: Prostitution and Pornography in Australia since 1945* (Cambridge University Press, 1997); Barbara

Sullivan, "When (Some) Prostitution Is Legal: The Impact of Law Reform on Sex Work in Australia," *Journal of Law and Society* 37, no. 1 (March 1, 2010): 85–104. For Austria Maggie O'Neil, "Prostitution, Feminism and Critical Praxis: Professional Prostitute?," *Austrian Journal of Sociology* Winter (1996); Birgit Sauer, "Taxes, Rights and Regimentation: Discourses on Prostitution in Austria," *The Politics of Prostitution: Women's Movements, Democratic States and the Globalisation of Sex Commerce*, 2004. For the United States Barbara G. Brents, Crystal A. Jackson, and Kathryn Hausbeck, *The State of Sex: Tourism, Sex and Sin in the New American Heartland*, New Ed (Routledge, 2009).

28. Alain Corbin, *Women for Hire: Prostitution and Sexuality in France after 1850* (Cambridge, Mass.: Harvard University Press, 1990); Petra de Vries, "Josephine Butler and the Making of Feminism: International Abolitionism in the Netherlands (1870–1914)," *Women's History Review* 17, no. 2 (2008): 257–77.

29. Outshoorn, "Pragmatism in the Polder: Changing Prostitution Policy in the Netherlands," 167; Annemarie Houkes and Maartje Janse, "Foreign Examples as Eye Openers and Justification: The Transfer of the Anti-Corn Law League and the Anti-Prostitution Movement to the Netherlands," *European Review of History: Revue Européenne D'histoire* 12, no. 2 (July 1, 2005): 321–44.

30. Annemieke van Drenth, "The City and the Self. The Case of Girls' Protection in the Netherlands around 1900," *Educational Review* 54, no. 2 (2002): 125–33.

31. Gert Hekma, "The Decline of Sexual Radicalism in the Netherlands," in *The Present of Radical Sexual Politics* (Amsterdam: Mosse Stichting, 2003); Hekma, "How Libertine Is the Netherlands?"; Amy T. Schalet, *Not Under My Roof: Parents, Teens, and the Culture of Sex* (Chicago: University Of Chicago Press, 2011); Cas Wouters, *Sex and Manners: Female Emancipation in the West* (Thousand Oaks, CA: Sage, 2004).

32. Outshoorn, "Pragmatism in the Polder: Changing Prostitution Policy in the Netherlands," 167–168.

33. e.g. Ibid., 172.

34. Daalder, "Prostitution in the Netherlands Since the Lifting of the Brothel Ban," 63.

35. Mariska Majoor, *When Sex Becomes Work* (Amsterdam: Prostitution Information Center, 2002).

36. Marieke van Doorninck and Rosie Campbell, "'Zoning' Street Sex Work: The Way Forward?," in *Sex Work Now* (Collompton, U.K.: Willan Publishing, 2006), 62–90.

37. quoted in Daley, "New Rights for Dutch Prostitutes, but No Gain."

38. dé Weekkrant Amsterdam, "Extra Geld Voor de Zorg Voor Prostituees," Dé Weekkrant, October 19, 2010, http://www.deweekkrant.nl/.

39. Daalder, "Prostitution in the Netherlands Since the Lifting of the Brothel Ban," 87.

40. These classification disputes are at the core of labor market disputes around the world in what Jennifer Chun *Organizing at the Margins: The Symbolic Politics of Labor in South Korea and the United States*, 1 edition (ILR Press, 2011). calls the symbolic politics of marginalized labor.

41. Daalder, "Prostitution in the Netherlands Since the Lifting of the Brothel Ban," 64.

42. Ibid.

43. Ibid., 66.
44. Ibid., 67.
45. Gail Pheterson, "The Whore Stigma: Female Dishonor and Male Unworthiness," *Social Text* 37, no. Winter (1993): 39–64.
46. Daalder, "Prostitution in the Netherlands Since the Lifting of the Brothel Ban," 66.
47. Ibid., 67.
48. Ibid., 70.
49. Barbara Meil Hobson, *Uneasy Virtue: The Politics of Prostitution and the American Reform Tradition* (New York: Basic Books, 1988), 231.
50. Daalder, "Prostitution in the Netherlands Since the Lifting of the Brothel Ban."
51. van Dongen, "Prostitutiewet: Bestuurders Te Naïef."
52. Outshoorn, "Debating Prostitution in Parliament: A Feminist Analysis," 473.
53. James Kennedy, "The Moral State: How Much to the American and the Dutch Differ?," in *Regulating Morality: A Comparison of the Role of the State in Mastering the Mores in the Netherlands and the United States* (Antwerp: Maklu, 2000), 9–22; Lechner, *The Netherlands*.
54. Daalder, "Prostitution in the Netherlands Since the Lifting of the Brothel Ban," 84.
55. Wim Huisman and Edward R. Kleemans, "The Challenges of Fighting Sex Trafficking in the Legalized Prostitution Market of the Netherlands," *Crime, Law and Social Change* 61, no. 2 (2014): 215–28.
56. Daley, "New Rights for Dutch Prostitutes, but No Gain."
57. Outshoorn, "Pragmatism in the Polder: Changing Prostitution Policy in the Netherlands," 171.
58. Kennedy, "The Moral State: How Much to the American and the Dutch Differ?"
59. Hekma, "How Libertine Is the Netherlands?"; Buruma, "Dutch Tolerance."

Chapter 4

1. Claes Britton and The Swedish Institute, *Sweden and Swedes* (Stockholm: The Swedish Institute, 2003), ii.
2. http://www.RFSU.se/our_history.asp, retrieved 3/26/2008
3. Aftonbladet 12/25/02; 11/30/00, 2/9/05, 5/28/06; 11/21/04
4. Kajsa Claude, *Targeting the Sex Buyer: The Swedish Example: Stopping Prostitution and Trafficking Where It All Begins* (Swedish Institute, 2010).
5. Gunilla Ekberg, "The Swedish Law That Prohibits the Purchase of Sexual Services," *Violence Against Women* 10, no. 10 (2004): 1210.
6. Aftonbladet March 12, 2007.
7. Newsmill.se 11/18/09
8. Claude, *Targeting the Sex Buyer*, 46.
9. Aftonbladet, Feb 7, 2001; October 29, 2002.
10. Sullivan, Tom. 2009. "In 30 years without spanking, are Swedish children better behaved?" *Christian Science Monitor*, October 5.
11. http://www.systembolaget.se/English, July 6, 2013.

12. Newsmill.se, December 31, 2009.
13. Aftonbladet March 20, 2009.
14. While there is scholarly disagreement over which comes first, the feminist movement or the shape of the welfare state see Dorothy E. McBride and Amy G. Mazur, *The Politics of State Feminism: Innovation in Comparative Research* (Temple University Press, 2012). What I wish to call attention to is their mutual reinforcement such that social democracies nurture radical feminism and corporatist states, liberal feminism. I discuss this further in Chapter 6.
15. "The Swedish Law That Prohibits the Purchase of Sexual Services," 1187–1188.
16. Newsmill.se November 3, 2008 e.g. Catherine A. MacKinnon, "Trafficking, Prostitution, and Inequality," *Harvard Civil Rights Civil Liberties Law Review* 46 (2011): 271.
17. Aftonbladet, January 3, 2004; e.g., January 8, 2004.
18. Britton and The Swedish Institute, *Sweden and Swedes*; Christine Ingebritsen, "Norm Entrepreneurs: Scandinavia's Role in World Politics," *Cooperation and Conflict* 37, no. 1 (2002): 11–23.
19. Hasselgren, Karin. Tal hållet av Karin Hasselgren vid FNEU:s torgmöte. Aug 25, 2007.
    Hasselgren, Karin. 2010. OM ÖKANDE MAKT INOM EU OCH EMU HÖSTEN 2010.
20. "Tyskland legaliserar prostitution." 2001. Nyheter Om EU. No. 14 November.
21. Prostituerade ges arbetstillstånd i Ungern. 2007. Nyheter Om EU. Oct.
22. Ekberg, "The Swedish Law That Prohibits the Purchase of Sexual Services," 1210.

Chapter 5

1. This has changed little since observed by Laura María Agustín, "Review of The Politics of Prostitution by Joyce Outshoorn," *Labour / Le Travail* 55 (April 1, 2005): 313–15.
2. BMFSFJ, "Report by the Federal Government on the Impact of the Act Regulating the Legal Situation of Prostitutes" (Berlin: Federal Ministry for Family Affairs, Senior Citizens, Women and Youth, 2007), 9.
3. Michaela Freund, "Ein Mädchen Kostet Einen Mercedes," *Welt Online*, October 21, 2001, http://www.welt.de/print-wams/article616417/Ein-Maedchen-kostet -einen-Mercedes.html; Vereinte Dienstleistungsgewerkschaft, "Arbeitsplatz Prostitution in Hamburg" (Hamburg, Germany: Verdi, 2003).
4. Ira von Mellenthin and Wolf von Hirschheydt, "Milde Strafen Im Hell's-Angels-Prozess Verhängt," *Welt Online*, October 5, 2001, http://www.welt.de/ print-welt/article479663/Milde-Strafen-im-Hells-Angels-Prozess-verhaengt .html.
5. Nikolaus Frei, "Polizei Zerschlägt Bordell-Kartell," *Welt Online*, July 14, 2001, http://www.welt.de/print-welt/article463231/Polizei-zerschlaegt-Bordell-Kar tell.html.
6. Carsten Holm, "Der Triumph Der 'Puffmutti,'" *Der Spiegel*, 2000.

7. Runder Tisch zur Prostitution in Frankfurt am Main, "Empfehlungen an Die Stadtverordnetenversammlung" (Frankfurt am Main, 2002).

8. e.g. Frankfurter Allgemeine Zeitung, "Tod Im Luxusbordell: Keine Tat Der Russen-Mafia," 1995; Frankfurter Allgemeine Zeitung, "Toedliche Schuesse Aus Verletzter Ehre," 2000.

9. Susanne Dodillet, "Cultural Clash on Prostitution: Debates on Prostitution in Germany and Sweden in the 1990s," in *First Global Conference: Critical Issues in Sexuality, Salzburg, Austria, October*, 2004, http://www.inter-disciplinary .net/ci/transformations/sexualities/s1/Dodillet%20paper.pdf.

10. Michael Mielke, "Wie Das Café 'Pssst!' Zum Politikum Wurde," *Welt Online*, December 1, 2000, http://www.welt.de/print-welt/article550585/Wie-das-Cafe -Pssst-zum-Politikum-wurde.html.

11. Peter Dausend, "Prostituierte Im Bundestag - Vorerst Nur Als Zuschauer," *Welt Online*, May 12, 2001, http://www.welt.de/print-welt/article450648/Prostitui erte-im-Bundestag-vorerst-nur-als-Zuschauer.html.

12. Ronald John Weitzer, *Legalizing Prostitution: From Illicit Vice to Lawful Business* (New York University Press, 2012), 116–119.

13. CITE the distinction between being a business but not an occupation

14. Myra Marx Ferree et al., "Abortion Talk in Germany and the United States: Why Rights Explanations Are Wrong," *Contexts* 1, no. 2 (2002): 27–34.

15. Weitzer, *Legalizing Prostitution*, 119.

16. BMFSFJ, "Report by the Federal Government on the Impact of the Act Regulating the Legal Situation of Prostitutes," 8.

17. Timo Fleckenstein, "The Politics of Ideas in Welfare State Transformation: Christian Democracy and the Reform of Family Policy in Germany," *Social Politics: International Studies in Gender, State and Society* 18, no. 4 (2011): 543–71; Franz-Xaver Kaufmann, *Variations of the Welfare State: Great Britain, Sweden, France and Germany Between Capitalism and Socialism*, 2013 edition (Heidelberg; New York: Springer, 2012).

18. Solveig Bergman, *The Politics of Feminism: Autonomous Feminist Movements in Finland and West Germany from the 1960s to the 1980s* (Åbo, Finland: Åbo Akademi University Press, 2002).

19. BMFSFJ, "Report by the Federal Government on the Impact of the Act Regulating the Legal Situation of Prostitutes," 9.

20. Richard J. Evans, "Prostitution, State and Society in Imperial Germany," *Past and Present* 70 (1976): 106–29; Patric Fouad, *Frauenzimmer: Brothels in Germany* (Heidelberg: Kehrer Verlag, 2004); Margarete von Galen, "Prostitution and the Law in Germany," *Cardozo Women's Law Journal* 3 (1996): 349; Isabel V. Hull, *Sexuality, State and Civil Society in Germany, 1700–1815* (Ithaca, NY: Cornell University Press, 1996).

21. von Galen, "Prostitution and the Law in Germany."

22. Mielke, "Wie Das Café 'Pssst!' Zum Politikum Wurde."

23. Weitzer, *Legalizing Prostitution*.

24. Interviewees frequently glossed the city council by reference to the name of its building, in the same way Americans make reference to the actions of the "White House."

25. Unlike Berlin or Hamburg, Frankfurt is not a city-state in Germany's federal system; the Romer operates more like a parliament than a city council.

26. John Friedmann and Ute Angelika Lehrer, "Urban Policy Responses to Foreign In-Migration: The Case of Frankfurt-Am-Main," *Journal of the American Planning Association* 63, no. 1 (1997): 61–78, doi:10.1080/01944369708975724; Frank-Olaf Radtke, "Multiculturalism in Germany: Local Management of Immigrants' Social Inclusion," *International Journal on Multicultural Societies* 5, no. 1 (2003): 55–76.

27. Runder Tisch zur Prostitution in Frankfurt am Main, "Empfehlungen an Die Stadtverordnetenversammlung."

28. It is difficult to distinguish interrupting voices from two of the three men in the group interview of department officials that included Heiko Kleinstuber.

29. European Court reports, 2001, page I-08615.

30. E.U. Network of Independent Experts in Fundamental Rights, "Report on the Situation of Fundamental Rights in the European Union and Its Member States in 2002" (Brussels: European Commission, Unit A5 of DG Justice and Home Affairs, 2003).

31. BMFSFJ, "Report by the Federal Government on the Impact of the Act Regulating the Legal Situation of Prostitutes," 79.

32. John Torpey, *The Invention of the Passport* (Cambridge University Press, 2000).

33. Stephanie Klee, "Comments from Hydra," in *Hearing on Draft Act to Improve the Legal and Social Situation of Prostitutes in Germany* (Berlin: Bundestag Committee for Family, Elderly, Women and Youth Affairs, 2001).

34. Ann Taylor Allen, *Feminism and Motherhood in Western Europe, 1890–1970: The Maternal Dilemma* (Palgrave Macmillan, 2005); Masako Yuki, "The Women's Movement within Trade Unions in Germany," *Signs* 33, no. 3 (March 1, 2008): 519–27.

35. Bergman, *The Politics of Feminism: Autonomous Feminist Movements in Finland and West Germany from the 1960s to the 1980s*.

36. Myra Marx Ferree, "Making Equality: The Women's Affairs Offices in the Federal Republic of Germany," *Comparative State Feminism*, 1995, 95–113; Myra Marx Ferree, "Patriarchies and Feminisms: The Two Women's Movements of Post-Unification Germany," *Social Politics: International Studies in Gender, State & Society* 2, no. 1 (1995): 10–24.

37. Alice Schwartzer, "Der Große Unterschied," *Emma*, 2003; Alice Schwarzer, *Prostitution—Ein deutscher Skandal!* (Köln: Kiepenheuer & Witsch GmbH, 2013).

Chapter 6

1. Helsingin Sanomat International Edition ("Helsinki News," abbreviated here as HSIE). "Amended prostitution bill likely to pass." June 11, 2006. See summary in Johan Karlsson Schaffer, "Finland's Prostitution Law and the Hope of Nordic Unity | Nordic Prostitution Policy Reform," *Nordic Prostitution Policy Reform*, October 12, 2009, http://nppr.se/2009/10/12/; see also Elina

Penttinen, *Corporeal Globalization: Narratives of Subjectivity and Otherness in the Sexscapes of Globalization* (Tampere: Tampere Peace Research Institute, 2004); May-Len Skilbrei and Charlotta Holmström, *Prostitution Policy in the Nordic Region : Ambiguous Sympathies* (Farnham, Surrey, GBR: Ashgate Publishing Group, 2013).

2. Of course, prostitution controversies have a long history in Finland Antti Häkkinen, *Rahasta—Vaan Ei Rakkaudesta: Prostituutio Helsingissä 1867–1939 (For Money—But Not For Love: Prostitution in Helsinki)* (Helsinki: Kustannusosakeyhtiö Otava, 1995). Regarding the 1986 repeal of the vagrancy act, see Margaretha Järvinen, "Prostitution in Helsinki: A Disappearing Social Problem?," *Journal of the History of Sexuality* 3, no. 4 (1993): 608–30.

3. The term red whore was used to slur women supporters of the socialist side of the Finnish civil war Markku Kangaspuro, *Neuvosto-Karjalan Taistelu Itsehallinnosta. Nationalismi Ja Suomalaiset Punaiset Neuvostoliiton Vallankäytössä 1920–1939*, Bibliotheca Historica (Helsinki: Suomalaisen Kirjallisuuden Seura, 2000).

4. *Pilu* [sic] *50 markka.*

5. Järvinen, "Prostitution in Helsinki: A Disappearing Social Problem?"

6. 2004 interview with Antti Häkkinen *Rahasta—Vaan Ei Rakkaudesta: Prostituutio Helsingissä 1867–1939 (For Money—But Not For Love: Prostitution in Helsinki).*

7. Sari Näre, "Libertarianism in the Discourse of Sex-Bar Customers," in *Who's Buying? The Clients of Prostitution* (Helsinki: Council for Equality: Ministry of Affairs and Health, 1999), 29–33; Sirpa Tani, "'That Kind of Girl in This Kind of Neighborhood . . .' The Potential and Problems of Street Prostitution Research," *City* 5, no. 3 (2001): 311–25.

8. Sari Näre, "Pornografiakeskustelusta Bordellikeskusteluun. Kaupallinen Seksi Vietti- Ja Rakkauseetoksen Taistelukenttänä (From Pornography Debate to Brothel Discussion. The Battlefield of Commercial Sex Drive and Love Ethics," in *Sex, Snack'n Pop* (Helsinki: Titanik Galleri, 1997); Näre, "Libertarianism in the Discourse of Sex-Bar Customers."

9. Sirpa Tani, "Whose Place Is This Space? Life in the Street Prostitution Area of Helsinki, Finland," *International Journal of Urban and Regional Research* 26, no. 2 (2002): 343–59.

10. Technically most street prostitution took place in the Harju neighborhood; most discussions generalized to the broader Kallio district, e.g. HSIE. 2000. "Street Prostitution Clearly Disturbed Helsinki Residents before Clean-Up." Nov. 1. http://www.helsinki-hs.net, Accessed Jan. 12, 2004.

11. (*Prostituutio pois kaduilta—kansanliike*).

12. HSIE. 2000. "Street Prostitution Clearly Disturbed Helsinki Residents before Clean-Up."

13. Gail Pheterson, "The Whore Stigma: Female Dishonor and Male Unworthiness," *Social Text* 37, no. Winter (1993): 39–64.

14. Ollikainen, Marjo. "Children in Viipuri Attest to Sex Trips by Finns." *Helsingin Sanomat International Edition*, 2001. http://www.helsinki-hs.net. Accessed Jan 12, 2009. HSIE. 2000. "Campaign against Sexual Abuse of Children Begins

along Eastern Border," Apr. 5. http://www.helsinki-hs.net. Accessed Jan 12, 2009. Lahdenmäki, Ari, and Riku Rantala. 2001. "Russian Mafia Ships Prostitutes to Helsinki." *Helsingin Sanomat International Edition*, Jun 19. http://www.helsinki-hs.net. Accessed Jan. 12, 2009. HSIE. 2000. "Street Prostitution Clearly Disturbed Helsinki Residents before Clean-Up." HSIE. 2003. "Finns Deny Swedish Claim of Widespread Prostitution on Passenger Ferries." May 12. http://www.helsinki-hs.net. Accessed Jan. 12, 2009. HSIE. 2003. "U.S. Report on Human Trafficking Shows Finland in a Poor Light." June 13. http://www.helsinki-hs.net. Accessed Jan 12, 2009.

15. Finnish law made separate provisions for refusal of entry, prohibition of entry, and deportation. Refusal of entry describes many circumstances beyond stopping someone at the border to Finland, including ordering a ten-year illegal resident to leave the country immediately. I use deport for ease of understanding in English because although the legal procedures are different, the practical result is the same.

16. See HSIE. 2000. "Directorate of Immigration prepares for the new Aliens Act," Jul. 6. http://www.helsinki-hs.net. Accessed Jan. 12, 2009. The Schengen common travel area in 2004 was the EU-15 minus the UK and Ireland, plus Norway, Iceland, and Switzerland.

17. Johan Bäckman, "'The Wolf Has a Hundred Paths': The Organised Crime of St. Petersburg in the Framework of the Russian Culture of Criminal Justice" (Helsinki: Oikeuspoliittinen Tutkimuslaitos, 1999); Ari Lahdenmäki and Riku Rantala, "Russian Mafia Ships Prostitutes to Helsinki."

18. HSIE. 2000. "Interior Ministry to crack down on public drinking," Nov. 15. http://www.helsinki-hs.net. Accessed Jan. 12, 2009. HS. 2002. "Jukinen prostitutuutio, juominen ja virtsaaminen rangaistaviksi," Mar. 14. http://www.hs.fi, Accessed Jan 11, 2009.

19. Hautamäki, Jaakko. 2002. "Hallitus haluaa kieltää julkisen prostituution ja alkoholin käytön." *Helsingin Sanomat*. www.hs.fi, Accessed Jan 11, 2009. HSIE. 2000. "Helsinki Prostitutes Move to Vantaa," Jan. 24; "New Helsinki ordinances reduce street prostitution and public drinking," Aug. 10. http://www.helsinki-hs.net. Accessed Jan. 12, 2009.

20. HS 2/8/2002, "Tavallaan Helsinkiä koskeva järjestyssääntö tulee nyt koskemaan koko maata."

21. Academic titles are more nuanced in Finnish than English; his actual title is *rikosoikeuden assistenttia oikeustieteen lisensiaatti*, or Assistant Criminological Licenciate of Law.

22. HS. 1999. "Ari Hirvonen: Järjestyksestä pitää säätää laissa." September 17. http://www.helsinki-hs.net. Accessed Jan. 12, 2009; HS 1999. "Helsingin järjestyssäännön uudistus on juridinen soppa." "Hirvonen epäili Helsingin Sanomien yleisönosastossa, että katujuopottelun ja prostituution täyskielto järjestyssäännössä on sekä hallitusmuodon että eräiden Suomea sitovien kansainvälisten ihmisoikeussopimusten vastainen."

23. HSIE.1999. "Helsinki comes down hard on public drinking and soliciting," Sept. 16; HSIE. 2000. New Helsinki ordinances reduce street prostitution and public drinking," Oct. 8. http://www.helsinki-hs.net. Accessed Jan. 12, 2009.

24. Kerkelä, Lasse. 2004 "Seksin Ostajat Saaneet Sakkoja Ensimmäistä Kertaa Suomessa." *Helsingin Sanomat*, Feb 13. Accessed Jan. 12, 2009.
25. HSIE 2/5/2004. HSIE 9/4/2004. HSIE 10/20/2011, see also Näre (1997). Pornografiakeskustelusta Bordellikeskusteluun. Kaupallinen Seksi Vietti- Ja Rakkauseetoksen Taistelukenttänä.
26. Aura Korppi-Tommola, *Tahdolla Ja Tunteella Tasa-Arvoa: Naisjärjestöjen Keskusliitto 1911–2001 (Equality Through Will and Emotions: The National Council of Women of Finland)* (Jyväskylä: Gummerus Kirjapaino, 2001); Stephanie Limoncelli, *The Politics of Trafficking: The First International Movement to Combat the Sexual Exploitation of Women* (Stanford University Press, 2010).
27. *"Nuolen ja imen kuin seksi-imuri." "Nuoret tytot tarjoavat seksiseuraansa." "Virolaistytaret PK-seura."*
28. Penttinen, Elina. 2008. Globalization, Prostitution and Sex Trafficking: Corporeal Politics. New York: Routledge, p. 149.
29. *Svenska folkpartiet i Finland / Suomen ruotsalainen kansanpuolue* (SFP/RKP). Finland's bilingualism is enshrined in the constitution, and the party representing the interests and culture of Swedish Speakers, while small, has participated in every governing coalition since 1979.
30. *Sociaali- ja terveysalan tutkimus- ja kehittämiskeskus* (STAKES), now called THL (*Terveyden ja Hyvinvoinnin Laitos*).
31. Oikeusministeriön työryhmämietintö, "Ihmiskauppa, Paritus Ja Prostituutio" (Helsinki: Ministry of Justice, 2003). Working group meetings were covered, for example, in: HSIE October 22, 2002, November 15, 2002, November 14, 2005, December 16, 2005, April 7 2006.
32. HSIE. 2006. "Finland's ranking improves in US report on human trafficking," June 11; "Amended prostitution bill likely to pass," June 11; June 14, 2006. HSIE June 19, 2006. HSIE. 2012. "Government divided on total ban on buying sex," Jul 25. http://www.hs.fi/english. Accessed Jan 12, 2009.
33. Skilbrei and Holmström, *Prostitution Policy in the Nordic Region*.

Chapter 7

1. Claude S. Fischer, *Made in America: A Social History of American Culture and Character* (University Of Chicago Press, 2010), 10.
2. Patricia Ewick and Susan S. Silbey, *The Common Place of Law: Stories From Everyday Life* (University of Chicago Press, 1998); James C. Scott, *Seeing Like a State*, Yale Agrarian Studies (Yale U., 1998).
3. Gøsta Esping-Andersen, *The Three Worlds of Welfare Capitalism* (Princeton, New Jersey: Princeton University Press, 1990).
4. For debates about incorporating gender into conceptions of welfare states, see e.g.: Gøsta Esping-Andersen, *Incomplete Revolution: Adapting Welfare States to Women's New Roles*, 1st ed. (Polity, 2009); Lynne A. Haney, "Engendering the Welfare State. A Review Article," *Comparative Studies in Society and History* 40, no. 4 (October 1, 1998): 748–67; Jane Lewis, "Gender and Welfare State Change" (Oxford: Department of Social Policy and Social Work, 2002);

Ruth Lister, "A Nordic Nirvana?: Gender, Citizenship, and Social Justice in the Nordic Welfare States," *Social Politics: International Studies in Gender, State and Society* 16, no. 2 (2009): 242–78; Julia S. O'Connor, "Gender, Class and Citizenship in the Comparative Analysis of Welfare State Regimes: Theoretical and Methodological Issues," *British Journal of Sociology* 44, no. 3 (1993): 501–18; Ann Shola Orloff, "Gender and the Social Rights of Citizenship," *American Sociological Review* 58 (1993): 303–28.

5. e.g. Margot Canaday, *The Straight State: Sexuality and Citizenship in Twentieth-Century America* (Princeton University Press, 2009); Nancy Cott, *Public Vows: A History of Marriage and the Nation* (Cambridge, Mass.: Harvard University Press, 2002); David T. Evans, *Sexual Citizenship: The Material Construction of Sexualities* (New York: Routledge, 1993); Ann Shola Orloff, "From Maternalism to 'Employment for All,'" *The State after Statism, Ed. Jonah D. Levy*, 2006, 230–68.

6. Framing meanings: John W. Mohr and Vincent Duquenne, "The Duality of Culture and Practice: Poverty Relief in New York City, 1888–1917," *Theory and Society* 26, no. 2/3 (April 1, 1997): 305–56.; "intellectual processes:" Ann Shola Orloff and Bruno Palier, "The Power of Gender Perspectives: Feminist Influence on Policy Paradigms, Social Science, and Social Politics," *Social Politics: International Studies in Gender, State and Society* 16, no. 4 (2009): 405–12.; "policy imagination:" Mary Daly, "What Adult Worker Model?: A Critical Look at Recent Social Policy Reform in Europe from a Gender and Family Perspective," *Social Politics: International Studies in Gender, State and Society* 18, no. 1 (2011): 2. On the translation of abstract policy into bureaucratic action on the ground Michael Lipsky, *Street-Level Bureaucracy: Dilemmas of the Individual in Public Services* (New York: Russell Sage, 1980). On indexical concepts that frame shared cultural meanings, Andrew Abbott, *Methods of Discovery: Heuristics for the Social Sciences* (New York: Norton, 2004); William H. Jr. Sewell, "A Theory of Structure: Duality, Agency, and Transformation," *American Journal of Sociology* 98, no. 1 (1992): 1–29.

7. I refer here to the "weak" Foucauldian model of action described by Jana Matson Everett, "Governance Reforms and Rural Women in India: What Types of Women Citizens Are Produced by the Will to Empower?," *Social Politics: International Studies in Gender, State and Society* 16, no. 2 (2009): 279–302. This is theorized by Michel Foucault and Norbert Elias: *The History of Sexuality, Volume I* (New York: Vintage Books, 1978); Michel Foucault, *Discipline & Punish: The Birth of the Prison* (New York: Pantheon, 1977). Norbert Elias, *The Civilizing Process: The History of Manners* (Oxford: Blackwell, 1939); Foucault is not the only theorist who considers the history of socialization into national norms. See also Norbert Elias, *The Civilizing Process: State Formation and Civilization* (Oxford: Blackwell, 1982).

8. Welfare state self-regulation Morris Janowitz, "The Concept of Social Control," in *On Social Organization and Social Control* (University of Chicago Press, 1991), 73–85.; "normal troubles" Sherri Cavan, *Liquor License: An Ethnography of Bar Behavior* (Chicago: Aldine, 1966)., 18; Joseph R. Gusfield, *Symbolic Crusade: Status Politics and the American Temperance Movement* (Urbana: University of

Illinois Press, 1963); Joseph R. Gusfield, *Contested Meanings: The Construction of Alcohol Problems* (Madison: University of Wisconsin Press, 1996).; Thomas theorem (Thomas and Thomas 1928, 572), morality W. I. Thomas, *The Unadjusted Girl* (Boston: Little, Brown and Co., 1923), 43.

9. James M. Jasper, *Energy and the State: Nuclear Politics in the United States, Sweden and France* (Princeton University Press, 1990); David D. Laitin, *Language Repertoires and State Construction in Africa* (Cambridge University Press, 1992); Campbell, John L., and Ove K. Pedersen. The National Origins of Policy Ideas: Knowledge Regimes in the United States, France, Germany, and Denmark. Princeton University Press, 2014.

10. Scott, James C. 1998. *Seeing Like a State*. Yale University Press. The quote is from Fischer (2010, p. 10).

11. Penetrating Theda Skocpol, *States and Social Revolutions: A Comparative Analysis of France, Russia & China* (New York: Cambridge University Press, 1979).; legibility Scott, *Seeing Like a State*.; embracing John Torpey, *The Invention of the Passport* (Cambridge University Press, 2000).

12. "Institutions of mass representations" Morris Janowitz, *Social Control of the Welfare State* (New York: Elsevier, 1976), xii.; "policy entrepreneurs" Michael Mintrom, "Policy Entrepreneurs and the Diffusion of Innovation," *American Journal of Political Science*, 1997, 738–70.

13. Anne Lise Ellingsaeter and Arnlaug Leira, *Politicising Parenthood in Scandinavia: Gender Relations in the Welfare State* (The Policy Press, 2006), 7.

14. Ibid.; Eliina Haavio-Mannila et. al., *Unfinished Democracy: Women in Nordic Politics* (Oxford: Pergamon Press, 1985); Helga Maria Hernes, "The Welfare State Citizenship of Scandinavian Women," in *Welfare State and Woman Power: Essays in State Feminism* (Oslo: Norwegian University Press, 1987), 135–64.

15. Kees van Kersbergen, *Social Capitalism: A Study of Christian Democracy and the Welfare State* (New York: Routledge, 1995).

16. Ibid, p. 154.

17. On the weakness of the American welfare state Nancy Fraser and Linda Gordon, "Contract versus Charity: Why Is There No Social Citizenship in the United States?," in *The Citizenship Debates: A Reader* (Minneapolis: University of Minnesota Press, 1998), 113–27.; on sociological partisanship Alvin Gouldner, "The Sociologist as Partisan: Sociology and the Welfare State," *The American Sociologist* 3, no. 1 (1968): 103–16.; on civil society, markets, and states Michael Burawoy, "Public Sociologies: Contradictions, Dilemmas, and Possibilities," *Social Forces* 82, no. 4 (2004): 1603–18.

18. On bodies and control see Julia O'Connell Davidson, "The Rights and Wrongs of Prostitution," *Hypatia* 17, no. 2 (2002): 84–98; Carole Pateman, *The Sexual Contract* (Cambridge, Mass.: Polity Press, 1988). The poverty of property rights theory see e.g. Bruce G. Carruthers and Laura Ariovich, "The Sociology of Property Rights," *Annual Review of Sociology* 30 (2004): 23–46. Victims without court recourse P. M. & D. J. Warr Pyett, "Vulnerability on the Streets: Female Sex Workers and HIV Risk," *AIDS Care* 9, no. 5 (1997): 539–47; Lisa E. Sanchez, "Boundaries of Legitimacy: Sex, Violence, Citizenship, and Community in a Local Sexual Economy," *Law & Social Inquiry* 22, no. 3 (1997): 543–80.

19. Ananya Roy, "Paradigms of Propertied Citizenship: Transnational Techniques of Analysis," *Urban Affairs Review* 38, no. 4 (2003): 463–91.
20. Clem Brooks and Jeff Manza, *Why Welfare States Persist: The Importance of Public Opinion in Democracies* (U. Chicago, 2007).
21. Ann Swidler, *Talk of Love: How Culture Matters* (Chicago: University of Chicago Press, 2001); Ann Swidler, "Culture in Action: Symbols and Strategies," *American Sociological Review* 51 (1986): 273–86.
22. The role of sporting events in driving demand for prostitution has repeatedly been debunked (Kathleen Deering and Kate Shannon, "Fears of an Influx of Sex Workers to Major Sporting Events Are Unfounded," *BMJ: British Medical Journal* 345 (2012); Julie Ham, *What's the Cost of a Rumour?: A Guide to Sorting Out the Myths and the Facts about Sporting Events and Trafficking* (Global Alliance Against Traffic in Women (GAATW), 2011).
23. Benedict Anderson, *Imagined Communities* (London: Verso Editions, 1983).

Chapter 8

1. On employment protections, see Susan Edwards, "The Legal Regulation of Prostitution: A Human Rights Issue," in *Rethinking Prostitution: Purchasing Sex in the 1990s* (New York: Routledge, 1997), 57–82; Andrea Marie Bertone, "Sexual Trafficking in Women: International Political Economy and the Politics of Sex," *Gender Issues*, no. Winter (2000): 2. (Bertone 2000; Häkkinen 1997b). On globalization as the penetration of capitalism into intimate lives, see Ibid.; Michelle A. Clark, "Trafficking in Persons: An Issue of Human Security," *Journal of Human Development* 4, no. 2 (2003): 247–63; Dennis Altman, *Global Sex* (Chicago: University of Chicago Press, 2001). On the lack of agreement, see e.g. Sabine Grenz, "Conference Report: The Globalization of Sexual Exploitation," *Feminist Review* 67, no. Spring (2001): 111–32; Dorchen Leidholdt, "Sexual Trafficking of Women in Europe: A Human Rights Crisis for the European Union," in *Sexual Politics and the European Union: The New Feminist Challenge* (Oxford: Berghahn Books, 1996), 83–96; Laura Maria Agustin, *Sex at the Margins: Migration, Labour Markets and the Rescue Industry* (London: Zed Books, 2007); Laura María Agustín, "Sex Workers and Violence Against Women: Utopic Visions or Battle of the Sexes?," *The Society for International Development* 44, no. 3 (2001): 107–10. On the role of war in creating the conditions for the exploitation of migrants, see e.g. Ismo Söderling, Anneli Miettinen, and Anna Pajula, "Human Trafficking as a New and Extreme Type of Migration," in *Women's World: 8th International Interdisciplinary Congress on Women* (Kampala, Uganda: Makarere University, 2002); Ryszard Piotrowicz, "European Initiatives in the Protection of Victims of Trafficking Who Give Evidence Against Their Traffickers," *International Journal of Refugee Law* 14, no. 2/3 (2002); David Ould, "Slavery in General and in Relation to Trafficking in Persons, Especially in Women," in *Sklaverei Ohne Ende* (Berlin: Bundesweiter Koordinierungsreis gegen Frauenhandel und Gewalt an Frauen im Migrationsprozess e.V., 2002); Ministry for Foreign Affairs of

Sweden, "Statement of Government Policy in the Parliamentary Debate on Foreign Affairs" (Stockholm, 2001).

2. On the similarities between contemporary discourse and White Slavery see Frederick K. Grittner, *White Slavery: Myth, Ideology, and American Law* (New York: Garland Publishing, 1990); Jo Doezema, *Sex Slaves and Discourse Masters: The Construction of Trafficking* (London: Zed Books, 2010); Gretchen Soderlund, *Sex Trafficking, Scandal, and the Transformation of Journalism, 1885-1917* (University of Chicago Press, 2013). On most trafficking as chain migration outside of mafia control, see Agustin, Sex at the Margins: Migration, Labour Markets and the Rescue Industry; Khalid Koser, "Asylum Policies, Trafficking and Vulnerability," International Migration, no. 1 (2000): 90–111; John Davies, "The Role of Migration Policy in Creating and Sustaining Trafficking Harm," in European Conference on Preventing and Combating Trafficking in Human Beings—A Global Challenge for the 21st Century (Brussels: EU/IOM, 2002); Andrew Geddes, "Chronicle of a Crisis Foretold: The Politics of Irregular Migration, Human Trafficking and People Smuggling in the UK," British Journal of Politics and International Relations 7, no. 3 (2005): 324–39; Jo Goodey, "Migration, Crime and Victimhood: Responses to Sex Trafficking in the EU," Punishment and Society 5, no. 4 (2003): 415–31; Helka Mongard, "Report of the Working Group Mobile Prostitution and Access of Migrant Sex Workers to Health and Social Services at the Seminar AIDS & Mobility: New Policy Directions in Finland," in AIDS & Mobility: New Policy Directions in Finland, vol. 2002 (Tampere: The Migrants Association for Social and Health Promotion, 1999), http://www.map.vip.fi/working_group_2.htm; John Salt, "Trafficking and Human Smuggling: A European Perspective," International Migration, no. 1 (2000): 31–56; European Commission, "Proposal for a Council Directive on the Short-Term Residence Permit Issued to Victims of Action to Facilitate Illegal Immigration or Trafficking" (Brussels: Information and Communication Unit of the Directorate-General Justice and Home Affairs, 2002), http://europa.eu.int/.

3. Margaret E. Keck and Kathryn Sikkink, *Activists Beyond Borders* (Ithaca, NY: Cornell University Press, 1998).

4. Prostitution legalization was relegated to a footnote. For abolitionist success in the bill, see Janice G. Raymond, "Guide to the New UN Trafficking Protocol" (North Amherst, Massachussetts: Coalition Against Trafficking in Women, 2001).

5. James C. Scott, *Seeing Like a State*, Yale Agrarian Studies (Yale U., 1998); George M. Thomas and John W. Meyer, "The Expansion of the State," *Annual Review of Sociology* 10 (1984): 461–82.

6. Leena Ruusuvuori, "Prevention of Prostitution 1998–2002," March 5, 2002, http://www.stakes.fi/sexviolence/pp/en/; The quote is from Laura Keeler, "Work Group Four: How to Research Difficult and Sensitive Subjects," in *Recommendations of the E.U. Expert Meeting on Violence Against Women*, Reports of the Ministry of Social Affairs and Health (Jyväskylä, Finland: Finnish Ministry of Social Affairs and Health, 1999), 97.

7. Outi Ojala, "Address by Member of the Eduskunta," in *Seminar on Trafficking in Women as Modern Slave Trading* (Tallinn, 2002).

8. On prostitution legalization as social control, see Joyce Outshoorn, "Voluntary and Forced Prostitution: The 'Realistic Approach' of the Netherlands," in *The Politics of Prostitution: Women's Movements, Democratic States and the Globalisation of Sex Commerce*, 2004, 185–204; Joyce Outshoorn, "The Political Debates on Prostitution and Trafficking of Women," *Social Politics* 12, no. 1 (2005): 141–55. Regarding sex workers' rights, see Kamala Kempadoo and Jo Doezema, *Global Sex Workers: Rights, Resistance, and Redefinition* (New York: Routledge, 1998); Melinda Chateauvert, *Sex Workers Unite: A History of the Movement from Stonewall to Slutwalk*, 2014; Samantha Majic, *Sex Work Politics: From Protest to Service Provision*, 2014.

9. Plummer, Kenneth. 1995. *Telling Sexual Stories: Power, Change and Social Worlds*. London: Routledge, p. 173.

10. Ulrich Bech, "Beyond the Nation State," *New Statesman*, no. 6 December (1999); Manuel Castells, *The Power of Identity*, The Information Age: Economy, Society and Culture Vol II. (New York: Blackwell Publishers, 1997); Anthony Giddens, *Modernity and Self Identity* (Oxford: Polity Press, 1991); David Held, *Global Transformations: Politics Economics and Culture* (Stanford, California: Stanford University Press, 1999); Kenichi Ohmae, *The Borderless World* (London: HarperCollins, 1994); Saskia Sassen, *Globalization and Its Discontents* (New York: New Press, 1998); Yasemin Nuhoæglu Soysal, *Limits of Citizenship: Migrants and Postnational Membership in Europe* (Chicago: University of Chicago, 1994); Anna Tsing, "The Global Situation," *Cultural Anthropology* 15, no. 3 (2002): 327–60.

11. Lauren Berlant and Michael Warner, "Sex in Public," *Critical Inquiry* 24, no. 2 (1998): 547–66; Margot Canaday, *The Straight State: Sexuality and Citizenship in Twentieth-Century America* (Princeton University Press, 2009); Nancy Cott, *Public Vows: A History of Marriage and the Nation* (Cambridge, Mass.: Harvard University Press, 2002); David T. Evans, *Sexual Citizenship: The Material Construction of Sexualities* (New York: Routledge, 1993); Michel Foucault, *The History of Sexuality, Volume I* (New York: Vintage Books, 1978).

Chapter 9

1. Lynn Sharon Chancer, "Prostitution, Feminist Theory, and Ambivalence: Notes from the Sociological Underground," *Social Text* 37, no. Winter (1993): 146.

2. Janice M. Irvine, "Is Sexuality Research 'dirty Work'? Institutionalized Stigma in the Production of Sexual Knowledge," *Sexualities* 17, no. 5–6 (September 1, 2014): 632–56.

3. Ibid., On the stigmas of sexuality research generally see also Don Kulick and Margaret Willson, *Taboo: Sex, Identity, and Erotic Subjectivity in Anthropological Fieldwork* (New York: Routledge, 1995). For prostitution specifically, see Chancer, "Prostitution, Feminist Theory, and Ambivalence: Notes from the Sociological Underground," 146.

4. e.g. Ann Ferguson, "Sex War: The Debate between Radical and Libertarian Feminists," *Signs*, 1984, 106–12; Lisa Duggan and Nan D. Hunter, *Sex Wars: Sexual*

Dissent and Political Culture (London: Routledge, 1995); Wendy Chapkis, *Live Sex Acts* (New York: Routledge, 1997); Bernadette Barton, "Dancing on the Möbius Strip: Challenging the Sex War Paradigm," *Gender & Society* 16, no. 5 (October 1, 2002): 585–602; Gayle Rubin, "'Afterward,' 'Postscript' and 'Blood Under the Bridge' on "Thinking Sex: Notes for a Radical Theory of the Politics of Sexuality," in *Deviations: A Gayle Rubin Reader* (Duke University Press, 2011), 182–222.

5. Examples of Weitzer's work include Ronald Weitzer, "Flawed Theory and Method in Studies of Prostitution," *Violence Against Women* 11, no. 7 (2005): 934–49; Ronald Weitzer, "The Social Construction of Sex Trafficking: Ideology and Institutionalization of a Moral Crusade," *Politics Society* 35, no. 3 (September 1, 2007): 447–75; Ronald John Weitzer, *Legalizing Prostitution: From Illicit Vice to Lawful Business* (New York University Press, 2012), 7–18. On gender and names see Stanley Lieberson, *A Matter of Taste: How Names, Fashions, and Culture Change* (New Haven: Yale University Press, 2000). Chancer's (1993) quote is on p. 167.

6. Don Kulick, "Four Hundred Thousand Swedish Perverts," *GLQ: A Journal of Lesbian and Gay Studies* 11, no. 2 (2005): 205–35.

7. This foundational concept in sociology was introduced in W. I. Thomas's The Unadjusted Girl a study of female delinquency that discussed prostitution. *The Unadjusted Girl* (Boston: Little, Brown and Co., 1923), 42.

8. D. A Snow and L. Anderson, "Identity Work among the Homeless: The Verbal Construction and Avowal of Personal Identities," *American Journal of Sociology*, 1987, 1348; see also M. L Schwalbe and D. Mason-Schrock, "Identity Work as Group Process," *Advances in Group Processes* 13, no. 113 (1996): 47.

9. Ann Swidler, *Talk of Love: How Culture Matters* (Chicago: University of Chicago Press, 2001).

10. Schwalbe and Mason-Schrock, "Identity Work as Group Process," 117.

11. Laura Nader, "Up the Anthropologist—Perspectives Gained From Studying Up," in *Reinventing Anthropology* (New York: Vintage Press, 1974); For exceptions, see Rosanna Hertz and Jonathan B. Imber, *Studying Elites Using Qualitative Methods* (SAGE Publications, 1995); Luis L. M. Aguiar and Christopher J. Schneider, *Researching Amongst Elites: Challenges and Opportunities in Studying Up* (Ashgate Publishing, Ltd., 2012).

12. Zachary M. Schrag, *Ethical Imperialism: Institutional Review Boards and the Social Sciences, 1965–2009* (Baltimore: Johns Hopkins University Press, 2010).

13. Rose Laub Coser, "Review of The Flight from Ambiguity," *Contemporary Sociology* 16, no. 2 (March 1, 1987): 256.

14. Kenneth Plummer, *Telling Sexual Stories: Power, Change and Social Worlds* (London: Routledge, 1995).

15. Gail Pheterson, "The Whore Stigma: Female Dishonor and Male Unworthiness," *Social Text* 37, no. Winter (1993): 39–64.

Bibliography

Aalbers, Manuel B. 2005. "Big Sister Is Watching You! Gender Interaction and the Unwritten Rules of the Amsterdam Red-Light District." *Journal of Sex Research* 42 (1): 54–62.

Abbott, Andrew. 2004. *Methods of Discovery: Heuristics for the Social Sciences*. New York: Norton.

Aguiar, Luis L. M., and Christopher J. Schneider. 2012. *Researching Amongst Elites: Challenges and Opportunities in Studying Up*. Ashgate Publishing, Ltd.

Agustín, Laura María. 2005. "Review of the Politics of Prostitution by Joyce Outshoorn." *Labour / Le Travail* 55 (April): 313–15.

Agustin, Laura Maria. 2007. *Sex at the Margins: Migration, Labour Markets and the Rescue Industry*. London: Zed Books.

Alesina, Alberto, and Francesco Giavazzi. 2008. *The Future of Europe: Reform or Decline*. The MIT Press.

Allen, Ann Taylor. 2005. *Feminism and Motherhood in Western Europe, 1890–1970: The Maternal Dilemma*. London: Palgrave Macmillan.

Anderson, Benedict. 1983. *Imagined Communities*. London: Verso Editions.

Bäckman, Johan. 1999. *"The Wolf Has a Hundred Paths": The Organised Crime of St. Petersburg in the Framework of the Russian Culture of Criminal Justice*. Helsinki: Oikeuspolittinen Tutkimuslaitos.

Balibar, Etienne. 2003. *We, the People of Europe? Reflections on Transnational Citizenship*. Princeton, NJ: Princeton University Press.

Barton, Bernadette. 2002. "Dancing on the Möbius Strip Challenging the Sex War Paradigm." *Gender & Society* 16 (5): 585–602.

BBC News. 2003. "Anger over Greek Olympic Brothels." Manninen, Mari. 2003. "Sweden Fights Prostitution at Home and Abroad." *Helsingin Sanomat International Edition*. UK Reuters. 2003. "Sex Row Is a Storm in a Teacup Says Athens Mayor."

Bech, Ulrich. 1999. "Beyond the Nation State." *New Statesman*, no. 6 December.

Beisel, Nicola. 1997. *Imperiled Innocents: Anthony Comstock and Family Reproduction in Victorian America*. Princeton, NJ: Princeton University Press.

Bellier, Irène. 2000. "A Europeanized Elite? An Anthropology of European Commission Officials." *Yearbook of European Studies* 14: 135–56.

Berezin, Mabel. 2009. *Illiberal Politics in Neoliberal Times: Culture, Security and Populism in the New Europe*. 1st ed. Cambridge University Press.

Berezin, Mabel, and Martin Schain. 2004. *Europe Without Borders: Remapping Territory, Citizenship, and Identity in a Transnational Age*. Baltimore, MD: Johns Hopkins University Press.

Bergman, Solveig. 2002. *The Politics of Feminism: Autonomous Feminist Movements in Finland and West Germany from the 1960s to the 1980s*. Åbo, Finland: Åbo Akademi University Press.

Berlant, Lauren, and Michael Warner. 1998. "Sex in Public." *Critical Inquiry* 24 (2): 547–66.

Biaudet, Eva. 1999. "Opening Address by the Minister of Social Affairs and Health." In *Recommendations of the E.U. Expert Meeting on Violence Against Women*. Reports of the Ministry of Social Affairs and Health. Jyväskylä, Finland: Finnish Ministry of Social Affairs and Health.

Biaudet, Eva. 2002. "Summing up: International Co-Operation to Combat All Aspects of Trafficking in Women: The Outcome of the Campaign." In *Third Joint Seminar of the Nordic and Baltic Countries against Trafficking in Women*. Riga.

Biaudet, Eva. 2007. "Opening Address." In *Vienna: Organization for Security and Co-operation in Europe*. http://www.osce.org.

Billig, Michael. 1995. *Banal Nationalism*. New York: Sage Publications.

BMFSFJ. 2007. *Report by the Federal Government on the Impact of the Act Regulating the Legal Situation of Prostitutes*. Berlin: Federal Ministry for Family Affairs, Senior Citizens, Women and Youth.

Bourdieu, Pierre. 1990. *The Logic of Practice*. Stanford, CA: Stanford University Press.

Bourdieu, Pierre, and Loïc J. D. Wacquant. 1992. *An Invitation to Reflexive Sociology*. Chicago: University of Chicago Press.

Brants, Chrisje. 1998. "The Fine Art of Regulated Tolerance: Prostitution in Amsterdam." *Journal of Law and Society* 25 (4): 621–35.

Brents, Barbara G., Crystal A. Jackson, and Kathryn Hausbeck. 2009. *The State of Sex: Tourism, Sex and Sin in the New American Heartland*. New York: Routledge.

Brooks, Clem, and Jeff Manza. 2007. *Why Welfare States Persist: The Importance of Public Opinion in Democracies*. Chicago: University of Chicago Press.

Brubaker, Rogers. 1992. *Citizenship and Nationhood in France and Germany*. Harvard University Press.

Brussa, Licia. 2002. "Community Based Experience in Western Europe in Support of Trafficked Women." In *European Conference on Preventing and Combating Trafficking in Human Beings—A Global Challenge for the 21st Century*. Brussels: EU/IOM.

Brussa, Licia. 2004. "Migrant Sex Workers in Europe: The Experience of TAMPEP (Transnational AIDS/STI Prevention among Migrant Prostitutes in Europe)." *International Conference on AIDS* 15: 11–16.

Brussa, Licia, and Pia Covre. 2001. "A Brief History of TAMPEP." In *Services in the Window: A Manual for Interventions in the World of Migrant Prostitution*, 7. Trieste: Asterios Editore for the European Commission.

Burawoy, Michael. 2004. "Public Sociologies: Contradictions, Dilemmas, and Possibilities." *Social Forces* 82 (4): 1603–18.

Bureau NRM. 2002. *Trafficking in Human Beings; First Report of the Dutch National Rapporteur*. The Hague: Bureau of the Dutch National Rapporteur on Trafficking in Human Beings. http://www.dutchrapporteur.nl.

Burgsmüller, Claudia. 1998. "Necessity for and Limitations of Cooperation with Criminal Investigation Authorities and Specialized Counseling Centers from the Perspective of the Joint Plaintiff Counsel." In *European Strategies to Prevent and Combat Trafficking in Women*, 182–203. Berlin: Senatsverwaltung für Arbeit, Berufliche Bildung und Frauen.

Buruma, Ybo. 2007. "Dutch Tolerance: On Drugs, Prostitution, and Euthanasia." *Crime and Justice* 35 (1): 73–113.

Campbell, John L., and Ove K. Pedersen. *The National Origins of Policy Ideas: Knowledge Regimes in the United States, France, Germany, and Denmark.* Princeton, NJ: Princeton University Press, 2014.

Canaday, Margot. 2009. *The Straight State: Sexuality and Citizenship in Twentieth-Century America.* Princeton, NJ: Princeton University Press.

Carroll, Patrick. 2006. *Science, Culture, and Modern State Formation.* Berkeley: University of California.

Carruthers, Bruce G. and Laura Ariovich. 2004. "The Sociology of Property Rights," *Annual Review of Sociology* 30: 23–46.

Castells, Manuel. 1996. *The Rise of the Network Society.* The Information Age: Economy, Society and Culture Vol. I. New York: Blackwell Publishers.

Castells, Manuel. 1997. *The Power of Identity.* The Information Age: Economy, Society and Culture, Vol. II. New York: Blackwell Publishers.

Cavan, Sherri. 1966. *Liquor License: An Ethnography of Bar Behavior.* Chicago: Aldine.

CBS News. 2006. "Vatican Laments World Cup Prostitution." Jun. 8.

Chancer, Lynn Sharon. 1993. "Prostitution, Feminist Theory, and Ambivalence: Notes from the Sociological Underground." *Social Text* 37 (1): 143–71.

Chapkis, Wendy. 1997. *Live Sex Acts.* New York: Routledge.

Chapkis, Wendy. 2003. "Trafficking, Migration and the Law: Protecting Innocents, Punishing Immigrants." *Gender and Society* 17 (6): 923–37.

Chun, Jennifer Jihye. 2011. *Organizing at the Margins: The Symbolic Politics of Labor in South Korea and the United States.* ILR Press.

Claude, Kajsa. 2010. *Targeting the Sex Buyer: The Swedish Example: Stopping Prostitution and Trafficking Where It All Begins.* Swedish Institute.

Communication and Political Research Society, and Greek Helsinki Monitor. 2006. *Sex Workers Rights in Greece.* http://cm.greekhelsinki.gr.

Corbin, Alain. 1990. *Women for Hire: Prostitution and Sexuality in France after 1850.* Cambridge, MA: Harvard University Press.

Coser, Rose Laub. 1987. "Review of the Flight from Ambiguity by Donald N. Levine." *Contemporary Sociology* 16 (2): 254–56. doi:10.2307/2070752.

Cott, Nancy. 2002. *Public Vows: A History of Marriage and the Nation.* Cambridge, MA: Harvard University Press.

Cox, R. H. 2000. "Liberalising Trends in Welfare Reform: Inside the Dutch Miracle." *Policy & Politics* 28 (1): 19–31.

Daalder, A. L. 2007. *Prostitution in the Netherlands Since the Lifting of the Brothel Ban.* The Hague: Wetenschappelijk Onderzoeken Documentatiecentrum.

Daley, Suzanne. 2001. "New Rights for Dutch Prostitutes, but No Gain." *New York Times.*

Daly, Mary. 2011. "What Adult Worker Model?: A Critical Look at Recent Social Policy Reform in Europe from a Gender and Family Perspective." *Social Politics: International Studies in Gender, State and Society* 18 (1): 1–23.

Dausend, Peter. 2001. "Prostituierte Im Bundestag—Vorerst Nur Als Zuschauer."
Welt Online, May 12. http://www.welt.de.

Davidson, Julia O'Connell. 2002. "The Rights and Wrongs of Prostitution." *Hypatia*
17 (2): 84–98.

Davidson, Julia O'Connell. 2010. "New Slavery, Old Binaries: Human Trafficking
and the Borders of 'Freedom.'" *Global Networks* 10 (2): 244–61.

Deering, Kathleen, and Kate Shannon. 2012. "Fears of an Influx of Sex Workers to
Major Sporting Events Are Unfounded." *British Medical Journal* 345, p. e5845.

Derné, Steve. 2005. "The (Limited) Effect of Cultural Globalization in India:
Implications for Culture Theory." *Poetics*, 33 (1): 33–47.

Dettmeijer-Vermeulen, C. E. 2010. "Foreword." In *Trafficking in Human Beings:
Ten Years of Independent Monitoring*, 7–8. 2010: Bureau of the Dutch National
Rapporteur. http://www.bnrm.nl.

Dettmeijer-Vermeulen, Corinne. 2010. "Introduction." In *The Hague: National
Rapporteur on Trafficking in Human Beings and Sexual Violence against Children*.
http://www.dutchrapporteur.nl.

Dettmeijer-Vermeulen, Corinne. 2012a. "At the Occasion of Conference 'Putting
Rantsev into Practice.'" In *Amsterdam: National Rapporteur on Trafficking in
Human Beings and Sexual Violence against Children*. http://www.dutchrappor
teur.nl.

Dettmeijer-Vermeulen, Corinne. 2012b. "Press Conference." In *Sofia, Bulgaria:
National Rapporteur on Trafficking in Human Beings and Sexual Violence against
Children*. http://www.dutchrapporteur.nl.

De Vries, Petra. 2008. "Josephine Butler and the Making of Feminism: International Abolitionism in the Netherlands (1870–1914)." *Women's History Review*
17 (2): 257–77.

dé Weekkrant Amsterdam. 2010. "Extra Geld Voor de Zorg Voor Prostituees." *Dé
Weekkrant*. October 19. http://www.deweekkrant.nl/.

DG for Freedom, Security and Justice. 2007. *The Daphne Experience 1997–2003:
Europe Against Violence Towards Children and Women*. Luxembourg City:
European Commission.

Díez Medrano, Juan. 2003. *Framing Europe: Attitudes to European Integration in
Germany, Spain, and the United Kingdom*. Princeton, NJ: Princeton University Press.

Dobbin, Frank. 1997. *Forging Industrial Policy: The United States, Britain, and
France in the Railway Age*. New York: Cambridge University Press.

Dodillet, Susanne. 2004. "Cultural Clash on Prostitution: Debates on Prostitution
in Germany and Sweden in the 1990s." In *First Global Conference: Critical Issues
in Sexuality, Salzburg, Austria, October*. http://www.inter-disciplinary.net/ci/
transformations/sexualities/s1/Dodillet%20paper.pdf.

Doezema, Jo. 2010. *Sex Slaves and Discourse Masters: The Construction of Trafficking*. London: Zed Books.

Donovan, Brian. 2006. *White Slave Crusades: Race, Gender and Anti-Vice Activism,
1887–1917*. Urbana: University of Illinois Press.

Duggan, Lisa, and Nan D. Hunter. 1995. *Sex Wars: Sexual Dissent and Political Culture*. London: Routledge.

DW. 2005. "Scoring in the Soccer Love Shack." *Deutsche Welle*.

Ekberg, Gunilla. 2004. "The Swedish Law That Prohibits the Purchase of Sexual Services." *Violence Against Women* 10 (10): 1187–1218.

Elias, Norbert. 1939. *The Civilizing Process: The History of Manners.* Oxford: Blackwell.

Elias, Norbert. 1982. *The Civilizing Process: State Formation and Civilization.* Oxford: Blackwell.

Ellingsaeter, Anne Lise, and Arnlaug Leira. 2006. *Politicising Parenthood in Scandinavia: Gender Relations in the Welfare State.* Bristol, UK: The Policy Press.

Embassy of Greece. 2003.*Athens Municipality Denies Increase in the Number of Brothels.* Washington, DC: Press Office.

Esping-Andersen, Gøsta. 1990. *The Three Worlds of Welfare Capitalism.* Princeton, NJ: Princeton University Press.

Esping-Andersen, Gøsta. 2009. *Incomplete Revolution: Adapting Welfare States to Women's New Roles.* Cambridge, UK: Polity.

E. U. Network of Independent Experts in Fundamental Rights. 2003. *Report on the Situation of Fundamental Rights in the European Union and Its Member States in 2002.* Brussels: European Commission, Unit A5 of DG Justice and Home Affairs.

Evans, David T. 1993. *Sexual Citizenship: The Material Construction of Sexualities.* New York: Routledge.

Evans, Richard J. 1976. "Prostitution, State and Society in Imperial Germany." *Past and Present* 70: 106–29.

Everett, Jana Matson. 2009. "Governance Reforms and Rural Women in India: What Types of Women Citizens Are Produced by the Will to Empower?" *Social Politics: International Studies in Gender, State and Society* 16 (2): 279–302.

Ewick, Patricia, and Susan S. Silbey. 1998. *The Common Place of Law: Stories from Everyday Life.* University of Chicago: Press.

Favell, Adrian. 2011. *Eurostars and Eurocities: Free Movement and Mobility in an Integrating Europe.* Hoboken, NJ: John Wiley & Sons.

Ferguson, Ann. 1984. "Sex War: The Debate between Radical and Libertarian Feminists." *Signs,* 106–12.

Ferree, Myra Marx. 1995a. "Making Equality: The Women's Affairs Offices in the Federal Republic of Germany." *Comparative State Feminism,* 95–113.

Ferree, Myra Marx. 1995b. "Patriarchies and Feminisms: The Two Women's Movements of Post-Unification Germany." *Social Politics: International Studies in Gender, State and Society* 2 (1): 10–24.

Ferree, Myra Marx, William A. Gamson, Jürgen Gerhards, and Dieter Rucht. 2002a. *Shaping Abortion Discourse: Democracy and the Public Sphere in Germany and the United States.* New York: Cambridge University Press.

Ferree, Myra Marx, William A. Gamson, Jurgen Gerhards, and Dieter Rucht. 2002b. "Abortion Talk in Germany and the United States: Why Rights Explanations Are Wrong." *Contexts* 1 (2): 27–34.

Fischer, Claude S. 2010. *Made in America: A Social History of American Culture and Character.* Chicago: University of Chicago Press.

Fleckenstein, Timo. 2011. "The Politics of Ideas in Welfare State Transformation: Christian Democracy and the Reform of Family Policy in Germany." *Social Politics: International Studies in Gender, State and Society* 18 (4): 543–71.

Fligstein, Neil. 2008. *Euroclash: The EU, European Identity, and the Future of Europe.* New York: Oxford University Press.

Fligstein, Neil, and Doug McAdam. 2012. *A Theory of Fields.* Oxford University Press.

Fligstein, Neil, and Frederic Merand. 2002. "Globalization or Europeanization? Evidence on the European Economy since 1980." *Acta Sociologica* 45 (1): 7–22.

Fouad, Patric. 2004. *Frauenzimmer: Brothels in Germany.* Heidelberg: Kehrer Verlag.

Foucault, Michel. 1977. *Discipline and Punish: The Birth of the Prison.* New York: Pantheon.

Foucault, Michel. 1978. *The History of Sexuality, Volume I.* New York: Vintage Books.

Foucault, Michel. 2000. "Governmentality." In *Power: Essential Works of Foucault 1954–1984*, 201–22. New York: The New Press.

Frank, David John, Bayliss J. Camp, and Steven A. Boutcher. 2010. "Worldwide Trends in the Criminal Regulation of Sex, 1945 to 2005." *American Sociological Review* 75 (6): 867–93.

Frankfurter Allgemeine Zeitung. 1995. "Tod Im Luxusbordell: Keine Tat Der Russen-Mafia." Apr. 23.

Frankfurter Allgemeine Zeitung. 2000. "Toedliche Schuesse Aus Verletzter Ehre." Dec. 31.

Fraser, Nancy, and Linda Gordon. 1998. "Contract versus Charity: Why Is There No Social Citizenship in the United States?" In *The Citizenship Debates: A Reader*, 113–27. Minneapolis: University of Minnesota Press.

Frei, Nikolaus. 2001. "Polizei Zerschlägt Bordell-Kartell." *Welt Online*, July 14. http://www.welt.de.

Freund, Michaela. 2001. "Ein Mädchen Kostet Einen Mercedes." *Welt Online*, October 21. http://www.welt.de.

Friedmann, John, and Ute Angelika Lehrer. 1997. "Urban Policy Responses to Foreign In-Migration: The Case of Frankfurt-Am-Main." *Journal of the American Planning Association* 63 (1): 61–78.

Gellner, Ernest. 1983. *Nations and Nationalism.* Ithaca, NY: Cornell University Press.

Giddens, Anthony. 1991. *Modernity and Self Identity.* Oxford: Polity Press.

Goodey, Jo. 2003. "Migration, Crime and Victimhood: Responses to Sex Trafficking in the EU." *Punishment and Society* 5 (4): 415–31.

Gordon, Linda. 1990. *Women, the State, and Welfare.* Madison: University of Wisconsin Press.

Gorski, Philip S. 2003. *The Disciplinary Revolution: Calvinism and the Rise of the State in Early Modern Europe.* University of Chicago Press.

Gouldner, Alvin. 1954. *Patterns of Industrial Bureaucracy.* New York: The Free Press.

Gouldner, Alvin. 1968. "The Sociologist as Partisan: Sociology and the Welfare State." *The American Sociologist* 3 (1): 103–16.

Grandell, Tommy. 2003. "Northern Ministers Criticize Plans for Olympics Brothels." *Associated Press.* Jul. 23.

Grittner, Frederick K. 1990. *White Slavery: Myth, Ideology, and American Law.* New York: Garland Publishing.

Gusfield, Joseph R. 1963. *Symbolic Crusade: Status Politics and the American Temperance Movement.* Urbana: University of Illinois Press.

Gusfield, Joseph R. 1981. *The Culture of Public Problems: Drinking, Driving, and the Symbolic Order*. Chicago: University of Chicago Press.

Gusfield, Joseph R. 1996. *Contested Meanings: The Construction of Alcohol Problems*. Madison: University of Wisconsin Press.

Haavio-Mannila, Eliina, ed. et. al. 1985. *Unfinished Democracy: Women in Nordic Politics*. Oxford: Pergamon Press.

Häkkinen, Antti. 1995. *Rahasta—Vaan Ei Rakkaudesta: Prostituutio Helsingissä 1867–1939 (For Money—But Not for Love: Prostitution in Helsinki)*. Helsinki: Kustannusosakeyhtiö Otava.

Halonen, Tarja. 2003. "Address by the President of the Republic of Finland." In *Stop Child Trafficking: Modern Day Slavery*. Helsinki: United States Embassy to Finland.

Ham, Julie. 2011. *What's the Cost of a Rumour? A Guide to Sorting Out the Myths and the Facts about Sporting Events and Trafficking*. Global Alliance against Traffic in Women (GAATW).

Haney, Lynne. 1996. "Homeboys, Babies, Men in Suits: The State and the Reproduction of Male Dominance." *American Sociological Review* 61 (5): 759.

Haney, Lynne A. 1998. "Engendering the Welfare State. A Review Article." *Comparative Studies in Society and History* 40 (4): 748–67.

Hekma, Gert. 2003. "The Decline of Sexual Radicalism in the Netherlands." In *The Present of Radical Sexual Politics*. Amsterdam: Mosse Stichtung.

Hekma, Gert. 2005. "How Libertine Is the Netherlands?" In *Regulating Sex: The Politics of Intimacy and Identity*, 209–23. New York: Routledge.

Held, David. 1999. *Global Transformations: Politics Economics and Culture*. Stanford, CA: Stanford University Press.

Henley, Jon. 2002. "Defending Their Honorarium." *The Guardian*. November 6.

Hennig, Jana, Sarah Craggs, Frank Laczko, and Fred Larsson. 2007. "Trafficking in Human Beings and the 2006 World Cup in Germany." http://www.popline.org/node/200308.

Hernes, Helga Maria. 1987a. "The Welfare State Citizenship of Scandinavian Women." In *Welfare State and Woman Power: Essays in State Feminism*, 135–64. Oslo: Norwegian University Press.

Hernes, Helga Maria. 1987b. *Welfare State and Woman Power: Essays in State Feminism*. Oslo: Norwegian University Press.

Hertz, Rosanna, and Jonathan B. Imber. 1995. *Studying Elites Using Qualitative Methods*. Thousand Oaks, CA: SAGE Publications.

Herzfeld, Michael. 2005. *Cultural Intimacy: Social Poetics in the Nation-State*, 2nd ed. New York: Routledge.

Hix, Simon. 2008. *What's Wrong with the European Union and How to Fix It*. Malden, MA: Polity.

Hobson, Barbara Meil. 1988. *Uneasy Virtue: The Politics of Prostitution and the American Reform Tradition*. New York: Basic Books.

Holm, Carsten. 2000. "Der Triumph Der 'Puffmutti.'" *Der Spiegel*. Dec. 11, pp. 132–34.

Houkes, Annemarie, and Maartje Janse. 2005. "Foreign Examples as Eye Openers and Justification: The Transfer of the Anti-Corn Law League and the Anti-Prostitution Movement to the Netherlands." *European Review of History: Revue Européenne D'histoire* 12 (2): 321–44.

HS. 2002. "Jukinen prostitutuutio, juominen ja virtsaaminen rangaistaviksi," Mar. 14. http://www.hs.fi, Accessed Jan 11, 2009.

HSIE. 2000. "Campaign against Sexual Abuse of Children Begins along Eastern Border," Apr. 5. http://www.helsinki-hs.net. Accessed Jan 12, 2009.

HSIE. 2000. "Street Prostitution Clearly Disturbed Helsinki Residents before Clean-Up." *Helsingin Sanomat International Edition*, Nov. 1. http://www.hel sinki-hs.net, Accessed Jan. 12, 2004.

See HSIE. 2000. "Directorate of Immigration prepares for the new Aliens Act," Jul. 6. http://www.helsinki-hs.net. Accessed Jan. 12, 2009.

HSIE. 2000. "Interior Ministry to crack down on public drinking," Nov. 15.

HSIE. 2003. "Finns Deny Swedish Claim of Widespread Prostitution on Passenger Ferries." May 12. http://www.helsinki-hs.net. Accessed Jan. 12, 2009.

HSIE. 2003. "U.S. Report on Human Trafficking Shows Finland in a Poor Light." June 13. http://www.helsinki-hs.net. Accessed Jan 12, 2009.

HSIE. 2006. "Amended prostitution bill likely to pass." June 11. http://www.helsin ginsanomat.fi/english. Accessed Jan 12, 2009.

Huisman, Wim, and Edward R. Kleemans. 2014. "The Challenges of Fighting Sex Trafficking in the Legalized Prostitution Market of the Netherlands." *Crime, Law and Social Change* 61 (2): 215–28.

Hull, Isabel V. 1996. *Sexuality, State and Civil Society in Germany, 1700–1815.* Ithaca, NY: Cornell University Press.

Irigaray, Luce. 1985. *This Sex Which Is Not One*. Ithaca, NY: Cornell University Press.

Irvine, Janice M. 2014. "Is Sexuality Research 'Dirty Work'? Institutionalized Stigma in the Production of Sexual Knowledge." *Sexualities* 17 (5–6): 632–56.

Janowitz, Morris. 1976. *Social Control of the Welfare State*. New York: Elsevier.

Janowitz, Morris. 1991. "The Concept of Social Control." In *On Social Organization and Social Control*, 73–85. University of Chicago Press.

Järvinen, Margaretha. 1993. "Prostitution in Helsinki: A Disappearing Social Problem?" *Journal of the History of Sexuality* 3 (4): 608–30.

Jasper, James M. 1990. *Energy and the State: Nuclear Politics in the United States, Sweden and France*. Princeton, NJ: Princeton University Press.

Jenness, Valerie. 1993. *Making It Work: The Prostitute's Rights Movement in Perspective*. New York: Aldine de Gruyter.

Kangaspuro, Markku. 2000. *Neuvosto-Karjalan Taistelu Itsehallinnosta. Nationalismi Ja Suomalaiset Punaiset Neuvostoliiton Vallankäytössä 1920–1939*. Bibliotheca Historica. Helsinki: Suomalaisen Kirjallisuuden Seura.

Kaufmann, Franz-Xaver. 2012. *Variations of the Welfare State: Great Britain, Sweden, France and Germany Between Capitalism and Socialism*. 2013 edition. New York: Springer.

Keck, Margaret E., and Kathryn Sikkink. 1998. *Activists Beyond Borders*. Ithaca, NY: Cornell University Press.

Keeler, Laura. 1999. *Recommendations of the E.U. Expert Meeting on Violence against Women*. Jyväskylä, Finland: Finnish Ministry of Social Affairs and Health.

Keeler, Laura, and Marjut Jyrkinen. 1999. *Who's Buying? The Clients of Prostitution*. Helsinki: Council for Equality: Ministry of Affairs and Health.

Keire, Mara L. 2001. "The Vice Trust: A Reinterpretation of the White Slavery Scare in the United States, 1907–1917." *Journal of Social History* 35 (1): 5–41.

Kennedy, James. 2000. "The Moral State: How Much to the American and the Dutch Differ?" In *Regulating Morality: A Comparison of the Role of the State in Mastering the Mores in the Netherlands and the United States*, 9–22. Antwerp: Maklu.

Kennedy, James C. 2005. "Recent Dutch Religious History and the Limits of Secularization." In *The Dutch and Their Gods: Secularization and Transformation of Religion in the Netherlands since 1950*, Hilversum, Netherlands: Uitgeverij Verloren, pp. 27–42.

Klee, Stephanie. 2001. "Comments from Hydra." In *Hearing on Draft Act to Improve the Legal and Social Situation of Prostitutes in Germany*. Berlin: Bundestag Committee for Family, Elderly, Women and Youth Affairs.

Knocke, Wuokko. 2000. "Migrant and Ethnic Minority Women: The Effects of Gender-Neutral Legislation in the European Union." In *Gender and Citizenship in Transition:*, 139–55. New York: Routledge.

Knox, Noelle. 2003. "In Belgium, Brothels Are Big Business." *USA Today*, Nov. 4.

KOK. 2004. "Bundesweiter Koordinierungskreis Gegen Frauenhandel Und Gewalt an Frauen Im Migrationskreis e.V." January 6. http://www.kok-potsdam.de/.

Korppi-Tommola, Aura. 2001. *Tahdolla Ja Tunteella Tasa-Arvoa: Naisjärjestöjen Keskusliitto 1911–2001 (Equality Through Will and Emotions: The National Council of Women of Finland)*. Jyväskylä: Gummerus Kirjapaino.

Koser, Khalid. 2000. "Asylum Policies, Trafficking and Vulnerability." *International Migration*, no. 1: 90–111.

Krabbendam, Hans, and Hans-Martien ten Napel. 2000. *Regulating Morality: A Comparison of the Role of the State in Mastering the Mores in the Netherlands and the United States*. Antwerp: Maklu.

Kulick, Don. 2005. "Four Hundred Thousand Swedish Perverts." *GLQ: A Journal of Lesbian and Gay Studies* 11 (2): 205–35.

Kulick, Don, and Margaret Willson. 1995. *Taboo: Sex, Identity, and Erotic Subjectivity in Anthropological Fieldwork*. New York: Routledge.

Lahdenmäki, Ari, and Riku Rantala. 2001. "Russian Mafia Ships Prostitutes to Helsinki." *Helsingin Sanomat International Edition*. Apr. 5. http://www.helsinki-hs .net. Accessed Jan 12, 2009.

Laitin, David D. 1992. *Language Repertoires and State Construction in Africa*. New York: Cambridge University Press.

Lamont, Michele. 1994. *Money, Morals, and Manners: The Culture of the French and the American Upper-Middle Class*. Chicago: University of Chicago Press.

Laqueur, Walter. 2009. *The Last Days of Europe: Epitaph for an Old Continent*. New York: St. Martin's Griffin.

Laqueur, Walter. 2012. *After the Fall: The End of the European Dream and the Decline of a Continent*. New York: Thomas Dunne Books.

Lechner, Frank J. 2007. *The Netherlands: Globalization and National Identity*. New York: Routledge.

Leonard, Mark. 2006. *Why Europe Will Run the 21st Century*. annotated edition. PublicAffairs.

Lévi-Strauss, Claude. 1971. *The Elementary Structures of Kinship*. New York: Beacon Press.

Lewis, Jane. 2002. *Gender and Welfare State Change*. European Societies 4 (4): 331–57.

Lieber, Robert J., and Ruth E. Weisberg. 2002. "Globalization, Culture, and Identities in Crisis." *International Journal of Politics, Culture, and Society* 16 (2): 273–96.

Lim, Lin Lean. 1998. *The Sex Sector: The Economic and Social Bases of Prostitution in Southeast Asia*. Geneva: International Labor Organization.

Limoncelli, Stephanie. 2010. *The Politics of Trafficking: The First International Movement to Combat the Sexual Exploitation of Women*. Stanford, CA: Stanford University Press.

Lipsky, Michael. 1980. *Street-Level Bureaucracy: Dilemmas of the Individual in Public Services*. New York: Russell Sage.

Lister, Ruth. 2009. "A Nordic Nirvana?: Gender, Citizenship, and Social Justice in the Nordic Welfare States." *Social Politics: International Studies in Gender, State and Society* 16 (2): 242–78.

Lorber, Judith. 1994. *Paradoxes of Gender*. New Haven, CT: Yale University Press.

Loveman, Mara. 2005. "The Modern State and the Primitive Accumulation of Symbolic Power." *American Journal of Sociology* 110 (6): 1651–83.

Ludwig, Uta. 1998. "Experience Gathered from Cooperation with Government Authorities." In *European Strategies to Prevent and Combat Trafficking in Women*, 68–89. Berlin: Senatsverwaltung für Arbeit, Berufliche Bildung und Frauen.

Luker, Kristin. 1998. "Sex, Social Hygiene, and the State: The Double-Edged Sword of Social Reform." *Theory and Society* 27 (5): 601–34.

MacKinnon, Catherine A. 1989. *Toward a Feminist Theory of the State*. Cambridge, MA: Harvard University Press.

MacKinnon, Catherine A. 2011. "Trafficking, Prostitution, and Inequality." *Harvard Civil Rights Civil Liberties Law Review* 46: 271.

Majoor, Mariska. 2002. *When Sex Becomes Work*. Amsterdam: Prostitution Information Center.

Mann, Michael. 1990. *The Rise and Decline of the Nation State*. Oxford: Basil Blackwell.

Marquand, David. 2011. *The End of the West: The Once and Future Europe*. Princeton, NJ: Princeton University Press.

Marshall, T. H. 1950. *Citizenship and Social Class, and Other Essays*. New York: Cambridge University Press.

Mattson, Greggor. 2014. "Nation-State Science: Lappology and Sweden's Ethnoracial Purity." *Comparative Studies in Society and History* 56 (2): 320–50.

McBride, Dorothy E., and Amy G. Mazur. 2012. *The Politics of State Feminism: Innovation in Comparative Research*. Philadelphia, PA: Temple University Press.

Mellenthin, Ira von, and Wolf von Hirschheydt. 2001. "Milde Strafen Im Hell's-Angels-Prozess Verhängt." *Welt Online*, October 5. http://www.welt.de.

Mérand, Frédéric. 2004. "Soldiers and Diplomats: The Institutionalization of the European Security and Defense Policy, 1989–2003." University of California, Berkeley, Department of Sociology.

Meyer, John W. 1987. "The World Polity and the Authority of the Nation-State." In *Institutional Structure*. Malden, MA: Sage.

Mielke, Michael. 2000. "Wie Das Café 'Pssst!' Zum Politikum Wurde." *Welt Online*, December 1. http://www.welt.de.

Migdal, Joel S. 2001. *State in Society: Studying How States and Societies Transform and Constitute One Another*. New York: Cambridge University Press.

Ministry of General Affairs. 2014. "Prostitution." *Government of the Netherlands*. http://www.government.nl/issues/prostitution.

Mintrom, Michael. 1997. "Policy Entrepreneurs and the Diffusion of Innovation." *American Journal of Political Science*, 41 (3): 738–70.

Mitchell, Timothy. 1991. "The Limits of the State: Beyond Statist Approaches and Their Critics." *The American Political Science Review* 85 (1): 77–96.

Mitchell, Timothy. 1999. "Society, Economy, and the State Effect." In *State/Culture*, edited by George Steinmetz, 76–97. Ithaca, NY: Cornell University Press.

Mohr, John W., and Vincent Duquenne. 1997. "The Duality of Culture and Practice: Poverty Relief in New York City, 1888–1917." *Theory and Society* 26 (2/3): 305–56.

Mosse, George L. 1985. *Nationalism and Sexuality*. New York: Howard Fertig.

Mouffe, Chantal. 1995. "Feminism, Citizenship, and Radical Democratic Politics." *Social Postmodernism: Beyond Identity Politics*, 315–31.

Mudge, Stephanie. 2007. "Precarious Progressivism: The Struggle over the Social in the Neoliberal Era." University of California, Berkeley, Department of Sociology.

Murphy, Clare. 2003. "Making Sex Pay." *BBC News*.

Nader, Laura. 1974. "Up the Anthropologist—Perspectives Gained from Studying Up." In *Reinventing Anthropology*. New York: Vintage Press.

Näre, Sari. 1997. "Pornografiakeskustelusta Bordellikeskusteluun. Kaupallinen Seksi Vietti-Ja Rakkauseetoksen Taistelukenttänä (From Pornography Debate to Brothel Discussion. The Battlefield of Commercial Sex Drive and Love Ethics." In *Sex, Snack'n Pop*. Helsinki: Titanik Galleri.

Näre, Sari. 1999. "Libertarianism in the Discourse of Sex-Bar Customers." In *Who's Buying? The Clients of Prostitution*, 29–33. Helsinki: Council for Equality: Ministry of Affairs and Health.

NBTC. 2008. "Cityguide: Quaint Quarters, Red Light District." *The Amsterdam Site*. February 22.

Neilsen, Ruth. 1983. *Equality Legislation in a Comparative Perspective—Towards State Feminism*. Copenhagen: Women's Research Center in Social Science.

Nguyen, Katie. 2014. "Netherlands Leads Way in Battle Against Sex Slavery." *Pittsburgh Post-Gazette*.

O'Connor, Julia S. 1993. "Gender, Class and Citizenship in the Comparative Analysis of Welfare State Regimes: Theoretical and Methodological Issues." *British Journal of Sociology* 44 (3): 501–18.

Odem, Mary E. 1995. *Delinquent Daughters: Protecting and Policing Adolescent Female Sexuality in the United States, 1885–1920*. Chapel Hill: University of North Carolina Press.

Ohmae, Kenichi. 1994. *The Borderless World*. London: HarperCollins.

Oikeusministeriön työryhmämietintö. 2003. *Ihmiskauppa, Paritus Ja Prostituutio*. Helsinki: Ministry of Justice.

Ojala, Outi. 2002. "Address by Member of the Eduskunta." In *Seminar on Trafficking in Women as Modern Slave Trading*. Tallinn, Estonia.

O'Neil, Maggie. 1996. "Prostitution, Feminism and Critical Praxis: Professional Prostitute?" *Austrian Journal of Sociology* Winter, pp. 333–50

Ollikainen, Marjo. "Children in Viipuri Attest to Sex Trips by Finns." *Helsingin Sanomat International Edition*, 2001. http://www.helsinki-hs.net. Accessed Jan 12, 2009.

Orloff, Ann Shola. 1993. "Gender and the Social Rights of Citizenship." *American Sociological Review* 58: 303–28.

Orloff, Ann Shola. 2006. "From Maternalism to 'Employment for All.'" *The State after Statism*, Ed. Jonah D. Levy, pp. 230–68.

Orloff, Ann Shola, and Bruno Palier. 2009. "The Power of Gender Perspectives: Feminist Influence on Policy Paradigms, Social Science, and Social Politics." *Social Politics: International Studies in Gender, State and Society* 16 (4): 405–12.

Outshoorn, Joyce. 2001. "Debating Prostitution in Parliament: A Feminist Analysis." *European Journal of Women's Studies* 8 (4): 472–90.

Outshoorn, Joyce. 2004a. "Pragmatism in the Polder: Changing Prostitution Policy in the Netherlands." *Journal of Contemporary European Studies* 12 (2): 165–76.

Outshoorn, Joyce. 2004b. *The Politics of Prostitution: Women's Movements, Democratic States, and the Globalization of Sex Commerce*. Cambridge, UK: Cambridge University Press.

Pateman, Carole. 1988. *The Sexual Contract*. Cambridge, MA: Polity Press.

Paternotte, David, and Kelly Kollman. 2013. "Regulating Intimate Relationships in the European Polity: Same-Sex Unions and Policy Convergence." *Social Politics: International Studies in Gender, State and Society*, March.

Patterson, Tony. 2005. "Germany Backs Bigger Brothels to Fight World Cup Sex Explosion." *The Independent*, Dec. 9.

Penttinen, Elina. 2004. *Corporeal Globalization: Narratives of Subjectivity and Otherness in the Sexscapes of Globalization*. Tampere: Tampere Peace Research Institute.

Penttinen, Elina. 2008. Globalization, Prostitution and Sex Trafficking: Corporeal Politics. New York: Routledge.

Pheterson, Gail. 1993. "The Whore Stigma: Female Dishonor and Male Unworthiness." *Social Text* 37 (Winter): 39–64.

Pliley, Jessica R. 2014. *Policing Sexuality: The Mann Act and the Making of the FBI*. Cambridge, MA: Harvard University Press.

Plummer, Kenneth. 1995. *Telling Sexual Stories: Power, Change and Social Worlds*. New York: Routledge.

Povinelli, Elizabeth A. 1997. "Sex Acts and Sovereignty: Race and Sexuality in the Construction of the Australian Nation." In *The Gender Sexuality Reader: Culture, History, Political Economy*. New York: Routledge.

Radtke, Frank-Olaf. 2003. "Multiculturalism in Germany: Local Management of Immigrants' Social Inclusion." *International Journal on Multicultural Societies* 5 (1): 55–76.

Raymond, Janice G. 2001. *Guide to the New UN Trafficking Protocol*. North Amherst, MA: Coalition against Trafficking in Women.

Reid, T. R. 2005. *The United States of Europe: The New Superpower and the End of American Supremacy.* New York: Penguin.

Richter, Marlise, Stanley Luchters, Dudu Ndlovu, Marleen Temmerman, and Matthew F. Chersich. 2012. "Female Sex Work and International Sport Events—No Major Changes in Demand or Supply of Paid Sex during the 2010 Soccer World Cup: A Cross-Sectional Study." *BMC Public Health* 12 (1): 763.

Rifkin, Jeremy. 2005. *The European Dream: How Europe's Vision of the Future Is Quietly Eclipsing the American Dream.* New York: Tarcher.

Risse-Kappen, Thomas. 2010. *A Community of Europeans? Transnational Identities and Public Spheres.* Ithaca, NY: Cornell University Press.

RNW English Section. 2009. "FAQ—Prostitution in the Netherlands." *Radio Netherlands Worldwide.* September 18. http://www.rnw.nl.

Robertson, Roland. 2003. *Globalization: Social Theory and Global Culture.* New York: Taylor & Francis.

Rosen, Ruth. 1982. *The Lost Sisterhood: Prostitution in America, 1900–1918.* Baltimore, MD: The Johns Hopkins University Press.

Roy, Ananya. 2003. "Paradigms of Propertied Citizenship: Transnational Techniques of Analysis." *Urban Affairs Review* 38 (4): 463–91.

Rubin, Gayle. 2011. "Afterward," "Postscript" "Blood under the Bridge" and "Thinking Sex: Notes for a Radical Theory of the Politics of Sexuality." In *Deviations: A Gayle Rubin Reader,* 182–222. Durham, NC: Duke University Press.

Rubin, Gayle S. 1997. "Thinking Sex: Notes for a Radical Theory of the Politics of Sexuality." In *The Gender Sexuality Reader: Culture, History, Political Economy.* New York: Routledge.

Runder Tisch zur Prostitution in Frankfurt am Main. 2002. *Empfehlungen an Die Stadtverordnetenversammlung.* Frankfurt am Main.

Sanchez, Lisa E. 1997. "Boundaries of Legitimacy: Sex, Violence, Citizenship, and Community in a Local Sexual Economy." *Law & Social Inquiry* 22 (3): 543–80.

Sassen, Saskia. 1998. *Globalization and Its Discontents.* New York: New Press.

Sauer, Birgit. 2004. "Taxes, Rights and Regimentation: Discourses on Prostitution in Austria." *The Politics of Prostitution: Women's Movements, Democratic States and the Globalisation of Sex Commerce.*

Schaeffer-Grabiel, Felicity. 2010. "Sex Trafficking as the 'New Slave Trade'?" *Sexualities* 13 (2): 153–60.

Schaffer, Johan Karlsson. 2009. "Finland's Prostitution Law and the Hope of Nordic Unity | Nordic Prostitution Policy Reform." *Nordic Prostitution Policy Reform,* October 12. http://nppr.se/2009/10/12/.

Schalet, Amy T. 2011. *Not under My Roof: Parents, Teens, and the Culture of Sex.* Chicago: University of Chicago Press.

Schrag, Zachary M. 2010. *Ethical Imperialism: Institutional Review Boards and the Social Sciences, 1965–2009.* Baltimore, MD: Johns Hopkins University Press.

Schwalbe, M. L, and D. Mason-Schrock. 1996. "Identity Work as Group Process." *Advances in Group Processes* 13 (113): 47.

Schwartzer, Alice. 2000. "Der Große Unterschied." Cologne, Germany: Kiepenheuer & Witsch.

Schwarzer, Alice. 2013. *Prostitution—Ein deutscher Skandal!*. Köln: Kiepenheuer & Witsch GmbH.

Sciolino, Elaine. 2002. "Paris Journal: Streetwalking, en Masse, for Right to Tempt." *International Herald Tribune*, Nov. 6.

Scott, James C. 1998. *Seeing Like a State*. New Haven, CT: Yale University Press.

Sewell, William H. Jr. 1992. "A Theory of Structure: Duality, Agency, and Transformation." *American Journal of Sociology* 98 (1): 1–29.

Skilbrei, May-Len, and Charlotta Holmström. 2013. *Prostitution Policy in the Nordic Region: Ambiguous Sympathies*. Farnham, Surrey, GBR: Ashgate Publishing Group.

Skocpol, Theda. 1979. *States and Social Revolutions: A Comparative Analysis of France, Russia and China*. New York: Cambridge University Press.

Snow, D. A., and L. Anderson. 1987. "Identity Work among the Homeless: The Verbal Construction and Avowal of Personal Identities." *American Journal of Sociology*, 1336–71.

Soderlund, Gretchen. 2005. "Running from the Rescuers: New U.S. Crusades Against Sex Trafficking and the Rhetoric of Abolition." *NWSA Journal* 17 (3): 64–87.

Soderlund, Gretchen. 2013. *Sex Trafficking, Scandal, and the Transformation of Journalism, 1885–1917*. Chicago: University of Chicago Press.

Soysal, Yasemin Nuhoæglu. 1994. *Limits of Citizenship: Migrants and Postnational Membership in Europe*. Chicago: University of Chicago Press.

Stoler, Ann Laura. 2002. *Carnal Knowledge and Imperial Power*. Berkeley: University of California.

Sullivan, Barbara. 2010. "When (Some) Prostitution Is Legal: The Impact of Law Reform on Sex Work in Australia." *Journal of Law and Society* 37 (1): 85–104.

Sullivan, Barbara Ann. 1997. *The Politics of Sex: Prostitution and Pornography in Australia since 1945*. New York: Cambridge University Press.

Swidler, Ann. 1986. "Culture in Action: Symbols and Strategies." *American Sociological Review* 51: 273–86.

Swidler, Ann. 2001. *Talk of Love: How Culture Matters*. Chicago: University of Chicago Press.

Tani, Sirpa. 2001. "'That Kind of Girl in This Kind of Neighborhood . . .' The Potential and Problems of Street Prostitution Research." *City* 5 (3): 311–25.

Tani, Sirpa. 2002. "Whose Place Is This Space? Life in the Street Prostitution Area of Helsinki, Finland." *International Journal of Urban and Regional Research* 26 (2): 343–59.

Tasma, Eelco. 2010. *The Social Dialogue in the Netherlands*. Amsterdam: Dutch Trade Union Confederation (Federatie Nederlandse Vakbeweging). http://www.fnv.nl.

The Economist Global Agenda. 2003. "Sex for Sale, Legally." *The Economist*, Jul. 11

Thomas, George M., and John W. Meyer. 1984. "The Expansion of the State." *Annual Review of Sociology* 10: 461–82.

Thomas, W. I. 1923. *The Unadjusted Girl*. Boston: Little, Brown and Co.

Tilly, Charles. 1992. *Coercion, Capital and European States, AD 990–1990*. Oxford: Blackwell.

Torpey, John. 2000. *The Invention of the Passport*. New York: Cambridge University Press.

Tsing, Anna. 2002. "The Global Situation." *Cultural Anthropology* 15 (3): 327–60.

Vaisey, Stephen. 2009. "Motivation and Justification: A Dual-Process Model of Culture in Action." *American Journal of Sociology* 114 (6): 1675–1715.

Van de Pol, Lotte C. 2000. "The History of Policing Prostitution in Amsterdam." In *Regulating Morality: A Comparison of the Role of the State in Mastering the Mores in the Netherlands and the United States*, edited by Hans Krabbendam and Hans-Martien ten Napel, 97–112. Antwerp: Maklu.

Van Dongen, Menno. 2011. "Prostitutiewet: Bestuurders Te Naïef." *De Volkskrant*, March 1. http://http://www.volkskrant.nl.

Van Doorninck, Marieke, and Rosie Campbell. 2006. "'Zoning' Street Sex Work: The Way Forward?" In *Sex Work Now*, 62–90. Collompton, UK: Willan Publishing.

Van Drenth, Annemieke. 2002. "The City and the Self. The Case of Girls' Protection in the Netherlands around 1900." *Educational Review* 54 (2): 125–33.

Van Kersbergen, Kees. 1995. *Social Capitalism: A Study of Christian Democracy and the Welfare State*. New York: Routledge.

Van Seters, Paul. 2000. "Legal Moralism, Liberal Legalism, and the Tangled Web of Law and Morality." In *Regulating Morality: A Comparison of the Role of the State in Mastering the Mores in the Netherlands and the United States*, 23–34. Antwerp: Maklu.

Väyrynen, Raimo. 2002. "Illegal Immigration, Human Trafficking, and the Organized Crime." In *Poverty, International Migration and Asylum*. Helsinki: World Institute for Development Economics Research.

Vereinte Dienstleistungsgewerkschaft. 2003. *Arbeitsplatz Prostitution in Hamburg*. Hamburg, Germany: Verdi.

Von Galen, Margarete. 1996. "Prostitution and the Law in Germany." *Cardozo Women's Law Journal* 3: 349.

Wagenaar, Hendrik, Sietske Altink, and Amesberger, Helga. "Final Report of the International Comparative Study of Prostitution Policy: Austria and the Netherlands." The Hague: Platform 31, July 2013. http://www.platform31.nl.

Walkowitz, Judith R. 1983. "Male Vice and Female Virtue: Feminism and the Politics of Prostitution in Nineteenth-Century Britain." In *Powers of Desire: The Politics of Sexuality*. New York: Monthly Review Press.

Weber, Max, Hans Heinrich Gerth, and C. Wright Mills. 1946. "Science as a Vocation." In *From Max Weber: Essays in Sociology*. New York: Oxford University Press.

Weitzer, Ronald. 2005. "Flawed Theory and Method in Studies of Prostitution." *Violence Against Women* 11 (7): 934–49.

Weitzer, Ronald. 2007. "The Social Construction of Sex Trafficking: Ideology and Institutionalization of a Moral Crusade." *Politics Society* 35 (3): 447–75.

Weitzer, Ronald John. 2012. *Legalizing Prostitution: From Illicit Vice to Lawful Business*. New York University Press.

Wilson, Nicholas Hoover. 2011. "From Reflection to Refraction: State Administration in British India, circa 1770–1855." *American Journal of Sociology* 116 (5): 1437–77.

Woolf, Stuart. 1989. "Statistics and the Modern State." *Comparative Studies in Society and History* 31 (3): 588–604.

Wouters, Cas. 2004. *Sex and Manners: Female Emancipation in the West.* Thousand Oaks, CA: Sage.

Yuki, Masako. 2008. "The Women's Movement within Trade Unions in Germany." *Signs* 33 (3): 519–27.

Zukin, Sharon. 2012. "The Social Production of Urban Cultural Heritage: Identity and Ecosystem on an Amsterdam Shopping Street." *City, Culture and Society* 3 (4): 281–91.

Index

abjection, 25, 178
abolitionism, 10, 45, 57, 142, 151, 153, 174, 180
abortion, 16, 23, 99, 123, 126, 164
accession to the European Union, 32, 91
activism, 4–5, 34, 126, 140–141
addiction, 41, 47, 84, 120. *See also* alcohol abuse
administration, 6, 11, 34, 45, 70, 109–110, 119
advice, 35, 53, 71–72, 173
AGISRA (Frankfurt), 110, 120–121, 124
AIDS, 35, 42, 44, 89, 200–201. *See also* HIV
alcohol
abuse, 41, 73, 84
regulation, 73, 83–84, 95–96, 133, 140
see also addiction
Aliens Act (Finland), 9, 128, 136–138, 149, 210
Amann, Gregor, 107, 110, 112, 121–123
ambiguity, 13, 23, 74, 98, 169, 178, 190–191
Anderson, Benedict, 10, 195
antitrafficking, 30–31, 34, 37, 44, 50, 98, 170–172, 176, 189–190
anxieties. *See* globalization anxieties
Athens, 2–5, 30–31, 78, 172, 193, 197
Ausländerbehörde (German), 108, 113
Ausländergesetz (German), 118

Austria, 8, 30, 59, 63, 161, 198, 204
autonomous feminism, 126, 207.
See also feminism

Bahnhofsviertel (Frankfurt), 105, 107–108, 110, 112–113, 118–120, 122
Balkans, 171
battle of the sexes *see* gender relations
Belgium, 8–9, 20, 28, 49, 194, 201
benefits, 15–158, 162, 164, 174, 177, 180
Berlin, ix, 9, 20, 22, 98–9, 102–103, 125, 140, 177, 181, 197, 199, 206
Betrieb (German), 99, 101, 118, 161
Biaudet, Eva, 36–37, 56, 145–149, 152, 199–200, 203
Bik, Ruud, 72
Blaak, Metje, 68
BlinN, 43–45
Bolhaar, Martin, 55
Bonded Labor in the Netherlands. *See* BlinN
bordello. *See* brothel
border control, 44, 138, 179
borders, 2, 4, 12, 18, 29, 32, 36, 41–42, 49–50, 92–93, 158, 168
boundary, 16, 60, 95, 180, 185, 199
boundary work, 190, 199
Bourdieu, Pierre, 33, 199. *See also* field
boycott, 31, 128, 141–144
brothel, 2–5, 7, 9, 11, 22–23, 28, 30–31, 52–53, 55, 57, 59–68, 70–72, 74, 76, 78, 97, 99–100, 102–104, 108, 110–115, 117–120, 123–124, 168, 172, 198, 206–207, 209, 211

"Brothel Europe," 91
Brussels, 20, 27–28, 45, 47, 171, 176, 182, 200–201
bureaucracy of sex, 76, 95, 125
Buruma, Ybo, 56, 203, 205
business, 21, 23–24, 28, 31, 46, 52, 58–62, 64–65, 67–69, 72, 74, 88, 99–102, 104, 106, 111, 113–117, 123, 125, 133, 138, 161–162, 188, 190

Café Pssst, 99, 102, 207
Catholicism, 21, 45, 60, 102, 162, 176, 191
CATW. *See* Coalition Against Trafficking in Women
CDU. *See* Conservative Democratic Party
chain migration, 49, 171
chauvinism, 94
Christianity, 17, 99, 107, 110, 162, 203, 207, 213. *See also* Catholicism
citizen incorporation, 15–16, 19, 43, 60, 64, 71–72, 124, 129, 160, 211. *See also* inclusion roadmap
citizenship, 13–21, 25, 28–29, 32, 52, 63, 75–76, 95, 100–101, 108–109, 111–112, 116, 123–124, 126, 138, 152, 156–158, 160–165, 170, 176–177, 179–180
conceptualized, 13–21, 25
corporatist social citizenship, 52, 63, 75, 100–101, 161, 170, 176
European, 28, 32
and gender, 19, 24, 95
liberal-residual social citizenship, 19, 162–164
of prostitutes, 15, 75, 100–101
social citizenship, 76, 95, 100, 152, 156–158, 160–165, 170, 176–177, 179–180
social democratic, 19, 95, 160–161, 179–80
status of workers. *See* undocumented labor
welfare state, 18, 197, 213

city councils, 2, 108, 139, 153. *See also* municipal regulation
civil society, 4–5, 17, 21, 23, 34–35, 55, 71–72, 79, 157, 163, 165, 171
clients
of brothel managers, 105–106
of NGOs or social workers, 17, 43, 64, 66, 68, 120, 173, 185
of prostitutes, 9, 37, 43, 46, 48, 56, 61, 73–74, 80, 84, 87, 96, 99–105, 107, 113–115; 128–129, 137, 148, 150, 152, 161, 174, 191
of state protection, 170, 174
Coalition Against Trafficking in Women, 45, 194
coercion in prostitution. *See* pimping
Committee on Women's Rights and Equal Opportunities of the European Parliament, 46, 200
Common Foreign and Security Policy of the European Union, 29–30. *See also* European Union
common market, 50, 116–117, 120. *See also* European common market
common sense, 10, 20, 25, 48, 76, 156–157, 163
comparative research. *See* research methods
conflict, 4–7, 15–16, 19–20, 28, 32–34, 36, 44, 46, 56–58, 62–63, 73, 76, 79–80, 89, 94–95, 106, 109, 117, 178, 185, 196, 199
Congress of the United States, 34
consensus, 4–5, 11, 17, 24–25, 33, 35–37, 47, 81, 95, 99–101, 103, 105, 107, 109–113, 115, 117, 119, 121–125, 158, 161–162, 179–180
Conservative Democratic Party (German), 107, 109–110
constitutional rights, prostitution and, 12, 23, 31–32, 61, 199
Constitution for Europe. *See* European Union
constitutional rights, prostitution and
Dutch, vii, x, 8–11, 16–17, 23–24, 29, 44, 48, 52–68, 71, 73–76, 78,

91, 98–101, 116, 123–126, 148,
153, 162, 172, 174–175, 179, 185,
202–205
contract, 7, 15, 23–24, 52, 61, 99,
101–102, 108, 111, 116–117,
125, 138
contrarian feminisms, 34, 37, 149. *See
also* feminism
controversies, 4, 21, 44, 165, 189
cooperation, 23, 34, 48, 56–57, 65–67,
70–71, 98, 137, 171, 175
corporatist welfare state, 57, 60, 75,
125, 162, 179. *See also* citizenship
cosmopolitanism, 73, 134
Council of Europe, 39
crime, 7, 24, 29, 40, 49–50, 55, 58–59,
73–74, 78–79, 81, 90, 93–94, 99,
108, 120, 125, 128, 136–137, 150,
170–172
criminality, 32, 48, 52, 61, 76, 120
criminalization of prostitution
of buying, 7, 9–10, 24, 30, 43, 46, 48,
56, 74, 82, 100, 126, 128, 130, 137,
140, 145–152, 161, 163, 184
of buying and selling sex, 5, 9, 59,
163, 177
of selling sex, 4, 132, 176
cultural politics, iv, 2, 10–11, 156,
183, 186
culture
and citizenship, 164
Dutch, 57, 64–65
institutional infrastructures of, 79,
156, 158
and globalization, 12, 179
meanings, cultural, 2, 4, 8–17, 20,
33, 89, 156–158, 162–165, 171,
183, 187, 191
national, 9–10, 156, 159
political, 158–159
popular, 168
problematic uses as explanation,
9–10
as repertoire, 25, 157–158
shock, 165
sociology of, 12–13, 18, 33

and the state, 164–165
and structure, 33, 159
Swedish, 79, 83

DAPHNE Program (EU), ix, 30, 36,
38–39, 41–42, 44
de Graaf Foundation, Mr. A
(Netherlands), 71–72, 75, 204
De Rode Draad (Netherlands), 63, 71
de Wallen (Amsterdam), 72
decentralization,, 35, 100
decriminalization of prostitution, 5, 8,
11, 15, 35, 47, 76, 84, 163
denizens, 13, 117, 165, 177
Denmark, 8–9, 30
Department of Public Safety
(Frankfurt). *See* Ordnungsamt
Dettmeijer-Vermeulen, Corinne,
54–55, 202
Directorates General. *See* European
Commission
discourse, *also* stories, talk; 14, 21, 23,
25, 32–3, 38, 48, 56, 64, 70, 83, 85,
89, 91, 94, 98, 107–109, 111–112,
124, 129–130, 132–133, 135–137,
141, 147, 152, 154, 164, 168–171,
173, 178–180, 190. *See also* prostitution: discourse, trafficking:
discourse, talk
disorder. *See* public order
disorderly conduct, 139
dispositions, 33, 165. *See also* habits
divergence in prostitution policy, 5, 7,
9, 50, 161
Division of Gender Equality
(Sweden), 89
documentation of citizenship,
111, 122. *See also* undocumented
migrants
drugs, 8, 20, 23, 41, 54, 58, 60, 63, 73,
76, 83, 119–120, 164
Dutch. *See* Netherlands
Dutch Labor Movement Federation, 71
Dutch model, 48, 56, 98, 126
Dutch National Trade Union
Confederation, 56

Eastern Europe, 30–32, 78, 92, 94, 111, 136
egalitarianism, 19, 41, 147, 152
Ekberg, Gunilla, 89, 94, 197, 205–206
Elias, Norbert, 212
elites, 20, 28, 159, 171, 174, 188, 190
employees, 7, 15, 60–61, 66–70, 99, 104, 107, 114, 116, 118, 141, 173, 189
empowerment, 66–67, 183
Enlightenment, 178
ENMP, 44. *See* European Network for Male Prostitution
Eriksson, Marianne, 36, 46, 48, 200
Eros Centers, 103–104, 107, 110, 112–113, 120
escorts, 22, 69, 106, 144, 163
Esping-Anderson, Gøsta, 156, 163, 195, 197, 211
Estonia, 34, 38
Euro currency, 12, 28–30, 91, 129
European Central Bank, 112
European Commission, 34–35, 50, 92, 152, 176, 198, 200–201
    Directorates General of, 30, 35–36, 38, 41–42, 44–45, 200
    Employment and Social Affairs, 35
    Health and Consumer Protection, 30, 44
    Justice and Home Affairs (EU), 35–36, 39, 41, 201
European common market, 50, 116–117, 120
European Network for Male Prostitution, 44
European Parliament, 30–31, 35–36, 42, 46, 93, 200
European Union, 2, 6, 9, 20–25, 28–50, 91–95, 129, 136–137, 147, 152–153, 157, 164, 168–177
    anti-trafficking and, 150, 189
    anxieties about, 11–13, 27
    Common Foreign and Security Policy of, 29–30
    constitution for, 9, 12, 23, 28, 31–32, 61, 199

European Communities, 29. *See also* first pillar of the European Union
European Council, 35
European Court of Justice, 52, 117
EU-15, 8, 31, 38, 50, 161, 210
EU Network of Researchers on Fundamental Rights, 50, 117, 208
first pillar of the European Union, 29. *See also* European Communities
    law, 116–117. *See also* law: European
    norm of mutual noninterference, 3, 16
    second pillar of the European Union, 29
    third pillar of the European Union, 23, 29–30, 32, 40
    see also European Commission, European Parliament
European Women's Lobby, 36, 44–46, 141, 172
Eurozone. *See* Euro currency
EWL. *See* European Women's Lobby
exploitants (Dutch), 52, 58–59, 65–66, 68, 70
exploitation, 8, 24, 28, 38, 44, 46–50, 54–55, 58–59, 74, 89, 99–100, 119–120, 125, 145–146, 148, 150, 162, 176

FairWork. *See* Bonded Labor in the Netherlands
federalism, 102, 123
feminism, 6, 13, 19–20, 59, 79, 89, 101, 148, 152, 165, 172–174, 179, 182–187, 191
    autonomous, 126, 207
    contrarian, 34, 37, 126, 148–149
    Dutch, 101
    Finnish, 24, 130, 132–133, 138, 144–150, 152–153, 174
    German, 110, 126
    liberal, 19, 101, 148–149, 163, 165, 172–173, 206
    radical, 9, 20, 37, 45, 91, 106, 126, 148, 152, 172–173, 176, 184, 206

and research, 182–187
sex positive, 183, 186
state feminism, 19, 89
Swedish, 39–40, 79, 86, 91–92, 96
and welfare states, 25, 163, 165, 174
see also European Women's Lobby,
feminist sex wars
Feminist Party (Sweden), 92
feminist sex wars, 183, 185, 190–191
field, Bourdieusian, 28, 33, 36, 48, 184,
188, 191
fieldwork, 32, 182, 188, 191
Finland, 7–10, 16, 19–20, 22–24, 28,
30–31, 34, 36–38, 43, 47–49,
56–57, 66, 99, 99, 102, 126–154,
157, 161, 170, 172, 174–176, 179,
186, 188–189, 194, 199–201
Fischer, Claude, xi, 156, 211
Fligstein, Neil, xi, 198–199
forced, 19, 63, 72, 95–96, 113, 148,
160–162, 169–170
Foreigners Office, 108
Foucault, Michel, 13–14, 177, 195
framing, 19–20, 110, 125, 156, 183, 187
France, 8–9, 31–32, 56, 59, 78,
195–196, 204
Frankfurt, ix, 20–22, 97–108, 110–113,
116–118, 123–125
freedom, 14, 28–30, 32, 42, 48, 69, 85,
114, 148, 153, 175, 177

GAATW. *See* Global Alliance Against
Trafficking in Women
gay and lesbian rights, 14, 23, 76,
144, 154
gedogen (Dutch), 52, 58–59, 65
gender
and citizenship, 19
egalitarianism, 19, 24, 35, 38, 41
equality, 24, 35, 38, 41, 77, 80–82,
86, 89–90, 92, 95–96, 101, 132,
132–134, 141–142, 144–146,
151–152, 160, 180
and human rights, 35
inequality, 45, 89, 92, 99, 148
and legal protections, 15, 18, 156, 174

norms (*see* gender roles)
as political category, 57, 129
of politicians and officials, 3, 5, 40
and prostitution, 15, 18, 20, 41,
109, 126, 134, 153, 160, 165, 174,
182–183
relations, 132–134, 136, 147, 154
in research, 182–184
roles, 25, 32, 129, 131, 157, 177
and social movements, 13, 141–143
and violence, 3, 38, 45, 89, 107, 146
Germany, 7–10, 13, 16–17, 19, 22–24,
28, 30–31, 45–46, 48–49, 53,
56–57, 63, 76, 90–91, 93, 97–126,
128, 140, 148, 153, 155, 157, 161,
165, 170, 170, 172–176, 179, 185,
188–189, 193–194, 196, 198,
201, 206
Gewerbe (German), 99, 101, 117–118,
120, 161
Gezondheidscentrum (Amsterdam),
58, 63, 65. *See also* P&G292
GGD (Amsterdam). *See*
Gezondheidscentrum
gidsland (Dutch), 23, 52, 56, 59, 73, 203
Global Alliance Against Trafficking in
Women, 45, 193
globalization, 2, 7, 10–12, 25, 47,
75–76, 80, 129, 132, 136, 154, 156,
164, 168–171, 174, 176–180
globalization anxieties, 12, 129, 136,
168, 178–180
governing loose women, iv, 25
government, 5–6, 8, 10–18, 20–22,
28, 36–38, 40, 46–47, 52, 54–62,
64–72, 74–76, 78–79, 84, 86,
88–92, 98–101, 109, 114, 125,
128, 138–139, 145, 150–152, 165,
177–178, 186, 189
Gradin, Anita, 36, 38, 40–41, 91, 169
Great Britain. *See* United Kingdom
Greece, 3, 5, 8, 31, 161, 172, 193, 197
Green Party, 99, 124, 126, 131

Habermas, Jürgen, 199
habits, 33, 165. *See also* dispositions

habitus. *See* dispositions, habits
Halonen, Tarja, 36, 151, 199
Hamburg, 23, 98, 102, 206
harmonization of policies, 24, 32, 40,
    153, 164
Heinrichs, Christine, 120, 125
Helsingin Sanomat (Finland), 31, 141,
    193–194
Helsinki, 20, 22, 30, 36–38, 43, 128,
    131–134, 136, 139–140, 148,
    150–153, 193, 199–201
Hertell, Sirpa, 141–144, 147
Hesse, 98–99, 107–108
HIV, 120. *See also* AIDS
Holland, 22, 123, 175–176
homogenization, 25, 168, 180
Howe, Christiane, 110, 120–121, 124
HSIE. *See* Helsingin Sanomat
    (International Edition)
human rights, 4, 6, 8, 13, 17–18, 24,
    35, 39, 47, 49, 93, 129, 139, 152,
    174–177, 180
human trafficking. *See* trafficking

identity work, 185–187, 189–191
IGO. *See* intergovernmental
    organizations
illegal aliens, 121
illegal workers, 17–18, 108, 110,
    113, 120
ILO. *See* International Labor
    Organization
immigration law, 118
immigration policy, 32
Immigration Services (Finland), 137
immorality, 100, 115, 124
inclusion roadmap, 16, 19, 57, 101,
    152, 177
indexical concept, 157, 188, 212
individualism, 14, 125
Industrial Revolution, 178
inequality, 45, 76, 92, 99, 147, 162, 168
INGO. *See* international non govern-
    mental organization
integration, 12, 23, 27, 91, 168–169

intergovernmental organizations, 2,
    6, 152, 171. *See also* Council of
    Europe, OSCE, NATO, Nordic
    Council
international agreement, 168,
    170–172, 175
International Labor Organization, 2, 6,
    29–30, 76, 194
international non governmental
    organizations, 5, 39
Internet, 63, 85, 103, 142, 144
interviewing. *See* research methods
Ireland, 8
Italy, 8–9, 31, 161–162, 194

johns. *See* clients of prostitution
Judaism, 60
Justice and Home Affairs (EU), 35–36,
    39, 41, 201. *See also* European
    Commission
Justice Ministry, 31, 52, 128

Kallio, 133–134, 136, 140
Kauppinen, Jaana, 136–137, 149, 151
KEGE. *See* Movement of Greek
    Prostitutes
Kleinstuber, Heike, 108, 113, 117–118
Kram, 94
KtK, 80, 84, 87, 89–90, 93–94, 96
Kvinna till Kvinna, 80, 84–85
Kvinnoforum, 40, 169
kvinnofrid, 79, 81–87, 89, 91, 93, 95

labor market, 63, 162, 164, 204
labor protections, 57, 95, 99–100, 125,
    156, 163, 171
laissez-faire, 57–58, 61, 89, 163,
    176–177
law
    advice, 35, 40
    common law, 163
    conceptualizations of, 14, 16, 18,
        157, 165
    criminal, 23, 28, 50, 61, 75, 80, 83,
        99, 102, 115, 128, 138, 149, 163

Dutch prostitution, 24, 52–54, 57–58, 60–61, 65–68, 71–72, 75
enforcement, 32, 82, 91
European, 24, 28–34, 116–117, 120, 125, 153
failure of, 11, 176
Finnish prostitution, 7, 24, 128–129, 138–140, 144, 149–150, 210
German prostitution, 24, 98–101, 103, 108, 110, 115–118, 120–123, 125
gray areas of, 11, 15, 18, 53, 102, 113, 116–117, 123, 180
human rights, 13, 18, 174
immigration, 31, 50, 108, 100, 118, 138–139, 210
labor, 60, 68, 99–101, 108, 110, 115–116, 118, 123
lawmakers, 21, 71
lawyers, 33, 40
legal rights, 71, 158, 189
municipal bylaws, 5, 11, 30, 52, 57, 59–60, 118, 139–140 (*see also* municipal regulation)
and order, 32 (*see also* social control)
property, 163
prostitution reforms generally, 18, 24, 28, 31, 44, 46
and religion, 74
and sex work, 59, 110, 121–122
Swedish prostitution, 8, 24, 78–88, 90–91, 95–96 (*see also* women's peace)
trafficking in human beings, 8, 31, 86, 120
unwritten, 158, 165
welfare, 24, 73, 75, 95, 125
see also policy
Lechner, Frank, 56, 203, 205
legalization of prostitution, 5, 7–9, 16–18, 28, 31, 45–48, 161, 172–173, 176–177, 180, 187
Dutch, 52–53, 57, 59–60, 64, 66, 68, 71–72, 74
Finnish perceptions of, 152

German, 97–98, 100–101, 106, 112, 122–126
Swedish perceptions of, 89, 93
Leijonhufvud, Madeleine, 80
lesbians, 76, 144. *See also* gay and lesbian rights
liberal feminism. *See* feminism
liberal-residual welfare state, 19, 156–157, 159–164. *See also* citizenship
licensing, 2, 22, 57, 59, 72, 74, 99, 133, 140
Lilja-4-Ever, 168–169
Lindh, Anna, 92–93, 145
Lutheranism, 38, 176
Luxembourg, 8, 31, 161, 200

Maastricht treaty, 29–30
Mackinnon, Catherine, 92, 197
mafia, 76, 98, 137
Majoor, Mariska, 61–62, 72, 204
Månsson, Sven-Axel, 92
markets
    anxieties about, 15, 178
    citizenship and, 19, 157, 163–164
    European single, 28, 50
    free, 60, 75
    for prostitution, 52, 61, 74, 106, 120, 130–132
    vs. the state, 12, 46, 75, 101
marriage, 14, 121, 160, 190
massage parlors, 127, 133, 152. *See also* sex business
media, 2, 21, 37, 47, 61, 92, 95, 133, 145, 174
Member States of the European Union. *See* European Union
men as prostitutes. *See* prostitution: male
MEP. *See* Minister of the European Parliament
Meriläinen, Rosa, 148–149
methods. *See* research methods
migration, 6, 12, 22, 24, 30, 38, 40, 47–50, 93–94, 99, 108, 110, 121, 152–153, 171, 175–176
feminization of, 50

Minister of the European Parliament, 36, 42, 46, 93, 200
Ministry of Social Services, 75
Ministry of the Interior, 36–37, 138
Monika Naiset (Finland). *See* Multicultural Women's Association
moral language, 20
moral leadership, 24, 73, 78, 110
moralism, 82, 90, 95
morality, xi, 4, 11, 16–17, 20, 24, 52, 54, 56–57, 60, 73, 78, 82–83, 89–90, 92–93, 95–96, 108, 110, 119, 128, 137, 148, 153, 158, 162, 165, 168, 170, 174–176, 178, 180, 180, 186
Movement of Greek Prostitutes, 2–3, 6
Multicultural Women's Association (Finland), 134
municipal regulation, 2, 5–6, 11, 21, 30–31, 52–53, 55, 57, 59, 63, 78, 99, 100–102, 118, 123, 128, 139–140, 156. *See also* city councils
mutual consultation, 57, 63, 137

Nagel, Helga, 111–113, 119
naming and shaming, 7, 170
nation, 2, 10–15, 17–18, 22, 24–25, 28, 31–32, 50, 52, 56, 59, 61, 63, 78–79, 91, 94–96, 116, 123, 125, 128–130, 133, 136, 140–141, 152–154, 156–157, 165, 171–173, 177–180, 191
nation-state project, 11, 15, 94–95, 123, 129, 136, 140, 152, 165
National Bureau of Investigation (Sweden), 37, 80–81
National Bureau of Tourism and Conventions (Netherlands), 53
national chauvinism, 94
National Council of Women (Finland), 141, 142
national culture, 9–10, 13, 37, 156, 159, 168 *see also* culture
national differentiation, 23
national identity, 7–8, 10–11, 16, 23, 76, 95

National Organization for Women's Shelters in Sweden, 94
National Police Board (Sweden), 54, 72, 81
National Rapporteur on human trafficking, 80
national standards, 17, 29, 139, 180
nationalization, of prostitution, 16, 61, 165
nativism, 55, 160
NATO, 129, 152
NCW. *See* National Council of Women
neoliberalism, 25, 75, 132
Netherlands, 7–11, 16–17, 19, 22–24, 28–32, 43–46, 48–49, 52–76, 78, 89, 91, 98–102, 107, 110, 116–117, 123–126, 128–129, 148, 153, 157, 161–162, 170, 172, 174–175, 179, 185, 189, 195, 197–198, 201–205
new prostitution politics, 2, 4–7, 15, 76, 151, 171, 178
newspapers, 24, 63, 79, 86, 103, 114, 122, 127–128, 130, 133–134, 141–144, 153, 161, 189
NGOs, 6, 17, 22, 33, 35, 37–38, 44, 63, 72, 86, 88, 94, 108–109, 111, 117, 120, 134, 169–170, 173, 187, 189–190
Nilsson, Karin, 84, 87–88
Nordic Council, 31, 78, 172
normal troubles, 158
normalization, 47, 174–175
norms, 11, 15, 29, 32, 60, 136–137, 149–150, 157

objectification, 146
Office for Multicultural Affairs, 111
Olympic games, 2–4, 6–7, 31, 78, 165, 172
openness, Dutch, 61
opposition, 19, 25, 87, 91, 144, 146, 151, 173, 183
ordinances. *See* municipal regulation
Ordnungsamt (Frankfurt), 107–108, 110–113, 115–119, 121

Organization against International
    Sexual and Racial Exploitation
    (Frankfurt). *See* AGISRA
Organization for Security and
    Cooperation in Europe. *See* OSCE
organized crime, 29, 49, 74, 90, 93–94,
    99, 171
OSCE, 29, 31, 37, 45, 152

P&G292, 63–64, 70–71, 75. *See also*
    Gesondheidscentrum
Palermo Protocol, 6, 31, 45
pandering, 92, 115
paper marriages, 121
papers, 21, 40, 62, 93, 102, 121,
    141–142, 144
parliament, 9–10, 22, 28–30, 98, 109,
    128, 136, 139, 145, 150–152, 173,
    175, 184
pastoral NGO, 172
pensions, 60, 98, 156, 162
Persson, Göran, 91–92
PIC (Amsterdam), 61–62, 71, 204
pimping, 31, 53, 59, 98, 102, 144–145,
    151, 172
pimps, 5, 9, 40–41, 46–47, 67, 115,
    130, 172
Platform 1012 (Amsterdam), 72
Poland, 111
Polder, 56–57, 203–204
police, 2, 4–6, 20–22, 24, 53, 58, 67–68,
    71–72, 78–79, 84, 98, 105, 107–
    110, 113–115, 121, 134, 138, 140,
    151–152, 155, 158–159, 170–174,
    179, 184, 190
Police and Judicial Cooperation, 29.
    See also European Union third
    pillar
policing, 4, 15, 34, 110, 125, 127,
    160, 177
policy. *See* law
policy entrepreneurs, 159
policy makers, 12, 19–20, 162
policy paths, 28
polity, 29

Portugal, 8, 30
Post-Soviet, 29–30, 129–130, 132,
    140, 171
pragmatism, 8, 24, 56–57, 62, 73, 76,
    110, 152
Presidency, 152
Pretty Woman, 168–169
privacy, 13–14, 54, 62–63, 69, 100, 102,
    105, 127, 141, 159, 163, 175, 179
Pro-tukipiste (Helsinki), 36–38, 43,
    136–137
Prostitutes' Help Center (Helsinki). *See*
    Pro-tukipiste
prostitution
    discourse, 48, 91
    male, 15, 37–38, 41, 44, 89, 170
    politics, 2, 4–7, 15, 32, 76, 151, 171,
        178, 184
    professionalization of, 65–70
    promotion of prostitution (*see*
        pandering)
    "prostituted women," 13, 89, 94 (*see
        also* "voluntary prostitution")
Prostitution Information Center
    (Amsterdam). *See* PIC
Prostitution Roundtable (Frankfurt),
    107, 111, 122
public
    opinion, 12, 158
    order, 8, 30, 110, 128, 139, 173
    sphere, 4–5, 60, 81, 86, 92, 100, 138,
        140, 142, 149, 151–153, 160–164,
        174–175, 179, 189, 191, 197–199
Public Health Service (Amsterdam), 63
Public Order Act (Finland), 128,
    138–141, 144, 149
Public Order Office (Frankfurt). *See*
    Ordnungsamt

queer, 186. *See also* gay and lesbian
    rights

radical feminism. *See* feminism
rapporteur on human trafficking,
    54–56, 58, 80–81, 152, 202–203

rationalization, 13–14, 16, 18, 23,
178–179
Raymond, Janice, 47, 148, 194, 200
realism, 24, 152–153, 168
realpolitik. *See* realism
red light district, 51, 53, 109, 123–124
Red Thread (Netherlands), 68, 71
"red whores," 129, 209
Reeperbahn (Hamburg), 102
reforms. *See* laws
regulation, 2, 11, 16, 19–20, 22, 28–30,
45–46, 52, 57, 59, 61, 63, 68,
73–74, 98, 118, 123, 127–128,
138, 140, 156, 158, 164, 179–180,
185–186
religion, 60–61, 64, 74, 76, 102, 158,
203. *See also* Catholicism, Judaism, Lutheranism
research methods, 21, 62, 87, 148,
181–191
case studies, 19, 101, 156
comparative, 16, 18, 156, 158, 185
interviewing, 20–22, 73, 79, 134,
168, 184–186, 188, 190
and sexuality, 182–187, 191, 216
residency permits, 42
residual state. *See* liberal-residual
retrenchment, 76, 87, 165
RFSU (Sweden), 78, 84, 88
Rikskriminalpolisen (Sweden), 80–81
ROKS. *See* National Organization for
Women's Shelters in Sweden
Römer (Frankfurt), 98, 107, 109, 208
Rosea (Sweden), 85
roundtable, 22, 80, 109–110, 113,
117–119, 122, 124
Russia, 38, 129–130, 136, 146, 152,
154, 186
Russian, 24–25, 104, 129–137, 144,
146–147, 153–154, 168, 172, 174
Russian prostitutes, 25, 133

SALLI (Finland), 130, 138, 151
Salvation Army, 62, 64
Saukkonen, Ari, 131–133, 136, 144
Scandinavia, xi, 160, 197

schadenfreude, 130, 153, 172
Schengen Agreements, 30, 32, 49, 136
Schwartzer, Alice, 126
SDP. *See* Social Democratic Party
secularism, 28, 61, 203
seeing as a state, 95, 157, 159, 161,
163, 165
Seksialan Liito. *See* SALLI
self-control, 73
self-regulating individuals, 157
sex advertisements, 127–128,
141–144
sex bars, 132, 134, 140
sex business, 52, 61, 68
sex buyers, 11, 79, 90, 100, 126, 128,
140, 151–152
sex war. *See* feminist sex war
sex work, 6–7, 19, 23–24, 30, 32, 34,
43, 48, 59–61, 66, 69, 72, 78–79,
81, 91–92, 99–101, 103, 105–107,
109–111, 113, 115, 117, 119, 121,
123, 125, 170–171
sexköpslag (Sweden), 78–84, 86–92,
94–95
sexual commerce, 11, 120, 122, 132,
151, 156, 177, 185
sexual politics. *See* gender roles
sexuality
conceptualized, 13–15
feminist debates over, 183
and law, 13, 157
as nation-state project, 15, 17
and the public sphere, 14, 31, 60,
85–86, 128, 138–141, 153, 216
rationalization of, 13, 15, 174, 177
researching, 182–187, 191, 216
social movements and, 13
state regulation of, 17
and vulnerability, 24, 157
and the workplace, 19, 60, 75, 157,
160
Siegler, Stephan, 109
Sirkiä, Johanna, 130–132, 136, 138,
144, 149, 151
sittenwidrigkeit (German), 99
social citizenship. *See* citizenship

social control, 17, 48, 74, 158, 163, 216
  via social services, 63
social democracy, 73, 92, 141, 148, 164, 180
Social Democratic Party, 107
social good, 82
social isolation, 38
social movements, 5, 13, 171
social policy harmonization, 32
social problems, 20, 29, 73, 83, 96, 156–160, 164–165
social rights, 116, 157, 162, 168
social services, 37, 62–3, 135
social work, 4, 34, 38, 63, 78, 92, 151, 176
socialization, 15, 66, 142
solidarity, 12, 17–19, 25, 41, 66, 80–84, 94, 96, 148, 157, 160, 164–165
sovereignty, 12, 29, 92, 177
Soviet Union, 30, 129–130, 132
Spain, 8, 43, 161, 198
spanking children, 8, 205
sporting events. *See* Olympic games, World Cup
St. Petersburg, 38
stakeholders, 21, 28, 33–34, 48, 52, 100
STAKES (Finland), 34, 36–38, 147
State Department, U.S., 6, 29–30, 47, 150–151, 170
state feminism. *See* feminism
STOP Programme (EU), 30, 36–38, 42
stories. *See* discourse
streetwalking, 9, 57, 62, 78, 120, 127, 131, 139, 153, 171
structural dilemma, 8, 13, 112, 164–165, 188
structure, 5, 19, 33, 37, 100, 102, 111, 156, 158–159, 163, 174
STTV (Finland), 140
supranational, 29, 157, 168
surveillance, 7, 62, 140, 172, 177, 179
Sweden, 3, 7–11, 16–17, 19–20, 22–24, 28–31, 34, 36–39, 41, 44, 46–48, 54, 56–57, 66, 72–74, 77–96, 99, 101–103, 107, 124–126, 128–129, 136, 140–142, 144–145, 148–154,
  157, 160, 160–161, 168–170, 172, 174, 176, 179, 189, 193–194, 197, 200, 205–206
Swedish Association for Sexuality Education. *See* RFSU
Swedish Institute, 78, 80, 200, 205–206
Swedish legislation. *See* Swedish model
Swedish model, 8, 24, 37, 48, 56, 91, 96, 145, 148–150, 160–161. *See also* *sexköpslaget*, women's peace
Swedish People's Party (Finland), 145
Swedish Women's Lobby, 94
Swidler, Ann, xi, 195–196
Systembolaget (Sweden), 83–84

Tallinn, 38
TAMPEP (EU), 30–31, 36, 42–44, 46–47, 200
technology, 14, 178
ten Broeke, Christy, 63
terrorism, 29, 145
third pillar of the EU, 29. *See* Police and Judicial Cooperation
Thomas (theorem), W. I., 158, 179, 196, 198–199
TIP Reports. *See* Trafficking in Persons Reports
tolerance, 6–8, 52, 56–62, 64–65, 68, 73–74, 76, 174, 181
tolerance zones, 22, 31, 102–104, 106, 110, 119
tourism, 23, 53, 61, 72, 106
  sex, 135
tourist visas, 13, 111
trade, 24, 37, 40, 46, 50, 62, 69–71, 93, 99, 101, 106, 113, 115–118, 120–121, 125–126, 128, 132, 139–140, 151, 161, 164, 178
trafficking
  amount of, 36, 165
  concern over, 2–4, 6, 32, 165
  as discourse, 4, 7, 25, 32–33, 35, 40, 48–50, 167–168, 170–171, 178–180, 190
  in Finland, 128, 130, 136–137, 145, 147, 149–151, 161

trafficking (*continued*)
  in Germany, 98, 107, 120
  of men, 50
  in the Netherlands, 52–55, 57, 59,
    63, 71, 73–74, 162
  programs to address, 8, 21–24,
    29–31, 40, 170–171
  equated with prostitution, 35, 45,
    161
  in Sweden, 79–80, 86, 88, 90–91,
    93–94
  talk, 168, 170–171, 178
  in women, 9, 37, 47, 176, 179
  victims of, 21, 42, 49–50, 88,
    173, 190
  see also DAPHNE, European
    Women's Lobby, STOP, TAMPEP
Trafficking in Persons Reports (U.S.), 6,
  29–30, 150–151, 170, 176
Trafficking Victims Protection
  Act (U.S.), 45
transgender, 14
transnational politics, 2, 4–7, 13,
  21–23, 48, 72–73, 89, 156, 169,
  172–174, 176–179
treaties, 139, 180
Treaty of Amsterdam, 23, 28–30, 32
truly trafficked women, 167, 178, 190

UK. *See* United Kingdom
UN, 6, 29–31, 45, 172, 187, 194
undocumented migrants, 18, 63,
  110–112, 168, 180
undocumented workers, 19, 110,
  112, 117
United Kingdom, iv, 8, 28, 89, 157, 163,
  193, 198
United Nations, 2, 6, 29, 45, 76, 129,
  152, 172
United Sex Professionals of Finland.
  See SALLI
urban governance. *See* municipal
  politics
urination. *See* public order
USSR, 129. *See also* Soviet Union

Valvira (Finland). *See* STTV
van Doorninck, Marieke, 75, 204
Vatican, 3, 7, 161, 172, 194
veterans, 157
Vice Unit (Berlin), 125
victimhood, 170
victims of human trafficking, 32,
  41–42, 49, 52, 63, 161, 170, 184
violence against women, 7, 30, 32, 35,
  37, 45, 48, 79, 82, 90, 169, 175
visas, 13, 31, 52, 111, 176
"voluntary" prostitution, 32, 40, 46,
  59, 170, 216. *See also* "prostituted
  women"
vulnerability, 2, 11–12, 15–16, 18–19,
  23, 41, 157, 162, 164–165
vulnerable women, 12, 18, 20, 41, 47,
  79, 85, 94, 160, 165, 172

Wahlberg, Kajsa, 37, 81–83, 87, 90, 152
Weber, Max, 13–14, 16, 18, 178, 195
welfare policy, 25, 165
welfare state, 2, 16, 18–20, 24–25, 57,
  60, 75, 78–79, 87, 89, 95, 99–101,
  125, 128, 152, 156–158, 160,
  162–163, 165, 171, 173, 179,
  191, 206
welfare state citizenship, 18, 197, 213
welfare states, 16, 18, 28, 63, 101, 124,
  156–157, 159–164, 174
Western Europe, 43, 93, 200–201
White Slavery, 49, 193, 201
whore, as insult, 86. *See also* Red
  whores
whore stigma, 135, 205
women in public, 161
Women's Café, 120, 125
women's peace, 78, 82, 85. See also
  sexköpslag
work, 4, 6–8, 13, 16, 19–21, 23–24,
  30, 32–34, 36–38, 40–44, 47–48,
  52–53, 55, 59–61, 63–64, 66–67,
  69–73, 75, 78–81, 86–89, 91–93,
  98–103, 105–123, 125–126, 132,
  137, 146, 148–149, 151, 157–162,

165, 170–177, 179–180, 182,
184–187, 189–191, 199
worker protections, 95
workplace, 15, 19, 22, 60, 75, 106, 115,
157, 160, 162, 176
World Cup, 2, 7, 31, 193–194

xenophobia, 94, 130–131, 146

youth, of women or girls, 41, 60, 82, 86,
115, 142, 168

zoning. *See* municipal regulation